VISIBLE EVIDENCE, VOLUME 7

States of Emergency

Documentaries, Wars, Democracies

Patricia R. Zimmermann

University of Minnesota Press

Minneapolis

London

Portions of chapter 4 appeared in an earlier version as "Fetal Tissue: Reproductive Rights and Activist Amateur Video," in *Resolutions: Contemporary Video Practices,* edited by Michael Renov and Erika Suderburg. Copyright 1996 by the Regents of the University of Minnesota.

Published by the University of Minnesota Press
111 Third Avenue South, Suite 290
Minneapolis, MN 55401-2520
http://www.upress.umn.edu

Library of Congress Cataloging-in-Publication Data

Zimmermann, Patricia Rodden.
    States of emergency : documentaries, wars, democracies /
Patricia R. Zimmermann.
        p.   cm. — (Visible evidence ; v. 7)
    Includes bibliographical references and index.
    ISBN 0-8166-2822-X — ISBN 0-8166-2823-8 (pbk.)
    1. Documentary films—political aspects I. Title.   II. Series.
PN1995.9D6 Z56 2000
070.1′8—dc21   99-043758

11 10 09 08 07 06 05 04 03 02 01 00   10 9 8 7 6 5 4 3 2 1

In loving memory of my father,
Byron L. Zimmermann

Contents

Acknowledgments

This book bears the indentations of many people and institutions who keep the counterpublic sphere of independent documentary and experimental media in the United States alive despite the civil war dead set to annihilate it. I am grateful to them all. They have stoked my ideas and fired my imagination. They remind me that in these terribly privatized and isolating times, a community of like-minded souls around the country thrives, sustaining a kind of intravenous injection of hope and energy each day.

States of Emergency would not have been possible without this larger set of social and political relations propelling it along and insisting on its urgency and agency. These people and institutions kept me honest and helped me refrain from mere academic theorization. They remind me that whatever we write, these films, these institutions, and these movements are always bigger than the writer. The words that follow are then not definitive or final, but merely humble contributions to the larger struggle to reclaim a liberated space away from media-as-exchange.

Many of the films and videos discussed and ideas traversed in the pages that follow were incubated by my contact with colleagues who keep those somewhat sidelined infrastructures of independent film going with heart and guts despite overwhelming negativity and assault. Without these people and these institutions, I would never have experienced most of the films and film movements analyzed in this book. I consider these people to be on the front lines of the war to save independent media culture. I am grateful for their vision, their undervalued hard work, their courage.

Many film- and videomakers also left their mark on this book through conversations with me about their complex aesthetics, politics, and the power relations of representation. I am humble before the brilliance of their images and the force of their editing and arguments. I thank these artists for giving me a new set of eyes with which to see this work. For their ability to help me understand the potency of their images and to help me translate them into ever-inadequate words, I thank Austin Allen, Kelly Anderson, Craig Baldwin, Joan Braderman, Christine Choy, Norman Cowie, Tami Gold, DeeDee Halleck, Kathy High, Chris Hill, Mandy Jacobson, Philip Mallory Jones, Cara Mertes, Branda Miller, Meena Nanji, Lourdes Portillo, Daniel Reeves, Alex Rivera, Ellen Spiro, Melinda Stone, Igor Vamos, Edin Velez, Lise Yasui, and Pamela Yates for their time.

Although Ithaca is a small town in rural upstate New York, a tiny town by any metropolitan standard, the committed, passionate people who form the independent media sector here make it feel large, vibrant, and life sustaining. The filmmakers, videomakers, intellectuals, writers, political activists, and fellow travelers of political documentary and experimental work here demonstrate that regional ties indeed do bind, forming a barricade against nationalism, transnationalization, and defunding. For their contributions to making this community pulse with independent documentary and experimental media, and for wrestling with ideas in public debates about this work, the following need to be named: Barb Adams, Susan Buck-Morss, Ben Crane, Zillah Eisenstein, Mary Fessenden, Carla Golden, Jane Greenberg, Vincent Grenier, Slawomir Grunberg, Gil Harris, Jill Hartz, Richard Herskowitz, Carol Jennings, Jason Longo, Liz Lyon, Gina Marchetti, Nina Martin, Ann Michel, Danah Moore, Tim Murray, David Ost, Marilyn Rivchin, Megan Roberts, Anna Marie Smith, Steve Tropiano, Gossa Tsegaye, Amy Villarejo, and Phil Wilde.

A special place of tribute is reserved for curator Leslie Schwartz Burgevin, who died before this book was completed. She heard speeches I made at rallies against the Gulf War and the cutbacks to the arts. She always insisted on the necessity to keep on fighting. She contended that urgent writing propagates passion, like perennial cuttings that grow into a garden.

At the Museum of Modern Art, the ever-affable Sally Berger and ever-gracious Bill Sloan pointed the way to many works that figure prominently in this book. John Columbus, the committed director of the Black Maria Film and Video Festival, deserves special commendation for pushing me to consider new work that stretched the original conceptions of this project. Ruth Bradley, director of the Athens International Film Festival and editor of *Wide Angle*, kept me plugged into new work and new film/video movements with her insatiable appetite and exquisite taste for the most moving offerings that stir the soul. The journal *Afterimage*, and its editors, Michael Starenko and Karen van Meenen, encouraged my edgiest writing and provided a supportive home for it.

Debbie Zimmerman, chief ambassador for feminist film, and the staff at Women Make Movies not only provided preview tapes of more films than I can name, but also suggested works that significantly contributed to shifting the shape of two separate chapters. Kate Kirtz and Erika Vogt of Women Make Movies dug out photo illustrations to give my words some anchoring in the visual world. Mindy Faber, Jennifer Reeder, and the crew at Video Data Bank suggested titles and supplied stills.

As always, Jake Homiak and Pamela Wintle of the Human Studies Film Archive at the Smithsonian Institution, Karan Sheldon of Northeast Historic Film, and Jan-Christopher Horak of the Universal Studios Film Archive kept my spirits up by continually reminding me that history is the potent stuff of politics and the future. Freelance producer and footage researcher Rosemary Rotondi supplied inroads into work and images that ended up becoming the fulcrum for some ideas in this book about processed imagery. B. Ruby Rich, Debbie Silverfine, and Claude Meyer of the New York State Council on the Arts provided heavy doses of reality checking and fantasy production, demonstrating that a dialectic between both is necessary for any writing to happen at all. Helen DeMichiel and the National Association for Media Arts and Culture taught me wisely that writing critical theory makes a difference only if it is in conversation with debates that cross disciplinary, professional, and political borders.

The Robert Flaherty Film Seminar has functioned as a sort of ongoing postdoctoral fellowship program for me for the past twenty years. Each year, it revitalizes my senses. It instructs me that these heated debates and explosive conflicts about independent film are substantive, real, invigorating, and necessary. They unsettle the mind and spur thinking and writing. Several Flaherty curators in particular screened work that ended up changing my theoretical paradigms, changing this book, and changing how I think about documentary and experimental work: Richard Herskowitz, Bruce Jenkins, Marlina Gonzalez Tamrong, Somi Roy, Ruth Bradley, Kathy High, Margarita de La Vega Hurtado, Scott MacDonald, and Pearl Bowser. I thank them all for their daring. They are all warriors on the front lines.

At Ithaca College, the support services offered by various staff were indispensable in reminding me that intellectual work is not a solitary activity; it requires many helping and generous hands and all sorts of hidden labor. For ordering books and journals for research on this project, I thank Jim Meyer of the Ithaca College Bookstore for his flair and acumen in navigating the ever-changing rapids of contemporary publishing. For retyping and computing first aid, I am indebted to the Department of Cinema and Photography departmental assistants Karen Wheeler and Barbara Terrell. For help with illustrations, Fred Estabrook was indispensable and magnanimous. For their projection skills during public exhibitions and classroom screenings, I thank Dave Sill, Tommy Inman, Slade Kennedy, DeWitt Davis, Rodrigo Bellot, Rodrigo Brandao, and Elena Tsaneva for the gift of bestowing a beautiful technical dignity to often obscure and maligned documentary and experimental work.

Over the past five years, this book has also benefited from the hard work and creativity of a phalanx of research assistants supported through the Roy H. Park School of Communications graduate program and the Dana Student Internship Program at Ithaca College: Brian Beatrice, Lenore De Paoli, William Hooper, Jason Longo, Nicole Luce-Rizzo, Ulises Mejias, and Todd Williams. Their skill in digging through documents, archival materials, and cyberspace eased my writing. Finally, various research and curatorial grants from Ithaca College as well as the James B. Pendleton Endowment of the Roy H. Park School of Communications at Ithaca College supported the material base of this book. Skip Landen, former chair of the Department of Cinema and Photography at Ithaca College and longtime friend of independent documentary and the arts, deserves a special thanks for support and extraordinary resources.

During its gestation at the University of Minnesota Press, this volume has benefited from the shrewd sculpting of several editors: Janaki Bakhle, Micah Kleit, and Jennifer Moore. I am grateful in every way for their trust in this polemical project about such marginalized cinematic practices as documentary and experimental works, bucking the market trends for discussions of Hollywood and popular culture. I especially thank Jennifer Moore for her creativity as an editor and her clear-eyed vision of what the book could be after taking it on near the end, and for her friendship. For meticulous checking of filmmakers' names, titles, and dates, and for her copyediting that sharpened my prose, I thank Judy Selhorst.

Several friends and colleagues read the manuscript, discussed the arguments within it, and pushed me toward greater clarity and courage. I am grateful to Jane Shattuc, Diane Waldman, Paula Rabinowitz, and Gina Marchetti for their encouragement and their invaluable, sustaining friendships. Carla Golden kept me hiking on the gorgeous Finger Lakes trails and insisted on a politics of urgency and clarity. John Hess was and is always a comrade in arms in every way imaginable, from the workplace to the screening room to the picket lines; during the most oppressive and darkest of times, he kept insisting that writing matters.

Scott MacDonald's work for the past twenty years to chronicle experimental film provided a role model of respect for the rigorous critical work that makers do and a humility that artists are perhaps better theory producers than theorists. His soaring spirit and generous collegiality have led me to incredible places in our deep friendship. Laura Marks's writing, thinking, talking, and e-mails made writing about documentary and experimental work less lonely; I hope this book measures up to the grace and poetry of her political aesthetics.

In the isolating, mean-spirited, psychic, and physical brutalities of this new world order, it is more important than ever to feel continuity with a historical tradition of committed scholarly work. For twenty years, Erik Barnouw has functioned as a collaborator, cocurator, coeditor, cohort, colleague, and coconspirator. His landmark writing on documentary opened up a virtually unmined field of inquiry for younger scholars like me. But most important, his generosity, grace, and gumption taught by example: scholarly work is not about individual achievement but about joyous collective engagement and glorious unending exchanges between writers and makers. I only hope the small offerings in this book, inspired by his own work, make him proud.

This book is made possible not by corporate underwriting, like many public television documentaries, but by caregiver labor underwriting that stretches our nuclear family out into a larger, more encompassing collective project. A special word of recognition is necessary for the caregivers who help our family navigate domestic life, work, school, and pleasure. They gave the gift of their time with zest and imagination that made integrating parenting with intellectual work and teaching seem like a dissolve rather than a jump cut: Beverly Gobert, Sarah Rubens, Karen Smith, Rona Vogt, Shari Sobell, Thom Denick, and Joslyn Wilschek.

Stewart Auyash, as always, knew the gourmet recipe for writing support and mental equilibrium: equal parts writing space, good food, good humor, balmy sailing, hearty fun, and incredible love. I thank him for all of that, as well as for the parts that exceed words. Sean Zimmermann Auyash taught me that sometimes writing can only achieve deeper insights through pillow fighting, chess playing, dancing, swimming, drawing, or reading about fairies, knights, and monsters. He told me that I could not do a book without pictures, or pictures without words. I hope he likes how this one turned out.

More than anyone, my workout partner and soul mate Zillah Eisenstein immersed herself in this project, reading every word, imbibing nearly every film and video piece discussed, pushing me to clarify, expand, theorize, politicize. She encouraged—no, commanded—me to be bold and daring in body and mind, to make leaps and to execute pirouettes no matter what. Her generous fighting spirit and galvanizing vision of sisterhood infuse this book.

States of Emergency
An Introduction

We are poised on a crumbling, frightening precipice as we edge into the enigmatic morphing media landscapes of the twenty-first century. Whether stationed in the academy or outside of it in nonprofit media sectors, we have been defunded and delegitimated. We urgently need a new world image order. We need to think differently about independent documentary. Independent documentary is in danger of losing its oppositional edge to disturb the universe as all of its supports and infrastructures deteriorate. Shedding its older forms of argument and its allegiances to maintaining nation-states, documentary has the potential to shift the new world image order into more democratic spaces.

We are caught within the folds of intense political and aesthetic contradictions. It is far from easy to navigate the hurricane-force storms unsettling the independent media arts field, destabilizing its foundations and shaking its moorings. As a result, we live in continual states of emergency.

We need to explain an intricately layered set of contradictions: the changing transnationalized economic sphere of commercial media on the one hand and the emergence of new technologies, new subjectivities, new discourses, new wars, and new ambushes on the other. These contradictions oscillate between utter despair and ecstatic hope.

On one side, corporate underwriting of nearly all sectors of culture devastates any democratic public sphere. On the other side, the emergence of technologies like camcorders, public access television, image processing, digitality, and satellites suggests newly imagined public spaces. On one side, privatization and fragmentation by market forces dilute debate and controversy; on the other side, the formation of provisional new alliances across multiple identities and nations opposes the corporate transnationalization of the globe and nationalist wars of genocide.

We ricochet between both ends daily. These are difficult and demanding times for everyone, no matter where we are located and no matter what we do. These coiled politics and aesthetics of the new world order propagate volatile, problematized sites. Yet these same precarious sites can mold alliances from which new imaginings can emerge.

During the past decade, draconian reductions to federal and state arts budgets have eaten away at the noncommercial media sector in the United States. The infrastructures that incubate new cultural practices have been hobbled. Democracy—if defined as access to the means of production and to the production of engaged public spaces—seems suffocated by media transnationals larger than most nation-states.[1]

Transnationalization undergirds the twenty-first century. The transnational economy depends on flexibility and mobility, constantly mutating to changing social and political conditions beyond the borders of nation-states. It depends on new technologies such as computers and satellites to transmute the relationships between space and time, shearing capital from any location. It relies on media imagery/imaginaries. It is global.[2]

The transnational economy manifests a techno/media/political-scape.[3] Images are politics, politics are media, and the new politics are image/media. Work is downsized, deskilled, degraded. This ever-expanding transnational economy transforms identities into market segments, converting multiculturalism into a niche-market advertising strategy.[4]

In 1989, we witnessed the initial rumblings of the transnationalization of the entire media sector. Media merged across industries, forming behemoths that converged radio, cable, satellite, new digital media, film, video, and theatrical exhibition. The word *synergy* camouflaged conglomerization without any state regulation, operating beyond the scope of antitrust laws. Sony, the Japanese hardware producer known for creating the Walkman, bought Columbia Studios. Time bought Warner Bros. Later in the decade, Viacom purchased Paramount. Disney and ABC/Capital Cites merged. News Corporation bought Fox and branched out into cable and satellite.[5]

By 1998, this media concentration across national borders heralded the most intensive cross-media merger activity in history. Disney/ABC/Cap Cities and Time Warner/Turner now reign as the largest media combines in the world, spanning every continent and deploying nearly every media technology available. Always subsuming new technologies and new markets, they function more like empires than businesses.

Concurrently, 1989 saw not only the acceleration of media restructuring but also the precipitation of the global reorganization of media democracy. The decline of the economic nation-state drove the rise of destructive nationalism on every continent, from Rwanda to Bosnia to East Timor to

Mexico. The student protests for democracy and free speech in Tiananmen Square demonstrated the political power of low-end, accessible technologies such as the Internet, fax, and camcorders to move information across national borders. The fall of the Berlin Wall in Germany, the Velvet Revolution in Czechoslovakia, and perestroika in the former Soviet Union presumably opened up the East to democracy, permanently altering East-West relations. But ultimately, these momentous events unlocked Asia and the former Eastern bloc for Hollywood action-adventure films, multiplexing, the demise of national cinemas, and the end of state-supported culture.

Within our own borders, a series of civil wars commenced over race, class, sexuality, immigration, and gender. One of the most vitriolic and hateful attacks against the National Endowment for the Arts took place in 1989 when the NEA funded the posthumous Robert Mapplethorpe photographic exhibition. The Mapplethorpe episode underscored the depth of the right's offensive against sexuality, difference, and politicized art. Yet this infamous, heartbreaking case, which put a curator on trial and fueled demonstrations in front of art museums, was unfortunately only a smoke signal cautioning about an even more troubled future.

In the past decade, the situation has only worsened. Newt Gingrich and his congressional transnational corporate allies have campaigned against art in all its public forms. They have defunded the arts and demonized artists. Their offensive has constituted nothing short of a civil war against art made by white feminists, women of color, radical white men, men of color, gays and lesbians, the working class, the middle class, new immigrants, rural people, and the avant-garde—virtually everyone except privileged white males. It is a war against difference. As a consequence, independent documentaries are suspended within a constant struggle to revive and sustain our collective imagination.[6]

These various reorderings are not isolated. Together they paint a palimpsest of the new world order, with layers piled on layers, each shading the other. Economics, politics, and aesthetics fold into each other, sifting down differences, controversies, passions. Anything public—from museums to grammar schools, from national parks to public television, from film festivals to cyberspace—is auctioned off like suburban real estate to private enterprise. The collective and the public have shrunk into the individual and the private.

Documentary producers and media activists make a grave mistake if we only confront arts cutbacks without threading them with exponentially expanding transnationalization. Media scholars erase these massive changes if we disengage new complex forms of documentary from their social and political contexts. Media economists cannot decry the viral spread of market democracy to the former Eastern bloc, Latin America, and Asia without linking it to broadcasting deregulation and the severing of national support for public culture across the globe. The transnationalization of nearly all psychic, political, and aesthetic sites suffocates public culture and public spaces. The entire globe is up for sale, privatized. At the close of the twentieth century, privatization breeds not one meaning but many: the dismantling of the welfare state, the triumph of the market economy, a retreat into the self, and sitting alone at a computer sending e-mail rather than protesting in the streets.

So, to invoke novelist Toni Morrison, is there any space for an unofficial, samizdat culture of hope within this official culture of expanding transnational corporate empires and nationalist civil wars? Can independent documentary recover any place amid attacks against difference and increasingly inaccessible high technology?[7] What is to be done in the media arts field when Hollywood films like *Titanic* amass $200 million production budgets? And their computer-generated special effects cost more than the entire film and video budget for the New York State Council on the Arts?[8]

We need to resist the new world order that razes the arts and transnationalizes the econo/politico/aesthetic-scape. New alliances across differences and across borders are required. We need to rethink how we think about independent documentary: while functioning as a metacritical practice, it also produces histories as forms of historical agency.

In the decrepit remains of this degraded public sphere that demobilizes nearly all collective action, a new world image order of radical political documentary with newly hewn, pluralized aesthetic languages has bloomed, one where difference makes a difference. Nationalist wars and genocides are recorded so memory will not die. New technologies are appropriated. Corporate images are pirated and harvested. New producers remake our vision. Artists invent ways to work without grants. New spaces are squatted.

But perhaps most urgently we also need to aggressively, unceasingly take back public spaces for these new world image orders to flourish. We need to make space for difference, hybridity, and publicness. Independent documentary practice, then, produces places to mobilize larger communities and new imaginaries not yet considered.

However, a word of caution to the reader. My deployment of the term *independent film* in this volume does not align with contemporary popular culture celebrating "American indie film" as the nonsubtitled, English-only replacement for European and Latin American art films at the Sundance

Film Festival. Rather, I argue that the construct "independent film" marks a counterdiscourse to both transnational and nationalist media and their de facto privileging of commercial exchange values. Independent documentary functions as a zone of conscience and consciousness.

In 1981, the first year of Reagan's unraveling of the arts, the welfare state, and federal regulatory controls of media, the intensive economic and political restructuring engulfing us now was set in motion. Yet 1981 also represents a significant turning point for American feature-length narrative independent cinema, for it was in that year that these films first reached larger audiences in art cinemas and festivals.[9]

Nearly two decades later, the transnational media companies and their boutique distributors raid independent media, looking for low-budget work to attract new untapped audiences and large profit margins.[10] The independent narrative features so heralded by journalists and critics simply function as hip upgrades to the old B-picture system developed during the classical Hollywood studio era.[11] Once the elaborate sound mixes and special effects are stripped away, it is difficult to discern many significant distinctions between "indie films" and Hollywood studio productions.[12] Hollywood films and these independents are merely two sides of the same old/new global Hollywood: a perpetual quest for deals, dollars, and undeveloped niche markets.[13]

In contrast, this volume operates as a historical reclamation project for the term *independent film,* a rerouting of the current commodification of the term. My aim in this book is to revive independent film's oppositional political heritage of a committed documentary practice where the larger world matters.[14] But this resuscitation of radical independent film discourse and social activist practice should not be read as a nostalgic evocation of paradise lost, a time when politics and art served the more lofty ideals of social and political revolution. Rather, in this book I attempt to locate independent documentary within its historical legacies and its evolving futures in order to rethink how the dramatic contradictions of new global politics, new wars, new technologies, and new forms can recharge its purpose.

The works and movements discussed in the pages to follow envision public space as volatile and necessary. In these still-forming temporary places, works from different voices using a diverse range of aesthetic strategies can dislodge spectators, ideas, and pessimism. In this era of despair and isolation, these independent documentaries are resolutely works of hope.

As a political intervention and epistemological site, *States of Emergency* situates practices disenfranchised by transnational media corporations—radical political documentary as well as experimental forms, low-end as well as high-end technologies—at its center. As it decenters documentaries that circulate as part of commodity culture, this book focuses exclusively on documentaries that seek to remake public culture.[15] Consequently, I do not discuss here documentaries produced for venues such as the Discovery Channel, the Arts and Entertainment Network, or CBS, which secure ample space in *TV Guide* and sufficient airtime. Nor do I discuss big(ger)-budget documentary features that have attracted commercial distribution, such as *Roger & Me, Hoop Dreams,* or *The Thin Blue Line.*[16]

Instead, my aim in this volume is to restore public space to independent documentary practices positioned outside of the spheres of commercial exchange relations. These works operate within other, more oppositional networks of production, distribution, exhibition, circulation, and political struggle, necessary outposts that reject the silencing of discourse and dissent. Social, historical, and political contexts are inscribed and enfolded into these works. These documentaries cannot be categorized exclusively by genre, formal strategies, identity, mode of address, or content.

Rather, in these works difference makes a difference. Bodies—whose bodies and where—matter. In many ways, they are works at war. They battle the psychic numbing of commercial culture. They fire away at historical amnesia. They debunk hegemonic standardized visual norms circumscribing subjectivity. These documentaries seek to comprehend transnational economies and national imaginaries in order to dissect how they are both entwined.

States of Emergency is a political project to reclaim independent documentary as a fulcrum for producing reimagined radical media democracies that animate contentious public spheres. In this book, I examine the fissures between a series of contradictions: transnationalism and nationalism, the collapse of public funding for the arts and the rise of new forms of independent documentaries of difference, old technologies and new ones, realist documentary forms and more hybrid styles, political economy and aesthetics. I tentatively challenge more traditional ways of conceptualizing political documentary as having only one effective form, whether realist, modernist, or postmodernist.[17] I seek to interweave realms of independent media typically disconnected from each other by the spurious borders that separate genres, technical formats, argumentation, and aesthetic strategies.

Throughout, I interrogate how corporate transnationalization, together with changes in the conception and function of the nation-state, has systematically chiseled away public space. I examine how contemporary oppositional independent documentaries elaborate racialized, gendered, and sexualized discourses that destabilize the homogeneity of the nation with heterogeneity and hybridity. I trace how massive federal and state budget cutbacks in public arts funding—advocated by conservatives attacking postmodernism and marginalized discourses—have undermined the non-profit media sector.[18] Transnationalization, privatization, and deregulation of both public and private media structures across the globe have rewired the relationship between the nation-state and national culture. The national imaginary no longer requires the discourse of documentary and public affairs, what Bill Nichols has termed "the discourse of sobriety."[19]

In this volume, I analyze these pivotal changes in independent documentary film and video in this reordered and realigned post-1989 landscape. I argue that radical documentary practices graphing difference have been engaged in a civil war over the national imaginary: the vital and necessary link between adversarial documentary practices and reimagined democracies is endangered. I maneuver among the new political economies, the new histories, and the new theoretical constructs required for documentary to be rethreaded with pluralized democracies in the new world image orders of the new millennium.

However, at the same time transnationalization and alterations in national culture threaten independent documentary, new consumer technologies such as camcorders, digital imaging systems, and computers offer hope for democratization of access to production and for specification of cultural difference. In this volume, I explore how documentary practices deploy multiple technologies, aesthetics, and strategies to mount multifaceted counterattacks that invent new formations and create new ecologies for image making. In a break from earlier periods, the contemporary era utilizes a multiplicity of technologies, often in tandem—film, high-end video processing, satellites, cable access television, VCRs, computers.

This book is periodized not by the emergence of new documentary forms or technologies, but by the larger structures of global shifts in culture, the arts, and the new information economy precipitated by the overlapping global changes of 1989. It is a provisional undertaking to decode how these politics and aesthetics of the new world orders have transformed independent documentary in the United States in the post-Mapplethorpe, post-Tiananmen, post–Berlin Wall period. However, this periodization has a beginning, but no end point and no closure: this post–Cold War period is still ripening, not yet complete, itself a work in progress.

I have deliberately *not* imposed on this book a linear structure that advances chronologically from 1989 onward. The complexities of documentary practice within these new world orders demand a different organizational structure, a more open architecture allowing for layerings of ideas across chapters, for different kinds of probes into documentary strategies to unsettle and disturb smooth linearity, to produce cracks and openings.[20]

Rather than a unified chronology, the book is organized along the lines of a montage that brings forward ideas through collisions. Each chapter then serves as a form of hypertext to the other chapters, which circle back into each other and amplify different levels of discourses and practices.[21] The chapters advance from despair to hope, a structure adapted from many of the works analyzed.

In this volume I attempt to map some of the shifting topography of this new world image order. The book thus is organized into two parts: "Wars" and "Ambushes." This design suggests the political and social urgency of independent documentary during these times of turmoil. It also implies different levels of attack and counterattack, a multivocality of discursive moves and strategies.

In the "Wars" section, the first chapter examines how arts defunding has altered the political economy of the media arts landscape, in particular independent documentary. The two chapters that follow probe how documentary during this period developed new epistemological and aesthetic strategies to map nationalist wars both outside and inside our borders. These chapters traverse this global economic reconstruction of culture and the emergence of new forms of documentary counterdiscourse to bloody nationalism in Bosnia, Guatemala, Argentina, Chiapas, Vietnam, and the Gulf War. They also consider documentaries tracking civil wars within our own borders: Japanese internment, AIDS, health care, the Los Angeles rebellion, disability rights, homelessness, welfare rights. This section of the book also analyzes how experimental and formally innovative documentary forms—installations, digital imaging—rework the trauma of war through aesthetic interventions into psychic architectures.

The "Ambushes" section offers two interventions into these national and global media flows that detour emerging technologies in order to intervene into public discourse and national/transnational media flows. Whereas the first half of the book documents movements that are reactive responses, the second half looks at movements that are proactive ambushes, with one chapter assessing feminist camcorder formations on reproductive rights and the last chapter suggesting media piracy as a new form of political art.

States of Emergency performs an archaeology into practices of hope that break through these debilitating contradictions like flares in a storm. Postcolonial theory and multicultural feminist media and theory disrupt the anesthetizing of public cultures. Digital theory and practices alter the sobriety and stability of the real. New hybrid forms purge documentary realism, figuring sexualities and race as processes rather than fixities. Adversarial transnational work defies national borders.

Within this context, independent documentary desperately needs to abandon thinking in modes left over from the political and social struggles of the 1970s and 1980s in order to reinvent itself for the next century's formidable challenges. To decipher how to work in these new world image orders, we need reformulations of independent documentary. This is a nonnegotiable imperative.

We need to reimagine and reclaim public spaces with multiple technologies and pluralized ideas. We need to rescue collective will, energy, and passion from post–Cold War inertia. We need to denationalize documentary to create alliances across identities and nations. We need to pirate commercial culture to remake it. We need to remember that every contradiction is worth the conflict if something new can emerge.

New independent documentary strategies are required to expose these sedimentary layers of contradictions. One book such as this can never complete a process that is collective and ongoing. At best, it can perhaps unravel a few of the pieces to unsettle the gloom descending upon us. Perhaps it can open up some new dialectics that will exceed its own arguments.

In the end, we must retake public space, from wherever we are, whenever we can. We need to experiment more with how we think about and do independent documentaries. Everyone needs to summon up the courage to fight back fearlessly with many strategies and weapons to spawn democracies of which we can be a part. Finally, we must connect with other people of passion so that we are no longer alone as we invent, each day, the new world image orders in which we will live.

Wars

[1] *The War on Documentary*

▶

The Siege

By the 1990s, the siege on documentary intensified. Religious right and conservative policy groups such as the Christian Coalition, Accuracy in Media, the American Family Association, the Christian Action Network, the Heritage Foundation, and the Center for the Study of Popular Culture created a force field to reduce independent documentary into an even more marginal practice. The cumulative effect of these conservative tidal waves was to weaken the foundations and wash out the multiple layers of public infrastructures, universities, and art institutions that support and champion noncommercial media.

The cutting off of public funding created a form of ideological and financial quarantine for independent documentary work such that speaking from any racialized, sexualized, ethnicized, or engendered location risked endangerment and annihilation. Not only did this pantheon of organizations unleash a hurricane-like storm that weakened all forms of documentary, it also cleared the path for privatization of all mass communication sectors. Public accountability was wiped out, and most public space of any kind was eradicated.[1]

This is much more than a culture war. It is a war between the white nation and everyone else. It is a war for public spaces in the midst of the deterritorializing strategies of the media transnationals encircling the globe with the Internet, satellites, and videos. It is a war between fantasy and history, between the commodities of the media transnationals and the public discourse of independent documentaries.

These various groups have unleashed a blitzkrieg on radical documentary practice, invoking universal values, artistic standards, and a reliance on the free market rather than federal funds. They seek to amputate documentary—and the multiple rewritten histories it propagates and mobilizes—from the nation and from the national agenda. They envision a documentary nation that has no independent documentary or critical news reporting at all—only entertainment programs produced by massive media transnationals.[2]

Transnationalization has utterly redefined the media landscape in the 1990s, changing the political relationships between independent political documentary and the state. Masao Miyoshi has defined a transnational corporation as a corporation that is "no longer tied to its nation of origin but is adrift and mobile, ready to settle anywhere and exploit any state including its own, as long as the affiliation serves its own interest."[3] Mark Crispin Miller has observed in *The Nation*: "Thus we are the subject of a *national entertainment state,* in which the news and much of our amusement come to us directly from the two most powerful industries in the United States (e.g. defense contractors and entertainment conglomerates)."[4]

In the post–Cold War era, transnational capital—concentrated so heavily in the media sector—has dramatically realigned three of the central tenets underpinning an oppositional, independent documentary strategy: access, diversity, and a democratic public sphere. With massive deregulation of public telecommunications across the globe, the role of communications in the formation of the unified nation has shifted from nation building through language cohesion toward dismantling the communications component of the nation and rebuilding communications within the corporate transnational sector, which has no need for the nation-state and is supranational. Rather than a nodal point for the formation of a national identity and the construction of a national imaginary of democracy, the real and the imaginary have collapsed into each other and now circle the globe as transnational consumerism. Yet national identities are still crucial and are still the sites where the conflicts between the global and the local are enacted, as the cases of indigenous people's land claims against nation-states and the fight for environmental rights in the face of transnational pollution demonstrate.

For example, broadcasting deregulation in many countries of the West since the revolutions of 1989—United States, Great Britain, France, Germany, Italy—has gutted the national imaginary, whether defined democratically, fascistically, liberally, or even along socialist pluralist lines. It has severed communications from the purview of the nation-state and affixed it firmly within the domains of the mobile transnationals. It moves capital and cultural capital, rather than opening up a space for democratic agendas to redefine and expand the nation.

As a result, the nation-state's need for and connection to culture has shifted and changed in the post–Cold War era. Given the fluidity of economic borders and the migration of cultural commodities that displace local production, whether in the United States or Mexico, there is less need for a culturally and artistically inscribed national identity that maps out a shared history. In some developing countries, for example, handicraft production has replaced agriculture as a form of subsistence when transnational agribusiness has altered the ecology of farming with monocrop production. Yet the handicrafts produced are designed to circulate within the global flows and by necessity are cut out of their historical and social contexts, where they function with more aura, as the traffic in Mexican Day of the Dead artwork in North America evidences. Hybrid forms of indigenous art that comment on globalization—such as anti-NAFTA sculptures or Zapatista dolls—do not carry the cachet of more nostalgic and "primitive" pieces. Rather than the truly radical role of artistic production to reimagine the world and open up new horizons, cultural production within transnationalization is an endless recycling of ahistorical mythologies disconnected from place, like the Arts and Entertainment Network's documentaries on great figures in American history or supposed exposés on the making of classical Hollywood film products like *Oklahoma*. In this terrain, independent documentary is truly an endangered species.

▶ _____

The Enemies List: Marxist Agitprop and Elitist Avant-Garde

Conservatives want art that speaks to such high ideals that anything real seems a throwback to Communism and old world orders. "PBS has become a purveyor of leftist propaganda, arrogantly unresponsive to its audience most of the year and unwilling to balance its so-called 'educational' messages—mostly delivered in documentaries and dramatic presentations—despite repeated requests to do so," asserts *Between the Lines,* a conservative newsletter reporting on media.[5]

The enemies list includes any producer, director, lobbyist, or scholar operating within what Cornel West has named "a cultural politics of difference."[6] From their positions as researchers for the Center for the Study of Popular Culture, David Horowitz and Laurence Jarvik have attacked Pamela Yates, producer of *Nicaragua: Report from the Front* and a longtime activist for independent producers; Deborah Shaffer, director of *Fire from the Mountain,* a film about the Sandinistas; Marlon Riggs, director of *Color Adjustment* and *Tongues Untied*; William Miles and Nina Rosenblum, directors and producers of *Liberators: Fighting on Two Fronts*

Marlon Riggs performing in *Tongues Untied* (1991). Dir. Marlon Riggs. Photograph courtesy of Frameline.

in World War II, a film about a black battalion that liberated Buchenwald in 1945; Ellen Spiro, for *Greetings from Out Here,* about southern gay culture; Barbara Abrash and Esther Katz, for *Margaret Sanger: A Public Nuisance;* African American feminist Kathe Sandler's *A Question of Color;* Jon Moritsugu's *Terminal USA,* about Asian Americans; Danny Schechter and Rory O'Connor, producers of *Rights and Wrongs,* a global human rights magazine series; Larry Daressa and Lawrence Sapadin, policy advocates and lobbyists for independent film; film scholars Michael Renov and Lauren Rabinowitz, for making arguments in support of Newsreel and the avant-garde; and any public television series associated with African Americans and civil rights, including *Eyes on the Prize, Passin' It On,* and *Making Sense of the 60s.*[7]

    This enemies list is not limited to individual producers. It also targets any organization or institution advocating critical investigative journalism, independent documentary film, or the nonprofit sector that subsidizes these endeavors: public television, the Corporation for Public Broadcasting (CPB), the National Endowment for the Arts (NEA), the National Endowment for the Humanities (NEH), the MacArthur Foundation, the Benton Foundation, the Ford Foundation, the Rockefeller Foundation, Fairness and Accuracy in Reporting (FAIR), the Association of Independent Video and Filmmakers (AIVF), the Independent Television Service (ITVS), National Public Radio (NPR), and Public Broadcasting Service (PBS) series such as *Frontline, P.O.V., Alive from Off Center,* and even *The MacNeil-Lehrer Report.*[8] This enemies list does not simply marginalize radical interventions into representation or inhibit new voices. Even more insidiously, by castigating these organizations for various kinds of mismanagement and political bias, Horowitz and Jarvik hope to undermine all the nonprofit infrastructures that sustain important counteroffensives and provide counterpublics to the newly privatized, deregulated, and conglomerated free market for media commodities.

What do all these women, African Americans, Asian Americans, Native Americans, gays, internationalists, and producers interrogating U.S. foreign policy in Central America, Asia, Africa, and the Middle East and institutions have in common? They displace the fantasy construction of the U.S. nation-state as conflict-free, essential, homogeneous, universal, and beyond reproach. These independent producers and artists spurn the totalizing phantasm of the nation as a symbol of unity. They make space for histories to replace history, for pluralized visual and aural languages to evict a common language into the realm of nonfunctional mythology.

These makers working outside the hegemonic commercial media formations question the borders of nation, rerouting its psychic, political, and social geographies. Of course, in the transnational media era, it is more difficult to determine the borders between nonprofit and commercial media sectors, especially when works themselves navigate through multiple dimensions of economic relations. However, independent documentaries sustain a possibility to open up more contestatory spaces that reject the essentializing strategies of nation building. They do not argue for an expansion of the nation with diversity, but for a total remaking of the form of the nation that insists that the social and political be layered locally, nationally, internationally, and transnationally.

Conservatives and members of the religious right accuse independent documentaries and public television of plunging into special interests, partisan politics, and a rejection of balance and objectivity. Conservatives argue that the space taken up by these independent documentaries gobbles up space for equal time for conservative viewpoints. At a time when economic transnationalization is transforming all media structures beyond national borders through a variety of new technologies, such as satellites, computers, modems, and fax transmissions, the conservative attack against documentary demands that it remain cornered within national borders and therefore neutralized. The conservative siege on documentary has not only defunded it, but wants to declaw it, delegitimate it, and detach it from democracy in order to maintain the chimerical construct of the nation-state as conflict-free multiculturalism that is necessary for transnational capital.

This attack polices our national borders, putting public culture into solitary confinement.

In 1995, celebrating the triumph of the Republican takeover of Congress led by House Majority Leader Newt Gingrich, the Center for the Study of Popular Culture, a Heritage Foundation-funded conservative think tank dedicated to attacking all forms of publicly supported culture, published an anthology of essays titled *Public Broadcasting and the Public Trust.* Edited by David Horowitz, an author and former host of a Pacifica radio show, and Laurence Jarvik, a Ph.D. in film studies and a former independent documentary producer, the book is a collection of essays reprinted from *COMINT,* a conservative magazine launched in 1990 to assail what the editors identified as the liberal, Communist-inspired, special interest, elitist, postmodernist coup d'état of public television in the 1970s and 1980s.

The book supplies detailed analysis of almost every critical and political documentary produced in the five years preceding its publication, from single programs to larger series. It accuses ITVS, established by Congress to stimulate independent production, of being an overblown, inefficient bureaucracy that caters to special interests and is unable to produce programs. In effect, *Public Broadcasting and the Public Trust* supplied ammunition to Newt Gingrich's famous January 1995 salvo to zero out and privatize public broadcasting, the NEA, and the NEH.[9]

Horowitz and Jarvik rewrite the history of public television as an insidious, leftist-inspired, Communist takeover of public funds promoted by liberal agendas set forward by the Kennedy, Johnson, and Carter administrations. These arguments are in line with many of the attacks on the arts in the past five years by various conservatives, ranging from Hilton Kramer to Jesse Helms, from the American Family Association to the Heritage Foundation. They constitute covert and coded attacks against the welfare state of the New Deal and Kennedy liberalism. They seek to dismantle the last vestige of the state that is connected to a larger notion of the public than consumerism, to reorder the state for integration with transnationalization that has no interest in a state that does anything more than open its borders to capital flows.

Horowitz and Jarvik accuse independent documentary producers of lack of balance and objectivity, deteriorating aesthetic standards, and alliances with radical organizations formed in the 1960s like Newsreel. Jarvik argues, for instance, that independents have committed a sin of misrepresentation and obfuscation of their agendas: "'Independent film' is really just another name for politically correct filmmaking—what was called in the '30's 'agitprop' and in the '60s 'alternative' or 'underground' media. It would be healthier to call its present incarnation just what it is—politically correct film—so that the taxpayers who pay for it would know what they're getting."[10]

Horowitz and Jarvik deploy a conspiracy theory, a tactic often identified with hard-core Marxist intellectuals in the Vietnam era, to demonstrate a concerted effort to warp the very foundations of the concept of the public. For example, Horowitz observes, "In fact, the protest culture that everywhere else had withered at the end the of '60s when its fantasies of revolution collapsed had found a refuge in public television."[11] In his discussion of the formation of ITVS, Horowitz asserts that "Congress had provided the extreme left with an institutional base in public television."[12]

For Horowitz and Jarvik, the revolutions of 1989 demonstrated two irrefutable historical truths: first, Communism and leftish politics had been extinguished across the globe, from Peking to Moscow to Prague, heralding the United States as the victor of the Cold War; and second, the triumph of the free market over any kind of state-supported enterprise showed how the very notion of the public was finally recombined with the freedoms of free enterprise. The demise of Communist states demanded the demise of the Communist-inspired structures within our own state.

Aimed almost exclusively at independent documentaries, which unevenly traverse the spaces between public and private, the state and the nation, Horowitz and Jarvik's argument is not just red-baiting, attacking these films for their left-wing analysis of U.S. politics; it is actually much more devious and geopolitically based. These authors accuse public television and documentary producers of operating under antiquated systems of thought found only under Communist regimes, which no longer exist. Their critique accuses these documentary producers of nostalgia for a world of right and left that no longer exists in the new world order of post-1989 global politics.

As such, their argument is that these institutions and works are trapped in an old world order fantasy that believes in a wider, more open notion of the word *public* that links democracy and diversity. They want the definition of *public* to shift into a consumer-oriented public accountability that sheds democracy for the marketplace and dispels diversity with universalism and standards, tropes reinvigorated from traditional nationalist fantasies. Horowitz, conducting a McCarthy-like witch-hunt for unreconstructed radicals who still believe in Communist ideals, pronounces, "The unchallenged proliferation of propaganda over taxpayer-supported airwaves in behalf of violent and extremist groups like the Panthers is a disservice to the American public, which pays for public broadcasting, and a violation of the laws that make public radio and television possible."[13]

In effect, Horowitz and Jarvik deploy accusations of an old-fashioned, outdated, nationally based documentary practice as a hangover from the Cold War to camouflage an assault against heterogeneity and difference. They use Communist bashing to defend the white nation without ever invoking the word *white*. They do an end run around deconstruction: they revive the binary opposition between capitalism and Communism, in itself a fantasy of stabilization, as a cover for race, sexuality, and gender bashing. In other words, their arguments insinuate that the new gender, sexual, and racial identities worked through in these various documentary practices are not new but old, remnants of the Cold War that have no room in the new post-1989 nation.

This strategy of lambasting heterogeneity through reinstalling couplets of East/West, Communist/non-Communist, standards/no standards is also located at the level of representation and form. Whereas independent documentary practice in the 1990s has been increasingly identified with hybrid forms that reject boundaries between genres and nation-states (for example, works by Trinh T. Minh-ha, Marlon Riggs, Rea Tajiri, Pamela Yates, Kathy High, Bruce and Norman Yonemoto, Philip Mallory Jones, Daniel Reeves), Jarvik separates independent film into two distinct genres that resuscitate film criticism from thirty years ago, before the systematic theories of psychoanalysis, Marxism, poststructuralism, and postcolonialism displaced auteur theory and connoisseurship.

He says, for example, that "'independent' films can be broken down into two basic types: agitprop and avant-garde. These are two sides of the same coin, as they are supposedly in opposition to capitalist Hollywood. The agitprop film contains revolutionary content, and the avant-garde film has a revolutionary form. Yet each of these conventionalized types are far less independent as *genres* than the despised Hollywood fare."[14] Jarvik's invective against independent documentary implies that official language should no longer be annexed to the state, but to free enterprise. Stated somewhat differently, the official language of the state is free enterprise media. By extension, from Jarvik's perspective, the unofficial, samizdat languages of political mobilization and formal experimentation have contaminated the mangled remains of state-supported official language.

▶

Independent Documentary: Marked for Death

Independent documentary's cultural and economic marginality has made it vulnerable to attacks by conservatives and the religious right for lack of objectivity, balance, and fairness and for an insistence on localized identities. Conservatives in Congress have tried to amputate public funding from documentary, always a politically contentious site. They argue that there is no longer a need for federal support of noncommercial media: such media should compete in the marketplace of the multichannel universe. They maintain that specialty channels such as Discovery and Arts & Entertainment now provide programming alternatives.

Critical, investigative documentary production has become extinct on cable television and at the networks; its remains, like those of the dinosaurs that have deteriorated into fossil fuel, are buried deep beneath the surface. Theatrically released feature-length documentaries, although making some inroads into commercial exhibition, often reproduce a realist style that focuses on the triumph or wackiness of unique individuals who flaunt overwhelming social and psychoanalytic structures.

Reviving a very traditional American trope of individualism that retains a homology to narrative film in its deployment of characters in whom larger social and political structures are condensed, most of these films do not critique larger governmental instititutions, policies, or national social and political agendas, nor do they seek to spur debate or controversy about the composition and viability of the nation. Films such as *Unzipped, Truth or Dare, Hearts of Darkness, A Brief History of Time, Crumb, Hoop Dreams,* and *Heidi Fleiss, Hollywood Madam* present a structure that is essentially a realist narrative garnished with postmodernist stylistic flourishes—disjunctive editing, mixed media, dramatic interventions. They do not imagine new social spaces, but rather affirm unique individuals— whether they are successes as in the case of Stephen Hawking or failures like Heidi Fleiss—as canny navigators of a basically unchangeable social and political landscape.

Frequently, these theatrical documentaries repress their connection to the real and to any form of nonlinear critical analysis by renaming themselves nonfiction, an example of using a negation to affirm allegiance to the tropes of classical realist narrative. One distributor even asserted in a 1996 *New York Times* piece on a theatrical documentary and home video release titled "Smile When You Say Documentary," "'Documentary' can be the mark of death for a film."[15] Only Barbara Kopple's *American Dream,* which chronicles the devastation of the Hormel strike in Minnesota, and Michael Moore's *Roger & Me,* which assails General Motors for its destruction of Flint, Michigan, confronted American corporate power by tracing its impact on communities, workers, and families.

Independent documentary, then, has become almost solely defined by the publicly funded and nonprofit sectors, two areas of national culture that argue that the state has a larger social and psychic function beyond its economic and regulatory supports for the circulation of transnational capital. Even to imagine independent documentary in the 1990s and beyond requires thinking through how public institutions can be structurally organized to support work outside of the market. When the national imaginary is not explicitly tied to the operations of the state, more particularly so in the context of transnational capital, where the functions of the state are being reduced to performative, symbolic, and instrumental functions, then culture's imperative is to float in a fantasy world articulated exclusively in the realm of the symbolic.

Although documentary constituted less than 1 percent of the box-office gross for commercial films for 1994, the amount of discursive space its warriors and enemies occupy in Congress, in the press, and in conservative and liberal think-tank publications by far outperforms conventional narrative film.[16] The question is, Why does documentary—a marginal area of film in the commercial as well as the scholarly sense—occupy so much discursive space during the post-1989 era?

Documentary—more than Hollywood narrative film, performance art, theater, or photography—signals the dissolution of the universal nation and its narrational strategies through its location within contestatory newly emerging identities and social collectivities. As Bhabha and others have demonstrated, the nation as a symbolic articulation of a mythologically hewn, ancestral common history depends upon the uninterrupted linear progression of a realist narrative that promotes identification and unification simultaneously, turning the multiple into one.[17] Through realist strategies that confirm social orders as well as limit psychic imaginaries, the novel stabilizes heteroglossia and multiplicities within realist strategies. It functions to narrate the nation as an imaginary space that contains competing discourses and subjects rather than provides space for them to rearrange the social order along less realist lines, as in the case of such postcolonial novelists as Salman Rushdie, Gabriel García Márquez, Chinua Achebe, or such postcolonial filmmakers as John Akomfrah, Ngozi Onwurah, and Haile Gerima.[18]

In contemporary documentary film and video, the explanatory function displaces and often reorganizes the realist narrative through a series of interruptions, jarrings, historiographic interrogations, and psychic reversals. History is not so simply pluralized; it is broken up into histories that create new social spaces and new social imaginaries. Much new documentary work therefore has insisted on an expanded formation of nation at exactly the time that transnational capital has required only an essentialized, symbolic nation.

Congressional debates, political targeting by conservatives, geopoliti-

A gay Southerner describes life as an out male in the South in *Greetings from Out Here* (1993). Dir. Ellen Spiro. Photograph courtesy of Video Data Bank.

cal restructurings in the telecommunications sector, and new technologies have turned documentary into a bloody political battlefield where the casualties are mounting daily in large and small, visible and invisible ways. It is on the discursive and institutional site of documentary where fantasies of the white, bordered, homogeneous, and stable nation are being dismantled and renegotiated by media work and institutional practices founded on racial and gender differences that interrogate the patriarchal state and its power. If it is to survive in its politically aggressive, analytically muckraking, and psychically disturbing variety, independent documentary needs public funding and public spaces—in short, publicness on multiple fronts and formulations, from access to debate, to argument, to set-asides, to protection from privatization, to the development of new imaginative zones.

This is a war over a discursive territory, a war over how the public spaces of the nation are defined and mapped, a war between the faux homogeneity of corporatist multiculturalism that absorbs and vaporizes difference and a radical heterogeneity that positions difference(s) and conflict(s) as a core of contestation over identity with frisson as its modus operandi. This is a globalized war between the imagined white nation-state and the new formations of diaspora, new subjectivities, exile. On this issue of the disruptions of emerging identities and locations, Homi K. Bhabha writes:

"The borderline work of culture demands an encounter with 'newness' that is not part of the continuum of past and present. It creates a sense of the new as an insurgent act of cultural translation."[19] It is a war about whether public spaces will exist: whether they will be zones of fantasy projections for the transnationals or zones of contestation, insurgency, and community with access to the means of production and distribution.

Culture has always mattered to the nation-state as a symbolization of unified identity and values. In the transnational era, culture matters, but differently and in new ways. Culture is no longer the place where the nation-state imagines and revitalizes itself away from the instrumentality of capital; it is now the place where transnational capital defines itself. In other words, culture has been subsumed by transnational capital, which fuels and drives it with computers, television shows, Hollywood films, faxes, the Internet. In older formations of the nation-state, culture was where dreams and nightmares, fantasies and realities, resided. In the current debates about noncommercial culture, it is precisely these dreams and nightmares refusing commodification that resurface as problematic sites, eruptions from older orders but in newer formations. The current wars are about whether the cultural and discursive space of the nation will become an empty signifier, a fantasy projection of community held together with narrativity, or whether it will be redefined by new makers, new practices, and new technologies as a more transnationalized space within which the nation itself is reconfigured as a fluid site of contestation, debate, and engagement with the emerging transnational globe. They are also wars between documentary form that relies on standardized and deductive structures that link them to the nation and new configurations that problematize textual, generic, national borders and seek transnational webs beyond the national.

The patriarchal nation writes itself by maintaining borders between inside and outside, inscribing bodies in blood, torture, and erasure, as Zillah Eisenstein has argued.[20] These documentary works and institutions eject the border and all the exclusions it implies. Trinh T. Minh-ha notes: "What is at stake is not only the hegemony of Western cultures, but also their identities as unified cultures. Third World dwells on diversity; so does First World. This is our strength and our misery. The West is painfully made to realize the existence of a Third World in the First World, and vice versa."[21]

As transnationalization across countries and borders has reduced the nation to fantasy representation and condensed the notion of the public into a nostalgic mythology, cultural practice itself has assumed center stage as just about the only function left for the nation. The consummate political activity of the United States has become its ability to manage how it narrates itself, a form of onanism that partially explains why the culture wars—particularly over documentary—have occupied so much discursive space. Because the nation is always in part fiction, all nonfictions are threatening. This new narration of the nation-state has been integrated in complex ways with a new form of economic transnationalization, specified by some of the most intensive media concentration activity across diverse industries of the past hundred years and the intensification of the mobility of capital. Documentaries repudiate the fictions of the nation with the real, the document, the historical, the particular, and it is these negations and refusals that provoke the offensives to close down all public cultures.[22] Bhabha contends that "counternarratives of the nation that continually evoke and erase its totalizing boundaries—both actual and conceptual— disturb those ideological manoeuvres through which 'imagined communities' are given essentialist identities."[23]

The fronts on which this war is waged also look different from those of earlier periods. Previously, radical media were defined in a series of oppositions, with independents located within alternative media in opposition to the corporate networks, a conflict pitched between the commercial and the noncommercial, between the monumental, historical sweep and breadth of public interest and the limitations of private interests. But in the 1990s, these very oppositions that have guided the independent film community and alternative media are being altered dramatically by increased concentration across industries in telecommunications; by a more fluid, layered transnational media flow; by the emergence of media products and telecommunications technologies as central players in geopolitical trade negotiations, such as GATT; by deregulation and privatization of public telecommunications across the globe; by proliferation of new technologies that loosen up the borders between high- and low-end productions and create new, unregulated public spaces; and by aggressive federal and state arts defunding.

A congealing of several important historical factors emerging during the 1980s created infrastructures and political spaces for the emergence of these new practices: federal mandates for funding for independents and diversity on public television; an increase in support for alternative arts institutions by state and local arts agencies; an explosion of new technologies that remapped access and distribution, such as VCRs, camcorders, satellite, and cable; mandates for diversity in the grant-making process for individual artists and organizations that stimulated a whole new set of producers; and the solidification of identity politics constituencies with specific political needs, structures, and demands for representation, such as feminists, gays and lesbians, Latinos, African Americans, Asian Americans, and Native Americans.

▶

1989: Before and After the Inquisition

The year 1989 marked the beginning of a new historical period for the triad of politics, democracy, and documentary. This watershed year re-organized and ruptured multiple fronts on a global scale: at the same time Tiananmen Square and the democratic revolutions in Czechoslovakia, the Soviet Union, East Germany, and Romania ostensibly created the tri-umph of democracy and the end of Communism, cutbacks in affirmative action programs in the United States seemingly closed democracy down, as Eisenstein has forcefully shown.[24]

In 1989 we also witnessed the eruption of controversies over federal funding of sexually explicit art in the United States, stimulated by the reli-gious right and by conservatives in Congress. The American Family Asso-ciation and Senator Jesse Helms questioned why the National Endowment for the Arts would fund public exhibitions of the works of Robert Mapple-thorpe, Andres Serrano, and Annie Sprinkle, invoking the moral purity of the American nation.[25] In his discussion of what he perceived as an explo-sion of "anti-American, anti-Christian, and nihilist art," Patrick Buchanan, the right-wing media pundit and sometimes presidential candidate, an-nounced, "Just as a poisoned land will yield up poisonous fruits, so too a polluted culture, left to fester and stink, can destroy a nation's soul."[26]

While images of protesters cascading over the Berlin Wall flooded tele-vision screens, representing the reunification of Germany as a popular de-mocratic movement, the discourse on arts funding in the United States was attempting to erect a symbolic Berlin Wall between art and politics to fend off gays, women, and ethnic minorities who had entered the once white male elite venues of art and destroyed the border between high and low art. For example, Maureen Dowd noted in the *New York Times*, "The un-easy coexistence of art and politics has temporarily collapsed, and it is not clear how the two sides will restore a balance in which the arts can have freedom of expression and the politicians can exercise control over the use of tax dollars."[27]

Independent radical documentary nearly always straddles art and poli-tics, nation and identity. In the post–Cold War era, the political position of documentary has intensified as nations reorganize themselves for the new world order of globalization. For example, when Mikhail Gorbachev began to open up the relationship between the state and the economy in the Soviet Union through perestroika, he enlisted cultural glasnost as his engine, particularly documentary practices in various Soviet states in multiple languages rather than exclusively in Russian. Glasnost's greatest impact was not felt by taxi drivers or farmers or miners, but by documentary producers in the state-run film and television studios. It was documentary productions that advanced the openness of the new Soviet state, rummaging through repressed archives of images to excavate history, reviving memory and languages other than Russian, exploring youth and minority cultures, and searching for ways to revive a concept of individuality and selfhood seemingly exiled from the more rigid Communist regimes.[28]

In Gorbachev's Soviet Union, state-financed documentary was the symbolic motor signifying democracy. Perhaps the most memorable project to emerge from this era was the highly touted *Glasnost Film Festival,* a collection of new Soviet documentaries that were more Flaherty than Vertov in style that toured the United States via theatrical distribution and home video between 1988 and 1990.

But many writers ignore that 1989 was also the year of some of the most intense transnational media merger activity in history, signaling a shift in the organization of communications along industry-specific lines into more synergistic global firms crossing technological and national borders. Time Inc. spent $14.1 million for Warner Communications, forming the largest media conglomerate in the United States. And the Japanese-owned hardware producer Sony bought the Columbia Pictures film studio for $4.8 billion.[29] Most of these new media conglomerates depended on globalization, multiple media technologies and industries merged within one supranational firm, and new information technologies.[30]

However, most discussions of 1989 separate the politics of the democratic revolutions from the struggles over culture and representation within the United States, framing them as inverses of each other, reinstituting Cold War binaries but this time by displacing them into separate realms of politics and culture—the changes in Eastern Europe are seen as political; the state repression of sexualities in art in the United States is figured as a cultural battle about identity politics.

Yet these observations neglect one other extremely significant event of 1989 in which the borders separating culture, politics, and nation-states were unraveled in a deadly way: the *fatwa* by Islamic fundamentalists in Iran against Salman Rushdie for his postcolonial novel *The Satanic Verses.*[31] In a *Wall Street Journal* piece responding to the congressional outrage at the federal funding of a Robert Mapplethorpe photographic retrospective, novelist John Updike was one of the few commentators in the United States to argue for an international outlook in analyzing the reasons for defunding the arts, attacking controversial art, and discrediting experimentation. He pointed out, "The most dramatic government sponsored event in arts and letters in the past year has been the promulgation by a head of state, the late Ayatollah Khomeini, of a death sentence upon the writer, Salman Rushdie, who was not then and had never been a citizen of Iran, but who instead was writing postmodernist fiction within the United Kingdom."[32]

The Rushdie affair, as it is now dubbed by media commentators, constitutes an important signpost for any understanding of post-1989 struggles over documentary in the United States because it demonstrates how relationships among the local, national, and transnational condense both a symbolization and a productive relation. Slavoj Zizek has analyzed how the symptom, as opposed to the more rigidified and inert construction of fantasy, materializes symbolic overdeterminations. He says, "What was foreclosed from the Symbolic returns in the Real of the symptom."[33] He analyzes how the wreck of the *Titanic* figures as a symptom elaborating the instabilities of immigration, labor unrest, nationalism, and changes in the structures of world capital. The Rushdie affair, then, can be read as a telling symptom wherein psychic and political fractures in the United States between documentary and nation, between the imaginary and the real, between nation and globalization, have been repressed in the symbolic register only to return in the real through a veritable inquisition into difference figured as death.

The *fatwa* against Rushdie shows how new aesthetic forms that refuse the standardized narration of realist temporal continuity and migrate between narrative space and the fantastic blast apart boundaries in dangerous ways, unleashing often murderous forces. These new forms of discourse and dream threatened the imaginary nation of Islam with hybridity marshaled on all fronts: aesthetic, geographic, narrative, psychic, structural. Reflecting in 1990 on the *fatwa*, Rushdie explained, "*The Satanic Verses* celebrates hybridity, impurity, intermingling, the transformation that comes of new and unexpected combinations of human beings, cultures, ideas, politics, movies, songs. It rejoices in mongrelization and fears the absolutism of the Pure."[34]

In the Rushdie affair, England, where the novelist resides, cannot be separated from Iran, which issued the death threat, nor can it be severed from the novel's aesthetic strategy of postmodernist pastiche of Englishness, Indianness, and Islam that redefines England. And the literary allusions to Indian film, Indian literature, and Western popular culture cannot be separated from the national literatures of English. The silencing and confinement of Rushdie for more than seven years cannot be separated from the closing down of public culture on a global scale.

Writing in a powerful collection of statements from Arab and Muslim writers titled *For Rushdie,* Anouar Abdallah recognizes the larger significance of the Rushdie affair: "Thus, the fatwa of Khomeini reveals to us the planetary character of this new tyranny that sets aside the laws and customs of other states."[35] In the same collection, echoing this theme of state tyranny and inquisitions of art, Etel Adnan remarks: "Above all, people have the right to their own lives and their own possessions, whether these possession are intellectual, ethnic, or religious. The time has come for dialogue to replace repression; the time has come for all the various inquisitions to disappear."[36]

The contradiction and interconnection between public broadcasting and its mandate for difference and the takeover of cultural production by transnational corporations working beyond borders of the nation-state also signify the enormous political and historical shifts of 1989. They are not simply a theoretical puzzle, but registers of how these larger geopolitical events and situations were worked through within the United States as an inquisition into the very coupling of the nation and culture. The local, the national, and the transnational are no longer distinct; rather, they now constitute different currents of a larger global flow.[37]

In 1988, two federal acts were passed within months of each other that graphically illustrate how issues of difference cannot be analyzed without a transnational context. To use Zizek, they double as symptoms of each other, showing how issues of the preservation of the national and the end of the national envelop documentary practice similarly. Both laws went into effect on January 1, 1989, anticipating the larger revolutions to follow.

On August 23, 1988, Congress passed the International Trade Act, which supported global growth for telecommunications trade. Less than three months later, on November 7, 1988, the 100th Congress passed the Public Telecommunications Act of 1988. This act was perhaps the most important piece of legislation for the independent film community in the past twenty-five years. It established the Independent Television Service to expand the "diversity and innovativeness of programming available to public broadcasting." This independent production service was established "for the production of public television programs by independent producers and independent production entities."[38]

The International Trade Act, on the other hand, recognized that the telecommunications industry would not survive within a national territory alone. The act recognized that "rapid growth in the world market for telecommunications products and services is likely to continue for several decades" and argued for "undertaking a program to achieve an open world market for trade in telecommunications products, services, and investment." The act acknowledged that telecommunications exports to foreign countries were inhibited by government intervention and restrictive trade practices, even though deregulation and divestiture liberalized U.S. trade with the rest of the world.[39]

Ushering in dramatic changes in the structure of private and public communications, these two laws should not be read as opposites of each other, where the Public Telecommunications Act constructs the nation as public and nonprofit and the International Trade Act confirms media as private and global, disintegrating trade barriers. Instead, they function more like a palimpsest, laminated into each other rather than distinct.[40] Like pictures painted over other pictures in layers, these laws imprint the nation and the globe by writing over and erasing each other within one frame, differing representations of the role of the state that bleed into each other. The inquisitions unleashed around independent political documentaries in the post-1989 era—whether on funding, visuality, distribution, or piracy—have concocted a fiction where the nation and the globe are distinct, while the documentaries (particularly the funding controversy surrounding the public television series *Globalvision*) in question have all cultivated the edges of the palimpsest between the nation and the globe, insisting on their blurred borderlands as an important political site in the post–Cold War era.

▶─────────────────────────────────────

ITVS and Documentary: Public Space for (an) Almost Extinct Public Affairs

For many documentary activists in the 1970s and early 1980s, it was almost unimaginable to think of defending public television, which was considered a bastion of bland, overly conservative, well-modulated, stultifying middle-class programs with no room for aesthetic innovation, political intervention, or connection with communities. The operative strategy involved using community-based, guerrilla media work to mobilize viewers to action, a strategy that developed out of the antiwar movement, the women's movement, and the black power movement.[41]

Although the Association of Independent Video and Filmmakers had lobbied intensely for increased funding and access for independents in the late 1970s and early 1980s, it did not focus its organizing energies exclusively on public television. Instead, it launched a multifront assault to open up film festivals, community centers, alternative media centers, cable access, tax incentives, film distribution, and even film schools to independent production outside of the networks and Hollywood by creating an alternative media system.[42] By the 1990s, the politics of culture were different. Media activists were defending the NEA, the NEH, and public television against total extinction.

But the politics of independent production—especially documentary—changed significantly by the end of the 1980s. A whole series of alternative infrastructures were firmly established with federal and state arts grants as well as with money from the Ford, MacArthur, and Rockefeller Foundations: distributors such as Asian CineVision, Visual Communication, Women Make Movies, Black Filmmakers Hall of Fame, Cine Acción, and the National Asian American Telecommunications Association, to cite only a few. As B. Ruby Rich has observed, "These groups were positioned to take advantage of eighties political life. The unprecedented emphasis on multiculturalism and the increased hunger of images of 'underrepresented' communities . . . created a space for new work and new practitioners."[43] The right would attack not just the films, but the emerging infrastructures fueled by state support.

By 1988, the only regularly scheduled program showing long-form, investigative documentaries on television—whether cable, the networks, or public television, whether nonprofit or for profit—was PBS's *Frontline*. Testifying before Congress during the reauthorization hearings, David Brugger of the National Association of Public Television Stations observed that public television offered "the most extensive schedule of regular and special public affairs programs on television, a schedule that includes *Washington Week in Review, Firing Line,* and *Eyes on the Prize.*"[44]

After nearly a decade of debate, lobbying, and testimony that independent producers required a separate producing organization to foster diversity and innovation, the Public Telecommunications Law of 1988 created a new, federally funded, separate infrastructure to create space for independent productions and mandated programming funds for minorities. This law created a public apparatus and funding structure that would be attacked by the right as a welfare program for artists and as a useless bureaucracy. Prior to this, CPB, PBS, and the independents, especially documentary producers, were locked in battles over how independent producers were defined and counted. The act installed a temporary truce. The 1988 act also required that the Corporation for Public Broadcasting assess the needs of minority, ethnic, and new immigrant populations, a provision that would also be attacked.

It is worth reviewing testimony from the hearings on the Corporation for Public Broadcasting in 1987 and 1988, precursors to the 1988 law, to see how documentary and public affairs programming were formulated as enterprises that expanded the nation through heterogeneity but were

Cover of the Corporation for Public Broadcasting's 1989 annual report, *Return on Your Investment*.

particularly vulnerable to extinction in the press toward commercialization, larger audience shares, and lack of long-term financing of public television. In his book *The Vanishing Nation: The Inside Story of Public Television*, James Day, past president of National Educational Television and WNET/ New York, describes the declining support for public affairs and documentary prior to the 1988 law. WNET's Independent Documentary Fund was discontinued in 1984. Conservative critics of public broadcasting in Congress increasingly unleashed charges of left-wing politics and lack of objectivity and balance against documentaries like *Tongues Untied*. The public television documentary series *Frontline,* established as a showcase for independent documentary in 1983, aired only about eight to ten films a year. Independent producers argued that a large percentage of the work selected was actually not independent, but produced by freelancers working for executive producers of the series.[45]

It is interesting to note that in the lengthy hearings, which produced nearly fifteen hundred pages of testimony and debate, the forces of conservatism were the Corporation for Public Broadcasting, the consortium of stations, and the Public Broadcasting System rather than right-wing think tanks. This cast of characters illustrates quite potently how the right's vociferous assaults on public television emerged only as a response to the political and economic restructurings of post-1989, when new producers and infrastructures were in place. In the 1987 and 1988 hearings, independents critiqued the PBS and CPB bureaucracies for operating as exclusively closed systems. However, producers as well as stations shared the ideas of the significance of the nonprofit, noncommercial sector and the urgency of protecting it, an ideology that would shift dramatically in the period from 1994 to 1996.

For example, Bruce Christensen, president of PBS, argued, "Public broadcasting is the only nationwide medium of communications organized for public service rather than private interest."[46] This issue of publicness was repeated over and over, an acknowledgment that space for public affairs had been chipped away. Lawrence Sapadin observed trenchantly: "For independents, public broadcasting represents the only major broadcast outlet for their work in this country. For the American public, public broadcasting is the only mass medium by which they can receive and appreciate independently produced programs."[47]

▶─────────────────────────────────────

New Cartographies, New Wars

The defunding of public television documentaries is not the whole story of independent documentary in the twilight of the twentieth century. Rather than documentary's simply flinging out a notion of democratizing communications through alternative media as an evocation of some idealized public sphere, the entire project of democracy itself has been contested by realignments and new developments in new communications systems, the state, and consumer culture. Democracy is no longer a given, it is an interrogation. There is not one democracy, but multiple democracies; there is not one form of documentary, but multiple documentary practices. Coupling these new documentaries with a notion of democracies requires a new cartography, one that is almost three-dimensional—like a hologram—composed of mobile, endlessly morphing layers of nation, borders, spaces, technologies, access, identities, transnationals, and pirates, where each layer is not parallel to any other, but all the layers are always in fact in relationships of varying impact and influence.

The new transnationalized media conglomerates—such as Disney/ABC/Cap Cities, Time Warner/Turner, Viacom, and Bertelsmann—materializing across the globe have defined both the post-1989 global economy and global politics as places where the divide between economy and representation has transformed into an almost totally symbolic landscape.[48] Consequently, the location adversarial media occupy within emerging geopolitical orders is quite different from the one they occupied twenty-five years ago: not as distinct, because it is sometimes subsumed as part of the transnationals themselves, as in the case of MTV's use of independent Pixelvision artist Sadie Benning for filler; and not as rigidly positioned in one visual, argumentative, or distribution strategy, because the mobility of imaging capital, people, and diseases (ATMs, *maquiladoras*, AIDS, illegal immigrants) across borders necessitates constantly shifting, provisional alliances between new politicized subjects occupying various ide/ntities and multiple strikes by a variety of media makers, ranging from low-end makers to quasi-independent commercial producers.

Independent documentary media are by-products of the social and political movements for social justice that have emerged over the last half of the twentieth century. These movements have opposed dominant, commercial U.S.-based media combines that restricted public debate, controlled access to production, operated within an industrialized mode of production, and neutralized political conflicts in the guise of objectivity and balance. Of course, the large media transnationals still retain vestiges of ideological control, but they have actually banked more—literally and figuratively—on loosening up strict hegemonic borders: ingesting racialized, gendered, sexualized, and nationalized differences, conflicts, and identities as new market segments to signal their vitality, hipness, and savvy.[49] Yet the transnationals' subsumption of identity politics and postmodern artistic strategies, while radicalizing form, mode of address, and subject positions, essentially eviscerates critique of the economic structures of transnationalism and political formations. Within this new symbolic universe, disjunctive editing replaces political debate. For most of its history, the epistemological foundation of alternative media assumed a greater diversity of voices would strengthen democracy and the nation, invigorating both with vigorous debate, public agendas, and social accountability. From about 1960 to the mid-1980s, when the three major television networks enjoyed nearly impenetrable monopolies on news and public affairs programming, it made political sense to think of independent documentary within the binary oppositions of dominant versus emergent, corporate versus nonprofit, bureaucratic versus autonomous, public versus private. The networks' exclusionary practices and ideological blackouts on Vietnam, El Salvador, civil rights, feminism, and AIDS activated independent media to expose omissions, elisions, and absences.

With the onslaught of corporate downsizing of the news, the dissolution of international news bureaus, and the demise of long-form, investigative documentaries on commercial television, documentary and public affairs programming are truly endangered species.[50] Congressional conservatives seeking to defund public television and especially public affairs programming frequently cite the Arts and Entertainment Network and the Discovery Channel as examples of how the marketplace has supplied diverse programming. However, despite celebrity profiles, historical documentaries, and wild-animal programs, these cable channels have for the most part assiduously avoided not only controversial programming, but anything resembling investigative public affairs documentary. Independent documentary has survived only by migrating into the public sector of art museums, film and video festivals, and public television. It is now almost entirely independently produced, and it is threatened with extinction as public culture in all forms is aggressively defunded.

The argument for independent production depended on a definition of the independent documentary community as significantly different in content, style, argument, textual practices, and institutions than its more bureaucratic and corporate foes: if they were tainted by profit, independents were anointed by purity. The very definition of independent media depended upon their offering up the structured absences of dominant media as interventions: dissent, voices and bodies made visible, critique, exposés, hidden histories, revisionist histories.

Independent media until about 1989 were constantly framed as a democratic and national given, where public arts funding and public television would salvage democracy by balancing out and supporting those voices denied access by the corporate agenda. They would expand and humanize the nation. There were always skirmishes over ideology. On a philosophical level, the term *independent media*, Kobena Mercer and others have pointed out, is a bit of a misnomer, an easy opposition of corporate and commercial versus independent and virtuous. Independent media in the United States have for the most part depended on infrastructural support from public funding and the stimuli of grants from liberal-minded private entities such as the Ford, Rockefeller, and MacArthur Foundations. They have always performed a sort of triage on a deteriorating democracy, rehabilitating the imagined nation with diversity. But this process of resuscitation is not without its own border wars over who speaks, how, and in what exhibition venues.

▶───

From Imaging to Imaging Space

The new politics, technologies, economics, and competing publics molding the last decade of the twentieth century have transformed independent documentary and the war against it. It can no longer be understood as merely a generic set of texts unraveled for formal complexities, structural nuances, political ideologies, and rhetorical organization. New documentary practices, reformulated older social and political formations, and the collapse between politics and culture have established a new media landscape. Independent documentary has been converted into a land-mined political space: the homogeneous, stable nation has been exploded, fortified, bombed to pieces, derailed, emboldened, pirated, protected, appropriated, bunkered. New, emerging, and pluralized ethnic, economic, social, and racial identities have shattered the nostalgia for the old material objectivity of the nation as a unified, exclusively territorial entity. They demand that the nation be remade as something more fluid, open, permeable.

This war on documentary by conservative think tanks and Republicans in Congress in the 1990s is tactically different from previous political and aesthetic controversies opened up by radical media in the 1970s and 1980s, which often entailed controversial content critiquing the state apparatus, as in the case of films criticizing U.S. intervention in Vietnam, El Salvador, and Nicaragua. These new hostilities toward innovative forms of work, alternative infrastructures, and public funding demand more variegated, fluid, and complex tactics, even though they in some ways rethread older tropes on democracy, free flow of information, vigorous debate, participation, and access from earlier periods into new constructs.

Congressman Newt Gingrich and transnational media corporations arguing for deregulation of all telecommunications laws have waged a civil war against publicly funded documentary and public visual art, against art made by new voices in new ways for new constituencies emerging within the new world orders. However, this civil war against documentary and public funding for the arts must not be framed solely as a freedom of speech or censorship issue, a strategy conjuring up classical tenets of liberal democracy and the nation-state that presumes the vitality of the nation depends on a plurality of voices given equal weight.[51] The fight for survival in this civil war against the arts and public broadcasting must deploy different tactics because the nation itself is being reengineered, downsized, and streamlined by the economic and geopolitical forces of transnationalization and by the decline of public space. In this civil war, there are similarities to and differences from the old world order independent media formations. Although the debate about access to technologies and the proliferation of diverse voices and forms is similar, the political landscape of public spaces/public spheres has shifted considerably with new communication technologies like the Internet, the World Wide Web, and other digital forms and with the changing terrain for corporatized media as a result of transnationalization. The relationship between the "nation" and "culture" has shifted within global corporatism, repositioning culture away from a zone of psychic and political autonomy into a zone of consumption configured with capital.

The war has shifted from defunding disruptive texts mapping difference—Mapplethorpe, Serrano, Finlay, Hughes, Riggs—that typified the post-1989 period to abolishing all nonprofit, public sectors through privatization.[52] This move signifies a shift from representations that destabilize psychically and formally to an economic destabilization of nonprofit infrastructures, a transfer from the image to the space for images, from representation as psychic places to more multilayered, politicized, and specific locations. Within these enormous shifts and reorderings, political documentary has been especially vulnerable. This strategic transposition attempts to sever the state from cultural production and to open up new enterprise zones for economic privatization while it simultaneously redefines privacy solely in economic terms.[53]

Images themselves, which can be appropriated and reconditioned for nearly any political agenda in postmodernity, are no longer the only realm of contention because they alone can no longer be contentious. The globalization of telecommunications has disassembled an entire range of cultural locations and productive aesthetic spaces within the nation of the United States.[54] Transnational capital—now more integrated, consolidated, and mobile, almost circumventing national borders—has reduced the symbolic and regulatory functions of the nation. The psychic and aesthetic moorings of the nation seem more and more useless within a system of global exchange that no longer requires that culture affirm a national identity. The nation-state is therefore increasingly defined economically, rather than culturally, a sort of intravenous system providing life support for transnational capital. In effect, nearly all cultural space has become or is in the process of becoming corporatized.

Indeed, the attacks on public funding for the arts signify how wars over culture, defining who constitutes the nation and how it is psychically mapped, are unhinged by the mobility of transnational capital. For example, the *New York Times* coverage of nationalist civil wars spanning the globe—Bosnia, Somalia, East Timor, Palestine, Ireland—constitutes psychic displacement of the civil war against the nation/culture couplet. These bloody wars stand in as horrific fetishes for the aggressive attacks on and dismantling of public funding for the arts, humanities, and public television, in themselves inscribing a war about national borders but displaced onto different territories and sites. The battles around independent political documentary for space, definition, and survival resonate as yet another inflection of stamping out heterogeneity and instituting confining borders.

The horrors of the murderous civil wars in Bosnia and Somalia over difference, territory, and survival are actually here and there at the same time: the battles over documentary here rework the denial of difference there; the issues of deregulation and privatization of all cultural infrastructures here perform the nation as economy shorn from cultural practices.

To situate these assaults exclusively in debates about sexually offensive content (the *Tales of the City* controversy, *Damned in the USA*) and disruptive, postmodernist style combined with emergent subjectivities (the *Tongues Untied* case) is to play directly into conservative agendas. The right has shrewdly instituted a strategy of diversion from the enormous changes in the structural and representational spaces a reimagined democracy requires into a strategy of containment that deploys a circular semiotic analysis of standards. While these debates invoke endless interpretation without resolution, public supports for alternative and popular cultural spaces have been stripped away, sold off, or shut down.[55]

This is not to say that these debates about content and form are not important and incendiary aspects of documentary, nor is it to minimize in any way the homophobia these debates disguise. It is to suggest, however, that lingering in the domain of the image alone detours the discussion away from how those images are circulated, regulated, produced, and consumed in the first place. In effect, the right has recruited Baudrillard at face value and shifted all discussion of cultural production into manifestations of hyperreal simulacra read only as consumption severed from social signification.[56]

In his book *Cultural Capital: The Problem of Literary Canon Formation,* John Guillory elaborates how this shift from textual signification to social production needs to be confronted analytically. He describes how the canon debates on inclusion and exclusion of texts in English departments in the late 1980s not only reaffirmed an older fantasy formation of nationhood, but, in their focus on texts, neglected the potential destabilizations and much larger social and political restructurings that new identities and subject positions can launch:

> For literacy is a question of the distribution of cultural goods rather than of the representation of cultural images. From the point of view of such a materialist critique, it would seem that pluralism can only apprehend the history of canon formation as a history of consumption, the history of the judgment of cultural products. But if the socially unrepresentative content of the canon really has to do in the first place with how access to the means of literary production is socially regulated, a different history of canon formation will be necessary, one in which social identities are historical categories determined as much by the system of production as by consumption.[57]

▶ ───

The Enemies Within: Defunding and Privatization

In 1982, the Reverend Donald Wildmon, who in the 1990s assumed the directorship of the media-harassing American Family Association (AFA), observed that the new cultural struggle was "not with an enemy from beyond our shores," but against the enemy "inside our borders."[58]

More than a decade later, in 1992, People for the American Way, Channel 4, the Association of Independent Video and Filmmakers, Human Rights Watch, the Independent Feature Project, and several other media organizations filed a $4 million federal lawsuit against Donald Wildmon and his American Family Association for attempting to block showings of *Damned in the USA*, an impressively researched, interview-style documentary produced for Channel 4 in England. The film chronicled the controversies over the NEA's funding of sexually explicit and politically controversial art and the issue of censorship. It shows Christian fundamentalists fuming over the work of Mapplethorpe, Serrano, and Madonna.[59]

Produced by Paul Yule and Jonathan Stack, the film featured a panoply of luminaries from all sides of the culture wars of 1989: Dennis Barrie, Luther Campbell of 2 Live Crew, Senator Alfonse D'Amato, Senator Jesse Helms, Andres Serrano, and the Reverend Donald Wildmon. Wildmon sued the producers for $8 million, claiming breach of contract. Reinterpreting a release, he claimed his interview could be shown only outside the United States and argued that no future screenings of the film in the United States could proceed without his permission. By the time of Wildmon's suit, *Damned in the USA* had been broadcast to great acclaim in England, Sweden, and Spain. The lawsuit effectively froze out potential distribution and exhibition of the film.[60] The courts ruled in favor of the producers, a momentary triumph for access to images and public exhibition against the religious right.

Since Wildmon's nationalist oratory and subsequent legal action against a documentary exposing the pernicious ideology of arts censorship campaigns against gays and people of color, the political battles over culture and nation have mutated from a religious and family values-inspired war against perverse, blasphemous, and homosexual imagery into a much larger and more ominous liquidation of all the nonprofit infrastructures that support noncommercial film and video, effectively forcing documentary to go underground.

Since 1989, media centers and state arts councils, organizations that often fund documentary to counter its economic marginalization in the private sector, have been imperiled. The Massachusetts House Ways and Means Committee proposed slashing funding for that state's Council on the Arts and Humanities from $19.5 million to zero, and then compromised at a 50 percent reduction. The largest state arts councils—those in New York, Massachusetts, Michigan, Ohio, Pennsylvania, Illinois, Texas, Minnesota, and California—have had their budgets slashed as little as 5 percent to as much as 70 percent. Governor Pete Wilson proposed a 50 percent cut in the California state arts council's funding in 1993, with a zeroing out the next year. Because California has a large multicultural population, arts activists saw Wilson's proposal as essentially racially motivated. When the Minnesota State Arts Board slashed its grant from $82,000 to $15,000 in 1993, Film in the Cities, a well-established media center offering artists grants and low-cost access to film equipment, shut down.

The two states with the most funding for media, New York and California, have not only been subject to attacks over the past fifteen years but also house the most multicultural populations and the densest populations of media producers.[61] New York and California also receive the largest percentage of NEA grants.[62] As the first state arts agency in the country with a systematic grants program, the New York State Council on the Arts (NYSCA), formed in 1960 by a bill passed by the New York State Legislature, was the model for the National Endowment for the Arts five years later. A year later, in 1961, NYSCA inaugurated its first year of funding film. It was also one of the first state arts agencies to fund film and video in the early 1970s.

The New York State Council on the Arts, the largest state arts agency in the country, has lost 50 percent of its budget and cut its staff by one-third. Of all the state arts agencies, NYSCA funds the highest number of media arts organizations. NYSCA was formed to support individual artists working outside the studio system and to sustain New York as a national and international cultural center. The film and media division of NYSCA is considered a model for the funding of independent film, video, and installation, providing access for artists and sustaining exhibition and critical writing as part of the infrastructure. For example, it was the first arts council to fund video in 1970.[63]

NYSCA's reduced appropriations have had a ripple effect on the budgets of media arts organizations and put them on a financial precipice, organizations such as Asian CineVision, Experimental Television Center, Millennium Film Workshop, Squeaky Wheel, Hallwalls, and Visual Studies Workshop. Begun in 1971 as an environment for video artists to explore new video technologies, the Experimental Television Workshop ended artists' residencies in 1993, in response to that year's cutbacks.[64]

If democratizing access to art and media making over the past thirty years of the endowments has restructured the national relationship between outside and inside, then the concerted effort to defund art and media institutions has in reality been a purge of the enemies within to purify the nation not only of difference, but of the nonprofit organizations that provide access to the production and public exhibition of this work as well.

The National Endowment for the Arts has without question expanded arts institutions and democratized access to the arts since its inception in 1965. The number of state arts agencies has grown from five to fifty-six, public arts agencies in small towns number more than 3,800, and nonprofit theaters, orchestras, and opera and dance companies have grown by bounds.[65] In effect, federal and state arts agencies, contrary to the myths perpetuated by the religious right, actually fund a greater number of arts institutions than actual artists, an often contentious point in the arts community, where some argue the importance of funding artists in the face of conservative attempts to excise individual artist grants from endowments. However, funding artists, although vitally important, does not significantly alter access and exhibition relations in quite the same way as funding institutions. In his analysis of the battle over federal funding for the arts and the attack against sexualities, George Yúdice has observed that "the very structure of institutions is what is being challenged," transforming all the material supports for independent cultural practices: the means of production, distribution, reception, and publicity.[66]

In 1991, People for the American Way began publishing an annual volume titled *Artistic Freedom under Attack* in an effort to document arts censorship around the United States. Tracing the years from 1991 to 1995, these volumes evidence how the majority of art attacked has been in visual arts, photography, mixed media, and theater—work that often appears in public spaces such as campuses, malls, public parks and other facilities, and office buildings.[67] The volumes document that the religious right, in the form of such groups as the American Family Association and the Christian Action Network (CAN), has been behind a large number of the offensives against art. Three trends emerge. First, censorship on the local level has escalated year by year, often outstripping national uproars over public television programs or major museum exhibitions in their intensity and effectiveness. Second, controversies concerning art have for the most part revolved around issues related to sexuality, such as AIDS and abortion, as well as race and immigration. And third, a majority of the attacks against photography, film, and mixed media have not criticized the aesthetic merits of the works of art outright, but have targeted the infrastructures that exhibit them, such as schools, galleries, museums, and film festivals.[68]

The religious right's strategy has been to raise moral questions of obscenity, family values, decency, and morality about the institutions that support independent documentary rather than to question the films themselves. In 1991, conservative religious groups such as AFA and CAN as well as the Catholic Church attacked the NEA's support of the San Francisco Gay and Lesbian Film Festival, the New York International Festival of Lesbian and Gay Film (for screening a safe-sex video by DIVA-TV called *Jesus Christ Condom*), and the PBS documentary series *P.O.V.* (for scheduling a broadcast of *Stop the Church*, a video about an ACT UP and WHAM! [Women's Health Action and Mobilization] protest against New York City Cardinal John J. O'Connor's opposition to abortion, AIDs education, and homosexuality and for deciding to air *Tongues Untied*, Marlon Riggs's critically acclaimed film essay on the lives of black gay men).[69]

In 1992 and 1993, Hallwalls, an alternative media center in Buffalo, New York, was threatened with reduced local funding from the city government for controversial programming about AIDS and abortion. A right-wing organization demanded that Hillsborough County in Florida withdraw funds from the Tampa Gay and Lesbian Film Festival for showing documentaries about children and gays. And Donald Wildmon asked the NEA to withdraw funds for Film in the Cities, claiming it was using NEA grants to show sexually explicit films. It was later revealed that Wildmon's charges were inaccurate, as only one of the films on his list of five was in fact screened.[70] By 1994, with the Republican takeover of Congress, the attacks intensified even further, with concerted efforts not only to defund NEA, NEH, and the Corporation for Public Broadcasting but to enact legislation allowing for even more media merger activity and control over the Internet.

The attack against all public funding for art and documentary is not new; rather it is the culmination of efforts inaugurated by President Reagan

ACT UP protest against Cardinal O'Connor, from *Stop the Church* (1991). Dir.
Robert Hilferty. Photograph courtesy of Frameline.

in 1981 to eliminate public support for culture by defunding the endowments by 50 percent and decentralizing all federal funding to the states.[71]
Reagan argued that arts funding is tantamount to a "welfare program for
artists," a position congruent with his other position on getting the government out of public life.[72] Reagan's offensive was highly effective: between
1979 and 1989, the endowments experienced a 40 percent decline in financial resources, taking into account inflation and reduced appropriations.[73]

   Internationally, the United States maintains one of the lowest arts funding levels of any industrialized nation of the North. France and Germany
spend an average of twenty dollars per person and Canada and England
spend an average of thirty dollars per person, compared with approximate-
ly one dollar per person in the United States.[74] The United States also has
the shortest history of arts funding of any industrialized nation: the endowments were formed by President Johnson in 1965 during the height of the
civil rights movement and during the escalation of the war in Vietnam as
a "Cold War weapon."[75] In *Art Lessons,* a detailed history of the endowments, Alice Goldfarb Marquis argues that although the endowments were
initially set up to boost "national character" during the Vietnam War and
the Cold War, their authorization engendered intense debates about whether
federal funding would promulgate mediocrity in the arts and inhibit artistic
productivity, arguments rehabilitated thirty years later by the Heritage
Foundation.[76]

Ironically, the most exciting and productive partnership between the government and artists occurred during the Great Depression in the 1930s, when regional, local, and experimental arts production flourished under President Roosevelt's Works Progress Administration.[77] Consequently, it is not much of a stretch to read the arts defunding debate as a dismantling of the democratic welfare state epitomized in the Roosevelt, Kennedy, and Johnson administrations, a point made by various feminist political theorists in discussions of issues ranging from affirmative action to military spending and welfare reform.[78]

The attacks by conservatives in Congress and various religious and conservative organizations against the National Endowment for the Arts and the National Endowment for the Humanities that commenced with a fury over the Mapplethorpe photographic exhibitions in 1989 have, in almost every sense, been border wars about what and who can be inside the nation, and what and who should be outside. As contemporary media practices have rejected the division between art and politics as not only false, but a universalizing, racializing, and engendering position that delegitimates adversarial discourse and axes out new social subjects, these border wars have intensified. In these debates, the role of the newly redefined nation within transnationalization is to be attached both to the real of the economic and to the imaginary and the fantastic. In other words, these debates about art suggest that the nation-state should be shorn of political debate about the sites and positions of cultural practice. Increasingly, transnational media corporations and their cultural commodities are allowed inside the nation, whereas independent work by women, racial minorities, immigrants, manual laborers, children, disabled persons, and gays that provides inquiry into the formation of the nation and the transnationals is pushed outside, almost rendered invisible through its marginalization within domains marooned from the economy and public space.

The intensification of media merger activity has closed down access to public realms at exactly the same time new technologies are opening up access and dramatically reconfiguring the global media landscape itself. Slavoj Zizek, writing about the war in Bosnia, has contended: "Today's world is more and more marked by the frontier separating its 'inside' form its 'outside'—the frontier between those who succeeded in remaining 'within' . . . and the others, the excluded. . . . This opposition, not the one between capitalism and socialism, is what defines the world today."[79] The culture wars are misnamed. They are really civil wars. They are wars that are remaking the welfare state and its cultural practices into natural resources for transnationalization.

Independent documentary, new forms such as performance art and mixed media, and media arts have been on the front lines of the arts defunding movement in the 1990s. For example, Senator Robert Byrd of Virginia in 1994 proposed targeting specific grant areas such as theater and visual arts for reductions rather than the entire endowment. NEA officials countered that these cuts were aimed directly at controversial grants and would drastically diminish funding to individual artists by nearly 42 percent.[80]

Visual, media, and performing arts have been particularly vulnerable targets for a variety of reasons. These practices are both culturally salient and accessible to diverse audiences beyond white elites. The social and cultural position of media arts and performance forms differs significantly from that of elite art forms such as symphony and opera, high-cost endeavors in urban areas that receive the lion's share of public funding and attract high-profile corporate executives to their boards.[81] These practices all work to confound the borders between private and public, inside and outside, high art and popular art, nation and difference. They are propelled by civil rights, identity politics, feminism, and skepticism of traditional formats, foregrounding both the politics of representation and political context. Media arts also require high levels of funding compared with painting, opening up charges of misappropriation of taxpayers' money, even though the average documentary costs a fraction of what it takes to make a single Hollywood blockbuster. It is important to underscore here that traditional high-art, Eurocentric forms such as opera and symphonies, which demand high ticket prices, are located in major urban centers and attract the largest portion of corporate support, receive the major portion of endowment funds. Of all other categories of art, such as arts education, painting, and folk art, media arts receives the next-highest amount of funds.[82] Media arts, however, especially documentary, are positioned differently within the transnational corporate networks: they rarely attract corporate matching funds and are often dispersed to different geographic areas. Because they are associated with disruptive, polemical ideas rather than more neutral affirmations of higher aesthetic and less localized sensibilities, media arts, especially documentary, engage a political volatility and national instability of public space that conservatives want to defuse and derail.

Because of the labyrinthine structure of the nonprofit sector, ranging from state arts agencies to the endowments to the independent television service to private nonprofit organizations such as the Rockefeller, Ford, Lila Wallace, and MacArthur Foundations, it is nearly impossible to determine the exact configuration of grants supporting independent documentaries. The largest funder of documentary is actually the National Endowment for the Humanities, which typically disperses about $10 million a year, but almost exclusively to public television documentary series and individual shows. The National Endowment for the Arts funds more media arts centers than individual makers. The Independent Television Service, with an average annual budget of $8 million to fund independent production, is the largest funder of independent media in the United States, with direct grants to productions rather than institutions. Each of the members of the Minority Broadcasting Consortia (Native American Public Telecommunications [NAPT], National Asian American Telecommunications Association [NAATA], National Black Programming Consortium [NBPC], Pacific Islanders in Communication [PIC], and the Latino Public Broadcasting Project [LPBP]) has about $1 million available. However, it is important to recognize that not all of these budgets are awarded to independent documentary; out of these budgets these organizations must also fund experimental, narrative, and animated films.[83]

Most documentaries are funded over a period of many years, combining state, federal, and private foundation grants with a variety of commercial business deals ranging from private investment, gifts, and distribution and exhibition deals to sales to cable and foreign television. As of 1996, the average cost of a feature-length independently produced documentary—if all the crew is paid—was about $300,000. However, struggling to cover breaking stories and hard-pressed for capital, many independent documentary makers forgo their own salaries and ask crew members to donate their labor in the hopes of getting paid when the film gets broadcast or distributed. Of course, many, many independently produced documentaries are produced on low-end video for very low cost, by such organizations as Paper Tiger Television, Deep Dish T.V., DIVA-TV, and Not Channel Zero, and operate outside the grant system for individual productions. In contrast, a one-hour episode of *TV Nation,* which aired on NBC and Fox, cost about $500,000. Although HBO has emerged as a major producer of documentaries, it has tended to finance work that focuses on drugs, sex, and violence rather than on larger political issues. HBO's documentaries cost from $500,000 to $750,000.[84]

The NEA and NEH, however, provide a significant imprimatur to leverage other financial resources, although it is important to remember that the number of grants to producers with established reputations is still extremely small, averaging between twenty-five and thirty per year. For example, in 1993, the NEA funded thirty producers from a $725,000 program fund, a measly amount compared even to the catering costs for a Hollywood feature. Grants ranged from $10,000 to $50,000, a level of funding that would not cover the entire cost of a feature-length production. In the film and video production category, twenty-six grants were awarded to documentary, experimental, and installation filmmakers. Only four narrative productions, which often can more easily secure commercial foot-holds, received funding. Documentary and experimental forms, then, were clearly favored, reflecting the NEA's commitment to providing an antidote to commercial culture and demonstrating documentary's increasing marginalization within the nonprofit sector as well as its dependence upon that sector for sustenance.[85]

However, the NEA's 1993 annual report reveals that the major portion of media arts funds are directed not to individual producers, but to a variety of nonprofit institutions that support production, distribution, training, and exhibition. In contrast to the individual media artist category, the regional fellowships program administered by media centers received $350,000, Media Arts Centers received $1,512,000, National Services received $329,000, and the American Film Institute received $1,135,000, representing a total of nearly $3.5 million, more than four times the amount of money directed to individual makers.[86]

It is important to remember that many of these organizations support production through grant activities. However, these figures suggest that the conservatives' shift from discrediting publicly funded texts to defunding all the infrastructures in which independent work circulates will be even more devastating to the survival of public, nonprofit space. It is also important to superimpose another set of practices upon these federally and state-funded ones: there is a panoply of independent documentary producers who have elected or been forced to work outside of the federal and state funding apparatuses entirely, particularly camcorder activists working on projects about AIDS, reproductive rights, health, and labor.

Arts defunding is both backlash against difference and reorganization of the state's relationship to representation. A significant change has occurred since the Mapplethorpe and Serrano controversies of 1989, when the content of state-supported exhibitions was questioned on the grounds of obscenity, indecency, homosexuality, and religion. The expansion of arts funding to underserved communities in the 1980s—women, rural communities, labor, children, multicultural communities—dovetailed with two historical factors: the increased accessibility of new technologies such as camcorders, microradio, VCRs, and satellites that have democratized access to production and distribution and the emergence of a new multicultural immigrant demographics that shifted arts funding agendas.[87]

In the 1990s, numerous documentaries on a range of issues have been attacked as examples of a partisan misuse of public funds, collapsing the distinctions between political agendas and so-called objective journalism. The financing and production of these films often traverse several sectors of public funding, from NEA to NEH to public television. These films have

Sokly "Don Bonus" Ny poses with his amateur camcorder in a publicity photograph for *A.K.A. Don Bonus* (1995). Dir. Spencer Nakasako. Photograph courtesy of National Asian American Telecommunications Association.

included a wide range of identity politics, from *Tongues Untied* (black gay liberation) and *Stop the Church* (AIDS activism) to *Damned in the USA* (arts censorship), *Deadly Deception* (exposé of General Electric), *Building Bombs* (military-industrial complex), and *Days of Rage: The Young Palestinians* (the *intifada*).[88]

The religious right and cultural conservatives such as Hilton Kramer and Roger Kimball have put forward four arguments against public funding for the arts and humanities: elitism, lack of standards, welfare, and excessive bureaucracy. These categories operate as a smoke screen of populism, universal values, and aesthetic excellence that obfuscates a covert attack against multiculturalism and postmodernism, which are viewed as two similarly dense and arcane philosophical systems that debunk humanism. Media arts and the theoretical positions circulating within film and media studies have shouldered a large amount of criticism. Hilton Kramer has even expressed his abhorrence of the teaching of film in college classrooms, claiming that films and popular culture have usurped books.[89] Writing about the controversies concerning political correctness in his book *Public Access,* Michael Berube has argued that conservatives have attempted not only to cut off debate, but to reroute the flow of cultural capital away from new constituencies with charges of jargon, special interest, and destruction of values.[90]

Publicly funded culture has been charged with a curious brand of elitism. Interestingly, media activists have also accused the endowments and state arts agencies of elitism, pointing out that the largest federal and state arts appropriations, which are dedicated to opera, symphony, and theater, bolster white upper-class, urban, high-art forms that do not reach rural populations, the poor, and other underserved audiences at the expense of media arts and other new forms. Conservatives have redefined *elitism,* separating the term from its critique of class relations and remaking it into a moniker of art that attracts an audience. As Gene Edward Vieth has written in *The National Endowments: A Critical Symposium,* a collection of essays attacking the NEA and NEH published by the Center for the Study of Popular Culture, "As long as art is funded from the top down, it has no reason to appeal to anyone except the grant makers. This is bad for the public, and it is bad for art. . . . The current system of arts funding makes art elitist, trivial, and culturally irrelevant."[91]

In the arts defunding debates, elitism no longer signifies a critique of cultural capital and class insularity. The antidote to elitism is the consumer mass-media market and free enterprise, not democratizing access to the arts. In 1994, Newt Gingrich dubbed the NEA "a sandbox for the cultural elite."[92] Commenting on the Republican victory in 1994, Gary Bauer, president of the Family Research Council, asserted, "The liberal elite still controls the cultural high ground: the universities, the major media, Hollywood, Madison Avenue."[93] Almost a year later, in 1995, Gingrich proclaimed: "I don't understand why they call it public broadcasting. As far as I am concerned, there's nothing public about it; it's an elitist enterprise. Rush Limbaugh is public broadcasting."[94] When conservatives discuss the need for art to be "popular," conforming to the preferences of the "American people," they claim to reroute art away from the cultural elites and toward some populist notion of "the people." However, this conservative offensive has no populist formation whatsoever because the populace has shifted into communities of color, immigrants, women, displacing the white male hegemony of "populist" art sites. No matter how tattered and problematic, it is clear that public support for the arts has begun to decenter white male standards by reconnecting politics with art within a variety of emerging communities.

A second prong in this attack against the endowments has been to argue that they are sustaining a program of "arts welfare." Hilton Kramer, for example, has railed against grants to individual artists, suggesting that the government is subsidizing a welfare program that destroys incentive to compete in the marketplace by creating a cushy financial haven for artists to languish in.[95] The Heritage Foundation has asserted, for example, that individual artist grants are beyond the NEA original charter. Representatives of the foundation claim abuse of the system: "Many individual grants have become bonuses for financially successful artists who do not need the money or a form of welfare for artists who produce unsalable works."[96] Much of the discussion of the endowments as welfare programs argues for policy initiatives: first, the end to individual artist grants from any federal and state arts agencies, thereby redistributing resources to urban, high-art endeavors such as opera, and the reinvigoration of the Renaissance patronage system, in which the wealthy would commission worthy artists of merit. Many writers contend that the free market should determine whether art meets artistic standards and is popular.[97] This patronage system in effect amounts to a privatization scheme for the arts, derailing culture further from the nation-state. *Welfare* is a heavily overdetermined word in the racialized, anti-immigration political atmosphere of the 1990s: the phrase *welfare reform* has masked what are essentially attacks against women, minorities, and the poor and their relationships to the state.

The third strand of the conservative attack against the arts involves a debate about "artistic standards." The conservative position aims to reinstitute classical realist artistic standards—read "white"—to counteract the perceived devolution of aesthetic beauty and sublimity into identity politics and postmodernism. Lambasting the National Endowment for the Humanities, Peter Shaw, a conservative cultural critic, queried: "The agency is charged with advancing humanities, but we are not told which humanities, whose humanities, are meant. Is it the tradition deriving from the humanists of the Renaissance? Or is it the postmodern repudiation of the human subject, as the current jargon has it, and the rejection of European and Western humanism?"[98] Conservatives have outed the intellectuals responsible for this shift into relativism: Michel Foucault, Raymond Williams, Jean Baudrillard, Paul de Man, Catherine Stimpson, Houston Baker Jr., Stanley Aronowitz, social constructionists, feminists, and multiculturalists, to name only a few infidels to Western culture.[99]

Within this debate, the assumptions behind the concept of standards braid several different trajectories together. First, Hilton Kramer of the *New Criterion* and the Heritage Foundation contend that good art is universal rather than particular, appealing to all people equally regardless of their gender, race, ethnicity, or region. The Heritage Foundation has blasted the NEA for "bias against traditional forms of art and traditional values in general," which has created a "platform for attacks on religion, traditional art forms, traditional families and traditional values."[100] Good art exhibits a standard of excellence, which is more often than not realist, representational work accessible to a wide population. The revival of artistic standards is counterposed as a unifying, stabilizing force to the fragmentations produced by postmodern consumer culture, which cuts off all imagery from any referent. Finally, conservatives have collapsed the aesthetic strategies of the avant-garde that critiques representation into identity politics, viewing any antirealist strategy as corrupted by elitist special interests, multiculturalism, and political agendas. The Heritage Foundation, for example, has lodged a charge of reverse discrimination against traditional, representational artists, claiming that the majority of grants are awarded to the conceptual, abstract, antirepresentational avant-garde.[101] Traditional artistic standards, in this argument, are tethered to traditional family values. In other words, the battle against experimental work is a battle to define the nation through pure, seamless imagery, not through imagery whose very construction and position within culture are questioned. "We need to distinguish between the national support of traditional cultural monuments and the subsidy of avant-garde art," Frederick Turner insisted at a conservative symposium convened at New York University in 1993 and sponsored by several conservative groups, including the Center for the Study of Popular Culture.[102]

Finally, conservatives charge that the National Endowment for the Arts and National Endowment for the Humanities are bloated bureaucracies that should be downsized for efficiency, emulating the transnational corporate model. The Heritage Foundation has accused the NEA of nepotism, mismanagement, and lack of accountability. Other conservatives view the peer panel system—justified by most arts administrators as one of the fairest grant evaluation processes because of the panel members' professional and regional diversity—as corrupt. They want grants determined by experts and "average" citizens with no experience in the arts who can judge the artistic merits of grants on their own grounds, ignoring gender, race, and region.[103]

This expurgation of difference within the nation operates within a much larger global context, however, than simply censorship of discordant sexual and political imagery. The quest to defund the arts infrastructures strips the nation of its histories, its imaginations, its visions, reducing its public functions at exactly the same time that transnational capital seeks to deterritorialize nations. Arts defunding strips politics and dissent out of the nation. Arlene Raven has observed, for example, that the skirmishes over public funding of controversial art are attempts to "roll back the clock to the fictive time when art and politics were a contradiction in terms."[104]

The transnationalization of corporate consumer culture has grown exponentially in the 1990s, ignoring national borders, arguing for free trade, and dismantling local communication systems.[105] Transnational cultural capital operates, as many writers, including Zillah Eisenstein, have pointed out, in a doubling move, homogenizing culture across borders and destroying the local while integrating the heterogeneity of difference. Consequently, the nation-state has shed its moral and ethical prerogatives to protect and enhance cultural difference. Instead, difference has now been exiled to the economic sites of the transnationals, where it is domesticated, neutralized, and commodified.

▶

Zeroing Out: Privatization, Commercialization, and the Demolition of the Public

The Republican takeover of the U.S. Congress in the 1994 elections propelled increased aggression in the civil war against culture and an even greater threat to the extinction of diverse documentary practices. In a now infamous vendetta, House Majority Leader Newt Gingrich vehemently exhorted the Congress to zero out the Corporation for Public Broadcasting and to privatize the National Endowment for the Arts and National Endowment for the Humanities. Invoking a fantasized populism, he also charged public television with elitism, declaring it a "sandbox for the rich."[106]

Responding to Gingrich, Marc N. Weiss, co-executive producer of a controversial PBS documentary series showcasing independent work, countered, "These programs would never be funded in a commercial environment because we involve scholars, historians." David Fanning, *Frontline* executive producer, observed: "Money is very tight right now in all areas, not just the government but corporate support too. Basically you piece things together. As a result, we operate very close to the edge. What the NEA gives is not a large amount, but it's a crucial one. It's the glue, as it were, to help you do the rest of the piecing."[107]

Gingrich's attacks signaled a strategic shift in the defunding crusades from defending traditional American morals from obscenity, homosexuality, and feminism to redeeming the national budget through cost-cutting measures and good accounting practices. Commenting on this tactical and discursive change in a *Village Voice* piece charting the Gingrich offensive against the arts and public broadcasting, C. Carr noted, "The old moral critique is simply wearing fiscal drag."[108] But cost cutting and financial management also emerged as coded language for racial cleansing of all publicly supported culture, preserving it not only for market forces but for the fantasies of the white nation composed entirely of obedient white families.

The discourse about privatizing the endowments and the Corporation for Public Broadcasting has political implications beyond morals and money. In throwing out publicly funded culture—especially documentary—to survive in the rapidly changing, increasingly economically concentrated communications marketplace, privatization amputates the state from history, memory, and imagination, reducing the nation to a fantasy of homogeneity secure from the disruptions of difference. The debate about privatization has not only pitted traditional family values against obscenity and economic excess, it has disguised an assault against women, people of color, regionalism, and the poor within instrumental and sanitized arguments about balancing the federal budget, a ridiculous unsubstantiated claim about accounting. As many arts advocates and their congressional allies have repeatedly pointed out, the portion of the federal budget devoted to military bands is higher than that for the NEA.[109]

But the move to zero out and privatize was not confined to Capitol Hill—it was bolstered by the Christian right. Many observers speculated whether the nasty offensives against the NEA and NEH were political payback to the conservative religious right for getting out the vote. The Christian Coalition, founded by Pat Robertson, issued a position pamphlet titled *Contract with the American Family* in 1995 that outlined a "bold plan to strengthen the family and restore common sense values." The contract included platforms on restoring religious equality, promoting school choice, ending tax penalties for mothers and homemakers, restoring antiabortion crusades, restricting pornography, and privatizing the arts. The contract asserted that "NEA dollars continue to go toward controversial works that denigrate the religious beliefs and moral values of mainstream Americans."

Arguing for the privatization of NEA, the contract further claimed that transforming it into a "voluntary, charitable organization would depoliticize one of the most controversial agencies in recent years." Not confining its agenda to the arts alone, the contract also advocated the privatization of the National Endowment for the Humanities, the Corporation for Public Broadcasting, and the Legal Services Corporation, which provides legal advice to the poor.

In reconnecting the survival of the traditional family to the reinstitution of an unregulated market economy, the contract in essence deployed "the family" and "traditional values" as a cover for a reorganization of the state that would block minorities, women, gays, and local regions from national access to the arts and media. A press release issued by People for the American Way opposed the idea that private firms such as Bell Atlantic should underwrite the Corporation for Public Broadcasting: "This kind of 'privatization' would risk the cannibalization of public television. . . . A corporate buy-out of PBS would signal a disturbing shift away from long-standing public policy that has encouraged a wide diversity of voices and viewpoints."[110]

The arts community, particularly independent producers, fervently assailed the idea of privatization. They stressed the hidden racializing of arts and the further homogenization and nationalization of mass communication embedded in the plan. In December 1994, Richard W. Carlson, president and CEO of the Corporation for Public Broadcasting, responded to Gingrich's salvos in a preemptive strike. He pointed out that if CPB were destroyed, many public radio and television stations in local areas would go off the air. Further, Carlson explained, valuable services for underserved groups would be abolished. Teacher training, preschool programs, closed captioning for the hearing impaired, descriptive video services for the blind, and free access to the information superhighway—provided by neither other public nor private sources—would be wiped out.[111] In testimony before the new Republican Congress in January 1995, the chair of the National Endowment for the Arts, Jane Alexander, argued that the sixty-four cents a year that the endowment costs each taxpayer is a small amount of money for a significant impact: it leverages funding from private sources, revitalizes urban areas, and extends arts education to small rural communities.[112]

Independent producers, who had throughout the 1980s criticized PBS for its excessive bureaucracy, conservative programming practices, and antagonism toward independents, rallied to defend PBS, NEA, and NEH as the last preserves of public, noncommercial media. With the acceleration of transnational media merger activities in the 1990s reducing the public space available for dissident viewpoints, these independent government agencies shifted from enemies to be criticized for their lack of responsiveness to the needs of independent producers to some of the last surviving public entities to be preserved against the onslaught of globalization and commercialization.

In an action alert to members, Martha Wallner, advocacy coordinator for the Association of Independent Video and Filmmakers, charged that Gingrich's privatization plan was a bold attempt to "destroy those programs that foster critical thought, creativity and community." She pointed out that ITVS and the Minority Broadcasting Consortia would be endangered with even more restrictions on funds, while the multichannel cable and satellite universe supported by Gingrich unfolded amid industrial consolidation, deregulation, and increased concentration in telecommunications. In a letter to supporters of public service media, James Yee, executive director of the CPB-funded Independent Television Service, underlined the devastation to underserved communities if CPB were to be eliminated: "The elimination of CPB . . . will inflict great injury to stations—rural and urban. It will savage, if not kill off, efforts by independent producers and minority communities to represent a whole America." Deann Borshay, executive director of the National Asian American Telecommunications Association, one of the five minority consortia funded by CPB, noted, "Though the system may not be perfect, public broadcasting in this country is the only viable means of ensuring quality programs that speak to the needs and concerns of minority communities across the country."[113] These organizations for independent producers shared a common assumption: the language of privatization masked the destruction of access to the arts and communications for racialized and sexualized identities and communities.

The Christian Coalition, Newt Gingrich, House Majority Leader Dick Armey, and others in Congress opposed to the NEA claimed they were not opposed to art or public broadcasting, just to the use of taxpayer dollars to support noncommercial enterprises. They asserted that private sector contributions far exceeded the contributions of the federal government: the NEA had a budget of $164 million in 1994, compared with the $9 billion contributed by corporations and private foundations. However, these private sector funds are not only concentrated in urban areas, they tend to go to high-profile elite institutions, such as opera companies, museums, and symphonies, not to individual artists or filmmakers. Cutbacks to the endowments would threaten programs in both inner cities and rural areas, thereby increasing the nationalization of culture. Many foundations cautioned that with their resources pulled in many directions, particularly because of the AIDS epidemic and the health care crisis, it was wishful thinking to imagine they could take up the slack if the endowments were to be defunded.

But the Gingrich plan to convince the private sector to fund the arts and public television again revealed a covert agenda to restore the nation to whiteness and heterosexuality. As David Mendoza, president of the National Campaign for the Freedom of Expression, wrote in a letter to the NEA, "America looks more like America—meaning the United States is a place where women and racial, ethnic and sexual minorities have a say and the voices of heterosexual, white males aren't the only ones heard." Mendoza further trenchantly observed that the "evolution of public arts funding (in 1965) coincided with the civil rights movements—the right of cultural expression was part of the prize."[114]

These debates about the sites of culture and the arts in the nation appear, on the surface, to be about art, but they are actually about race, gender, and family values, and how these are negotiated within the transnational media landscape. These attacks against public funding of the arts constitute a defense of inaccessible, official culture against the rapidly multiplying, increasingly more accessible unofficial cultures. However, it would be a mistake to analyze these attacks solely as elements of the war between homogeneity and heterogeneity: they also must be viewed as part of an affirmative, productive strategy to support globalization.

Although the attacks on various images by gays (Mapplethorpe, Riggs), women (Holly Hughes, Karen Finlay, Annie Sprinkle), and people of color (Andres Serrano, Guillermo Gómez-Peña) have mobilized anticensorship campaigns of great fervor and impact, to enter the defunding debates on the levels of images alone is to separate the complexity of these new politics from aesthetics by reducing everything to a romanticized modernist position of defending the freedom of expression of individual artists.

The defunding and privatization agendas of Gingrich, the Heritage Foundation, and the American Family Association sandbag the representational systems of the white nation against the invasions of an expanding multicultural society, experimental art forms, and increased access to and democratization of technologies and arts institutions that serve diverse communities. The reorganization of the state by transnationalization has meant that the state requires different cultural policies; because the state has new needs to ensure that capital can cross borders, the art form most linked to this new nation-state is that of consumption, the antithesis of artistic production. Thus this new form of nation-state has produced new positions for the arts. An example of this is the growth of blockbuster museum shows featuring acclaimed international masters, such as Picasso, Vermeer, or Rauschenberg, underwritten by transnationals such as Philip Morris.

The conservative offensives against public funding of the arts have accelerated since 1989, coinciding with the major transnationalization and concentration of media industries. Media companies are not only vertically integrating, they are moving horizontally across different media. In 1989–90 alone, Paramount, engulfed by an enormously diversified conglomerate, became Paramount Communications Inc.; Time Inc. bought Warner Communications to emerge as the largest communications company in the world; Sony, the Japanese electronic transnational, bought Columbia Pictures; and Matsushita purchased MCA/Universal.[115] By 1995, ABC/Cap Cities was in the process of merging with Disney, and Turner Broadcasting was negotiating with Time Warner. These mergers represented aggressive moves into new technologies, cable, video, and satellite, creating enormous conglomerates with their fingers in a multitude of media industries that require deregulation to increase their flexibility and speed. The necessity of deregulation was not lost on the Heritage Foundation, which issued a series of position papers on the necessity of deregulation to propagate and exploit new technologies and free trade in the communications industry, one of the largest sectors of the U.S. economy, in 1995 and 1996.[116]

It is important to put Gingrich's use of the word *privatization* into its proper context. By anchoring the debate about privatization in the arts and public broadcasting, Gingrich effectively utilized a rhetoric of nationalism to support one of the major fulcrums of transnationalization of communications. Hamid Mowlana has astutely recognized that in effect, deregulation, privatization, and liberalization all indicate a move by particular countries and communications industries to create a global free market economy with no trade barriers. He suggests that the term *privatization* has no meaning in the United States, because it has generally been used to refer to the dismantling of state communications enterprises typical of Eastern Europe.[117] For Mowlana, the battle has shifted from the geographic and physical to the cultural and informational. Cees J. Hamelink has maintained that the emergence of the new world order depends on what he calls the "gospel of privatization": "It declares that the world's resources are basically private property, that public affairs should be regulated by private parties on free markets, and that the state should retreat from most—if not all—domains that affect people's lives."[118]

Fredric Jameson has also argued that the deregulation of India, Brazil, and Eastern Europe has opened the way to globalization, but has also set the stage for what he terms a discursive struggle that appeals to political fear and delegitimates the welfare state.[119] The arts defunding debates and the advocacy of privatization wind around these concepts, galvanizing fears as they mobilize transnational capital.

Historically, arguments for cutting off funding for the Corporation for Public Broadcasting and the issuing of threats for its deauthorization began full tilt when President Richard Nixon, disturbed by documentaries on the Vietnam War, the poor, and blacks, and believing that the entire public television system was infected by a liberal/left bias, demanded a "purge of public affairs programming on public TV." By 1971, public affairs programming constituted about 33 percent of the PBS network schedule.[120]

By 1980, President Ronald Reagan, a vigorous advocate of privatizing government, opened the doors to increased corporate underwriting on public TV. Like Gingrich, he put forward the idea of defunding public television, which significantly reduced its appropriations. Historian Ralph Engelman has contended that public television's retreat from public affairs in the early to mid-1980s was a direct result of increased corporate underwriting: corporations such as Mobil Oil preferred less controversial dance and music programs.[121] During the decade of the 1980s, private sector funding increased from 41 percent to 54.4 percent.[122]

As transnationalization accelerates, particularly in the telecommunications sector, where capital and culture increasingly have no single home but are located everywhere at once, the necessity of cultural practices to produce, narrate, and imagine the nation dissipates. Cultural imaginaries become engulfed by the real of the transnational economy, which transfigures them into commodities of fantasy. As the regulatory functions of the economic state disintegrate under pressures of transnationalization, the state's relationship to culture also shifts.

Until the 1990s, the state served the function of protecting and enhancing activities outside the market to support diversity of viewpoints and to create spheres autonomous from capital as a way to ensure democratic agendas through cultural production. In the post–Cold War period, transnational telecommunications companies have subsumed diversity and marketplace democracy as their modus operandi by marketing multiculturalism and creating segmented and fragmented specialty markets on cable and satellite. Instead of public funding for PBS series like *Eyes on the Prize*, the epic masterpiece on the history of the civil rights movement, there is the Black Entertainment Network. Instead of experimental film and video, there is MTV. Instead of political muckraking into institutions, there are talk shows.

Therefore, one can no longer argue for public state support of cultural practices—whether through the schools, libraries, art, film, or television—by pointing to diversity, because diversity has been redefined as segmented markets. Both Herbert Schiller and Edward Hermann have noted that privatization mobilizes the state differently—whether in Latin America or the United States—by selling off public space and regulated markets to the private sector, effectively limiting the range of discourse and narrowing the space for dissent.[123]

Worldwide, deregulation, privatization, and liberalization have devastated news and public affairs programming. As formerly state-run television organizations are disbanded, cheap programming becomes a paramount goal. Reruns of American entertainment television eventually displace local-origination news and documentary.[124]

When the transnationals move into a country, whether it is Brazil or the United States, documentary moves out. As documentary production declined to minimal levels at the networks during the 1980s under advertiser pressure, documentary survived in two interconnected but separate domains, public television and the art museum and festival circuit, both of which rely on public support as nonprofit enterprises. Consequently, by

Publicity postcard announcing *Out at Work* (1997). Dir. Kelly Anderson and Tami Gold. Image courtesy of Anderson/Gold Films.

1989, the only long-form documentary series on broadcast or cable television, if we exclude the Discovery Channel and the Arts and Entertainment Network, was *Frontline* on PBS.

However, the lines between the transnationals and the independent documentary sector are not immobile; rather, they are constantly shifting, and they have often blurred in the post-1989 landscape. Sometimes the corporatized multiculturalism of the media transnationals creates a crack that can be widened for documentary distribution. HBO, owned by Time Warner/Turner, has emerged as a home for provocative and politically oppositional documentaries, showing work by venerable independents with long track records, such as Jon Alpert, Rene Tajima, Chris Choy, Rob Epstein, and Jeffrey Friedman.[125]

Kelly Anderson and Tammy Gold, for example, produced a $65,000 interview testimonial documentary titled *Out at Work* (1997) about three gay and lesbian workers who dealt with harassment and discrimination on the job through union activism. One of the workers had been fired from Cracker Barrel, one was fighting for domestic partner benefits from the New York Public Library, and one was an openly gay autoworker in Detroit. *P.O.V.* accepted the film for broadcast, only to be overruled by PBS, which contended that the funding supplied by the United Auto Workers and the ASTREA National Lesbian Action Foundation violated PBS underwriter guidelines.

A national controversy ensued, with editorials in *The Nation,* official statements of support from the AFL-CIO contending that corporate underwriters are never attacked for conflict of interest in PBS funding, and a special conference at New York University. HBO's senior vice president for documentary and family programming approached Anderson and Gold about producing a longer version of the film that would include more individual stories.[126]

To conclude: it is no longer possible to analyze attacks against independent documentary as simply an issue of maintaining "American" values when the entire landscape for publicly funded public affairs is rapidly deteriorating across the globe as a result of arts defunding, privatization, and intensive transnational media activity. The clear lines of distinction between public space and corporate space, between public affairs and private enterprise, between oppositional work and corporatist multiculturalism, between identity politics and niche marketing, between the nation and the globe, have become murky. Independent documentary producers, an endangered breed by even the most optimistic prognosis, are stuck defending some of the very systems they once despised in order to stake a claim on redefining the relationship between the nation and cultural practices in the post–Cold War new world order.

[2] *Mobile Battlegrounds in the Air*

▶

War Never Stops

World War II, Korea, Vietnam, El Salvador, Angola, Panama, the Gulf War, Rwanda, Somalia, Bosnia: these are some of the wars that have molded modernity and the twentieth century through images and imaginaries. Wars also rage within our nation: AIDS, antihomosexual campaigns, racism, the Los Angeles rebellion, homelessness. These wars are real and unreal, bloodless and bloody, fought in the air and on the ground, fought both here and there, in hearts and minds, in battlegrounds and in psychic imaginaries, inside and outside nations.

Wars always depend on both real and imagined projections, fantasies of white male power and nationalistic pride that blend easily with representations severed from the complexities of historical context. In his book *War and Television,* Bruce Cumings observes: "War is a national endeavor. War is an American tradition. War is manly. War is rational."[1] Although many cultural commentators have criticized media coverage of the Gulf War for sanitizing the carnage of battle through tightly controlled imagery, Cumings argues that during most of the wars the United States has engaged in during the twentieth century—World War II, Korea, El Salvador, Vietnam—the media have banished the "daily horror of modern warfare" from view to maintain nationalist agendas and to control public opinion. The physical and psychic horrors of war, its micropractices and dismemberments, its fragmentations and disruptions, must be repressed so that a unified national imaginary can pose as the ultimate authority and explanation.[2]

However, to analyze a war only from the point of view of the state and its propaganda machines is to miss the war entirely. A new location and practice is necessary, one that rejects this infinitely expanding imagery and deauthorizes the state. An unofficial documentary practice that dislocates from state fantasies is necessary. As Cynthia Enloe has argued, wars have always, simultaneously, had massive repercussions on women of all colors, blacks, Latinos, Asians, and others here and abroad in the real, not only in the realm of the imagined.[3] Nonmilitary women's lives are changed as they wait for men to return. Thousands of Bosnian women are raped. Families are devastated. Vietnamese, El Salvadorans, and Bosnians are murdered and maimed. Documentary film and public affairs formats have been so frequently conscripted by governments that it becomes almost impossible to separate them from state propaganda and psychological warfare.[4]

State- and corporate-produced documentary is one of the armed forces of war, the artillery that leaves no visible trace as it destroys bodies, relying increasingly on high technology such as computer imaging and lasers to secure distance from the enemy. Distance is mapped through the image, through the process of visualization that annihilates all conflict by compressing it into a spectacle. Conversely, independent documentaries function as negations, offering proxemics as the only way to travel between the inside and the outside, between history and memory, between damaged bodies and healing, resistant psyches. Against the completeness of the nationalized and aestheticized image, they propose a juxtaposition of fragments to write histories as continual processes of excavation, retrieval, and explanation. These documentaries are themselves historical acts.[5]

Wars are not so simply and reductively masculinist and nationalist; they recirculate in multiple registers as traumas and hallucinations, histories and memories, demobilizations and reconnaissance missions. By detaching documentary and war from their grounding in the state apparatus and relocating them to independent films produced within sexualized and racialized positions that see history and location as fluid, it is possible to counter the plenitude of the image with words, stories, histories, specificities, places, and new landscapes. Marita Sturken, in her book *Tangled Memories: The Vietnam War, the AIDS Epidemic, and the Politics of Remembering,* has argued: "Ironically, though, the image that allows the public to feel as though it participated in the event does not aid us in mourning. Rather we invest it with a truth it cannot reveal. It is the reenactment, the replaying, the fantasizing of the story that allow the mourning process to proceed and the event to acquire meaning."[6]

Inside and outside the borders of the United States, wars ravage people mercilessly. Through reclaiming images and the imaginary, independent documentaries that rework the psychic work of war constitute a refusal to be domesticated, neutralized, and separated. Ribbons tie us to each other, across great divides of differences, histories, and territories. Red ribbons for AIDS, yellow ribbons for the troops in the Gulf or for Cory Aquino's democracy movement in the Philippines, pink ribbons for breast cancer, black armbands to protest state and federal cutbacks to higher education: all of these ribbons are images, but they are also partial documents of the real that is in creation, in process of becoming. Independent documentaries rewrite wars in a way similar to these ribbons: they ask spectators to interrogate and to be disturbed, and, ultimately, to be connected to each other in this process of rewriting as renewal.

The physical fighting may stop, but the psychic and imaginary war never ends. Rather, the return of war in imagery, metaphor, language, trauma, and news stories breaks up this state-produced history into histories that are always inscribed by absence and incompleteness. These pluralized histories—often found in independent documentary—recover from the wounds of wars by reclaiming images from the state. They revision them, literally, with aesthetics, memory, historical context, political interventions, and personal locations. These histories etch the real, but also recognize the impossibility of representation. They suggest the dialectic between that which must be represented and that which is beyond representation.

Wars intensify both official mainstream and independent documentary functions, because images replace objects, subjectivities, and territories. The state increasingly blurs the boundaries between documentary and fiction, turning them inside out and disconnecting them from history, as Bill Nichols has cautioned.[7] In wars, the state exalts fiction as documentary evidence and explanation, as in Frank Capra's *Prelude to War* (1942), a film featuring rapid editing that visually illustrates every point about why the United States must fight the Axis powers. The state also deploys documentary form as a citadel for the visualization of fictions through structured absences, as in John Ford's *Battle of Midway* (1944), where no bloody bodies emerge, only triumphant air raids against the Japanese. Paul Virilio says, "There is no war, then, without representation, no sophisticated weaponry without psychological mystification."[8]

But to linger on the outside of the nation in these wars in others' lands is to deny how their representational tactics recirculate and attempt to nullify national crises. There are also wars at home, on the inside, that repeat and rethread the numbing, nationalistic strategies symptomatically, denying the pain and suffering of the others within. Avital Ronell has shown that what is unrepresentable elsewhere—the brown bodies of the Iraqis, for example—returns somewhere else as something else: Rodney King's black body demonstrates that the violence to bodies of color cannot be repressed, the amnesia cannot be maintained. "But the Rodney King event is also an eruption of the effaced Gulf War," Ronell says.[9] The outside and the inside, then, are not simply contradictions between the international and the domestic, but embody the traumas of the twentieth century as military power devastates nations, as new epidemics like homelessness, AIDS, and layoffs destroy lives.

Wars have been the excuse to define the nation as borders written in blood and defined by race, as Paul Gilroy has noted.[10] The images produced by the state and its ideological allies, such as the major television networks and CNN, have not only derailed independent, critical reporting about war, as so many have repeatedly and obsessively observed about the Gulf War in 1991. These images have done much more damage because the image has been drained of all its contradictions. The image has been etherealized. These phantasmagoric images repress the traumas, the amputations, the terrors, the bombings, the destruction, the deaths, the displacements, the rapes, the horrors, the racisms, the pain, the loss, the atrocities. Zizek writes of "the Real, that which resists symbolization: the traumatic point which is always missed but none the less always returns, although we try—through a set of different strategies—to neutralize it, to integrate it into the symbolic order."[11] In the independent documentaries discussed in this chapter, the real resists not only symbolization but also subordination. These films stalk the return of trauma with different strategies, opening up a space for it to unfurl and detonating it in the present to enact the future.

Wars manufacture enemies through imagery: the heartless Nazi, the vile Jap, the plotting Vietnamese, the obsessed guerrilla, the drug lord, the evil Arab, the impure Bosnian—unfathomable ancient ethnic hatreds.[12] The fighting ends, but the war never stops. Peace accords and partitions, treaties and truces, summit meetings and troop withdrawals only mark the public history of war as an altercation between nation-states. But the real of war returns in many ways: it is independent documentaries on war that execute the dream work of the real.

When documentary aligns with the state, it produces fantasies and coherent narratives, creating truths through facts that have beginnings, middles, and ends. War documentaries made by the state have closure: the war begins and it stops. It can be contained.[13] But independent documentaries tell a different story of war and tell the story differently, as a war that does not end in death but is remade in life. Trinh T. Minh-ha has described the story from the belly, the story that is always continually unfolding and has no end as the antithesis of the narrative and history that accumulate facts and collect events. The story is always being brought into life and nurturing others, the opposite of war; it constantly "needs us all, needs our remembering, understanding and creating what we have heard together to keep on coming into being."[14]

If state-produced documentaries of war operate as a series of reversals between fact and fiction, then independent documentaries on wars are, in the words of Trinh, "neither fact nor non-fiction, and can constantly invite the reader to either drift naturally from the realm of imagination to that of actuality or to live them both without ever being able to draw a clear line between them yet never losing sight of their differentiation."[15] Rather than reversals, the independent documentaries analyzed in this chapter constitute transversals: they move across official and unofficial languages, across traumas to testimonies, across anesthetized numbing to aesthetic sensing, across the air to the ground, across incomprehensibility to rationality and mobilization, across what can be represented and what cannot.

Blockades and Embargoes

Wars blockade and embargo unofficial languages. These samizdat languages evolve in the margins of war. They threaten the official language of the state, which is not simply language at all, only an image shorn of its territory and its meaning. Independent documentaries tracing war as stories from the belly operate as unofficial, minor languages, showing that the official language of the state is bankrupt, a lie, a half-truth, a monologue creating false unities. Rather than disruptive flows between the official and the unofficial, which is how these independently produced documentaries function, the state depends on blocking flows and dialogues to maintain the illusion of control during wartime.[16]

Gilles Deleuze and Félix Guattari claim that a minor language is always constructed within a major, official language. The minor language is deterritorialized, political, and collective; it revels in polylingualism and takes "flight along creative lines of escape."[17] The minor language awakens the senses, and thus is the only truly revolutionary language because it is the only one to cross and commingle different territories, refusing the purity of languages. "Since language is arid, make it vibrate with intensity," Deleuze and Guattari advocate.[18]

Traditionally, mass communication historians chronicling government control of media during wars in the twentieth century have viewed all wartime communications of the state as a series of distortions of the truth, limitations to freedom of speech, and a woeful reduction of the public sphere. This sort of analysis remains within the official language of the state, assuming that the state is capable of reforming itself internally through democratization, openness, and ethical improvement.[19] By centering analysis on the illusions, lies, and marginalizations propagated by the state, this line of attack circumnavigates the flows of minor languages that are always already in place, fighting for space, charting new ground, fighting a different war. Of course, wartime news and imagery operate within these restrained parameters, performing a series of denials. But they also enact a productive relation. The media are not separate from the state, a fourth estate, as the adage goes, keeping watch over democracy. The media and the state in fact produce each other, especially in wartime, which only serves to spotlight their interconnectedness.

Armand Mattelart, in his book *Mapping World Communication: War, Progress, Culture,* contends that communication systems have always developed in tandem with the wartime needs of the state, imbricated into its geopolitical functions. They are yin and yang to each other. He shows how World War I marked a new kind of war, in which "ideological warfare became as decisive as the operations on the battlefield."[20] Information was controlled, press censorship was instituted, and a public information committee was established to control film and press images. By World War II, the term *psychological warfare* took the place of the term *propaganda* and became highly integrated with the entire field of the sociology of mass communications.[21] By the time of the Cold War, the needs of the national security state materialized in the new field of international communications, an academic field almost completely defined by the government.

During the wars in Vietnam and El Salvador, the media and the state became even more intimately connected, according to Daniel Hallin. He contends that the culture of professionalism and objectivity induced reporters to adopt a technical and administrative point of view conducive to legitimating the state rather than to engendering engagement in public dialogue.[22] During these confrontations, events were analyzed in terms of strategy, success, and failure. During both wars, the press tended overwhelmingly to reflect official views and to depend almost entirely on state authorities for information and commentary.[23] Hallin's empirical research on news coverage of these wars illustrates the collapse between the state and the media: both are engaged in the same war and use the same tactics, wound around each other. Indeed, to stretch Hallin's point even further, the official language of the state resides in the dominant media. Todd Gitlin has shown, for example, that during the war in Vietnam, the press delegitimated the actions and words of the antiwar demonstrators through trivialization, marginalization, manufacture of individual celebrities within the movement, and overreliance on statements by government officials to the exclusion of dissenting voices.[24] The Gulf War intensified these attributes to such a degree that any disturbances to this system of state-media collaboration were evacuated.

I start at the other end, which locates me within the unofficial, the samizdat, the minor languages of war.

▶ ─────────────────────────────────────

Bombs Bursting in Air

Metaphors, discourse, and images of the air abound in war iconography from all wars of the twentieth century: the air war, the air force, the airplane fighter pilot, the parachutist, air defense, air raids, air attacks, air command. The air is everywhere and nowhere; it is here and there but never descends to the ground. One of the most horrifying examples of this convergence of air and war inhabits the image of the Hiroshima bomb: the mushroom cloud, photographed from the bomber *Enola Gay,* spreading across the sky as a spectacle of technological omnipotence. The burned bodies of the people of Hiroshima and Nagasaki are invisible, silenced, absent.

Analyzing how the very process of translating the lived experience of war into representation dematerializes war, Paul Virilio, in his wide-ranging polemic *War and Cinema,* observes, "The history of battle is primarily the history of radically changing fields of perception."[25] For Virilio, it is impossible to imagine war without cinema or cinema without war: each invokes the other and depends on the other for its own productivity. He says that the "war of objects" is increasingly replaced by images and sounds; it is etherized into the air. The state transposes war, in this instance, into images in order to maintain exclusive control over the weapons, the bombs, and the imaging technologies. For the Vietnamese, Bosnians, and El Salvadorans on the ground, the images are seen through blood and death.

Virilio contends that "war has finally become the third dimension of cinema."[26] The aerial dimensions of photography substitute for maps, according to Virilio. The airplane transports the imaging systems to the air, transforming geography itself into imagery and dislocating war from its spatial dimensions. In the twentieth century, weapons and the eye increasingly form a single unit, smelted together to create a variety of simulations, hallucinations, disintegrations, and dematerializations that culminate in live broadcasts of war.[27] The round-the-clock live coverage of the government-controlled representation of the Gulf War provides an example of this grafting together of war and cinema. Information and rationality, morality and ethics, argument and analysis, according to Christopher Norris, are no longer viable terms of debate.[28] The image smothers them.

The sky is the place where the advanced high technologies of war—radar, laser missiles, atomic bombs, napalm, computer imaging, stealth bombers, spy satellites—shed their mechanical and cybernetic functions as instruments of death and streamline into pure imagery, ritualizing and glorifying power. The hyperadvanced technology of war derives its political/psychic power through reductivist and simplified imagery that can be repeated endlessly, revived, recycled, rehabilitated, renewed as an engine of war.

If the image that condenses all war is floating high in the sky, then all spectators look up, craning necks and straining eyes for a view outside everything, above bodies and conflicts. These suspended images and metaphors double as advertisements for the impunity of the state in all moral questions. Language is never necessary for the images in the air; it intrudes and protrudes, creating dissonance by punctuating the sheer visuality of the aerated war image with speech.

It is the air and the images suspended in it that graph state domination in the visualization war: the only way to levitate into the air is by, quite literally, riding with the state. The image symbolizing the Gulf War, recounted repeatedly by all manner of critics on the right and left and in between, is the shot from the point of view of the laser-guided missile, where weapon and camera cruise silently toward destruction with no collateral damage, inserting spectators into the bomb itself.[29] Leni Riefenstahl's notorious paean to Adolph Hitler and the Nazi Party, *Triumph of the Will* (1935), opens with the celebrated descent of Hitler's plane from the clouds. The power and sweep of the party is visualized not only through the adoring masses reduced to patterns, but through the multitude of angles and access points for the camera.

The inevitability of the power of the Nazi Party is pronounced through a refusal of language: the aerial shots of Hitler walking through the crowd at the Nuremberg rally graph his command of the ground and the air. Brian Winston asserts that *Triumph* is nothing more than "an 'official' film obsessed with surface and dedicated to social integration."[30] During World War II, cameras were inserted into the wings of B52s to record bombing accuracy, merging vision with technology in order to produce bombardiers' accuracy.[31]

Perhaps one of the most evocative images from the Vietnam War, recycled in a multitude of documentaries and fiction films, is the aerial shot of napalm bombs dropping from planes over the green expanse of North Vietnam. Increasingly, the images of Buddhist monks' self-immolation to protest the war, of a Vietnamese child running down a road with napalm burns, and of antiwar protesters in the United States rebuking unbridled imperialism and racism have retreated into the shadows in representations of the war. These protests are not simply marginalized and trivialized, they evaporate like dewdrops into the air.[32] The image of napalm bombs dropped from planes has metonymically displaced everything else as the documentary image that survives the Vietnam War. It is not only an image exalting U.S. technology, but an image that repels proximity, people, geography, nations, conflicts.[33]

For images to mobilize, nationalize, and unify spectators, they must be recast as fetishes. These images of war in the air depend on repetition for their political solvency. Slavoj Zizek has observed that for Marxism, the fetish "conceals the positive network of social relations," whereas for Freud, it "conceals the lack around which the symbolic network is articulated."[34] The state then operates not in a war of containment and censorship, but in productive relation to the image, where it literally replaces all social and symbolic relations with fetishized images, whether they be Pixelvision images from the nose of a missile during the Gulf War, 16mm film wing-side views of bombs dropped over North Vietnam from B52s, or *New York Times* photographs of weeping Bosnian Muslim women burying their children. On this question of the dominance of visuality, Rey Chow cautions, "The privileging of vision as such is always the privileging of a fictive mode, a veil which remains caught in an endless repetition of its own logic."[35] Despite the different historical and geographic locations of these wars, these images inculcate a fetishistic relation for the spectator, using repetition to annihilate all differences and distinctions and to blunt our senses.

The fetishized, state-manufactured image of war functions as spectacle. Visual spectacles counterpose the story from the belly, which has location and temporality and moves through different histories and projections with different voices and registers. Dana Polan has described the aesthetic practice of the spectacle as a containment, a banishment of all the other senses through an explosion of sight and sound. For Polan, the spectacle removes itself from history by situating itself almost exclusively in the present. As non-sense and antinarrative, it relies on passive looking and a complete saturation of viewers' senses: "The world of spectacle is a world without background, a world in which things only exist or mean in the way they appear."[36] All meaning is destroyed by overwhelming presence.

Polan provides examples from several historical and contemporary Hollywood films, including, most interestingly, Steven Spielberg's rendition of the start of World War II, *1941*. Beyond Hollywood cinema, however, the state increasingly has depended on spectacle, conscripting images of war to induce further passivity and to close down rational debate. One of the hallmarks of war propaganda, for example, has been the generalization, glorification, and spectaclization of even the most mundane imagery to compensate and stand in for the repression of traumas. In propaganda, spectators look, but never analyze, experience sight but never feel, watch but never empathize, are moved but never move.

However, at the end of his essay, Polan proposes a remedy to the enervation and neutralization proffered by the spectacle. He advocates an analytic distance to transform the image, to instigate a critical sense "to situate aesthetic practice, its myths, its fiction, its spectacle, within a new and higher coherence: the coherence of history and its knowledge as a totalizing reciprocity of people and their world."[37]

As the spectacle elevates looking, it also silences. Language is exiled. bell hooks has described the necessity of speech for any political project of resistance. For her, speech is the essence of historical imaginings and entering into history and identity. She writes: "Moving from silence into speech is for the oppressed, the colonized, the exploited, and those who stand and struggle side by side, a gesture of defiance that heals, that makes new life, and new growth possible. It is that act of speech, of 'talking back' that is no mere gesture of empty words, that is the expression of moving from object to subject, that is the liberated voice."[38] The independently produced documentaries that counter war, then, accomplish much more than the simple dismantling of the spectacle effect, slowing down the image and rethreading it into history. They address the silencing strategies of the image through language and invent new minor languages rich with memory-in-the-making.

The fundamental question about the war in the air and the images suspended in it like apparitions is not, finally, about how it pacifies and defuses spectators. Nor is it ultimately about the visual designs of these smart bombs as postmodern images, a fetishistic critical strategy that has occupied much of the recent writing on the Gulf War as a media spectacle, focusing so much on the plentitude of the images produced by the state that the bodies of Iraqis have been wiped away. The few interventions by independent media producers into the state imposed restrictions on information—Jon Alpert illicitly sneaking behind enemy lines into Iraq and the Paper Tiger Gulf War programs—have received attention only as afterthoughts, shimmers of resistance. More important, a politics of war imagery and imaginaries must move beyond the spectacle, beyond the fetish, beyond the image that fills our eyes and dulls our senses into that place where more than images are produced. It must move into the small spaces and the still-forming cracks. What else is there? What else can be done?

Traumas and Testimonies

In the postmodern cyberspace era, words appear to have either no meaning at all or so many meanings that no referent or truth can be fixed. Words are forwarded and deleted ad infinitum. Words are severed from traumas and amputated from images. *Revolution* can describe the rebellion in Chiapas or Revlon makeup, with no reference to the monumental deprivations in people's living conditions in Mexico that propel revolutions in the first place.[39] Fragmented, pastiched, montaged, repossessed, reedited, recontextualized, the image holds a paradox: it is of consummate importance, and it is not important at all.

Although media transnationals have converted the image into a conveyor belt for globalized consumption, the image also retains its conservative function as a depository for pain and suffering elsewhere, beyond our own place, in civil wars in Bosnia, Rwanda, Somalia, Argentina, a holding tank for sorrow so that the horror will not seep into our consciousness and our psyches, so that our sympathy will always be inscribed by distance, demanding no metamorphoses and leaving our psyches intact.[40] The war and the pain are then always shanghaied to other landscapes.

Against this scene where words float and images restrain, documentary has driven a different course entirely, where words have been marshaled for expository purposes, convening evidence and arguments for persuasion in a logical system of proofs and counterfactual arguments, often in reference to the ethical or moral compunctions of the nation-state.[41] The interview with participants has been a central diagnostic tool of documentary as well as of the legal system, psychoanalysis, and social work. The reliance on the interview as evidence, a strategy historically based in social science's infusion of positivism in the 1920s and 1930s, has become a mainstay of journalism, emphasizing experience as verification and truth.[42] But the interview also served in those early years as a component of professionalization that drafted empiricism to dislodge subjectivity and partisanship.

Harvest of Shame (1960), *Report on Senator McCarthy* (1954), *Who Killed Vincent Chin?* (1988), and *The Thin Blue Line* (1988) are all expository films as well as films in which what people say and how they say it forms the films' political backbones. Through the words of subjects, these films enter into the world, the words materialize the subject, the place that is attended to, unwound, traversed, described. But even persuasion has become suspicious, corrupted by the perceived uselessness of words and the privileging of visual displays that open up play and performance between different representational modalities and different high and low cultures.

Zeroing in on Grierson's *Housing Problems* (1935) as an exemplary and prototypical text deploying the interview, Brian Winston has argued that the sync-sound interviews create victims who represent the "poetry of poverty and the exoticism of the underclass," expunging class consciousness and social relations by emphasizing individualism.[43] *Housing Problems,* as well as many other Grierson films for the Empire Marketing Board and the General Post Office, is organized around a problem/solution structure that has now become the mainstay of newsmagazine reporting on commercial television networks. Participants present the problem in interview, while the organizational structure of the film offers a solution, usually in the form of a state-sponsored remedy dependent on allegiance to the nation. For Winston, the filmmakers reneged on their responsibility to the people and the dire circumstances in which they found themselves. Because they used their interviewees almost exclusively to specify a problem, the filmmakers could maintain distance and dispassion. Winston rails against the victim documentary as an invidious form of depoliticization: "The victim documentary seeks to substitute empathy and sympathy for analysis and anger. The 'problem moment' structure removes any need for action, or even reaction, on the part of the audience."[44] The question posed for documentaries on war is how to move beyond a stagnant empathy to action, beyond distance to a more interactive relationship that demands that each side—the speaker and the listener—change.

Feminist filmmaking has also utilized the interview, but in a manner different from the early Grierson work. It has revived and rehabilitated the spoken word as a way to pound out space for women's voices. It has refused the position of the victim. As Julia Lesage has argued, a large strand of feminist filmmaking from the 1970s relied quite heavily on women discussing their experiences, either in talking-head interview films or in cinema verité films chronicling women's groups. Despite critical attacks on these formats for relying on realist conventions beholden to patriarchal representational models, Lesage defends these works by arguing that they provided a more subversive realism, one that moves from the domestic, interior zones of women's lives into more public political realms that critique and disrupt patriarchy. For Lesage, these works insisted on women's presence and speaking connected to the women's movement and to consciousness-raising strategies that are repeated as deep structures within many of these films. Lesage contends that these talking films, accessible to many audiences, demonstrate that "some women have deliberately altered the rules of the game of sexual politics."[45]

However, words that are marshaled for an argument built into a logical structure or consciousness-raising are different from words that in their very uttering enact a process of change and create an act of history by creating agents of historical memory. Bill Nichols has discussed the political implications of the testimonial as opposed to the traditional documentary interview: "Testimonial contrasts with the traditional essay or documentary where the authorial 'i' speaks to and on behalf of a universalized collectivity. The 'I' of testimonials embodies social affinities and collectivities. It is acutely aware of hegemonic discourse and social difference, historical conjuncture, material practice, and marginality."[46] The words that name the traumas of war do not operate as arguments at all, but instead argue with the very position of the spectator, undermining distance and passivity by creating an entirely new relational structure. They cultivate a more dialogical relationship with and alongside the spectator, as opposed to speaking to the spectator. Indeed, without the attentive, responsive listener, testimonies do not move out into the world, but remain sunk within the recesses of damaged self, inflicting even more pain.

In *Testimony,* their important study of trauma and testimony as the most important psychoanalytic and historical acts confronting World War II and the Holocaust, Shoshana Felman and Dori Laub argue that silenced traumas repeat in other forms: "An event that could not and did not proceed through to its completion, has no ending, attained no closure, and therefore, as far as its survivors are concerned, continues into the present and is current in every respect."[47] For them, the twentieth century is the century of testimony, that process of history as constantly evolving in witnesses and acts of witnessing.

Analyzing the words of Holocaust survivors in a variety of poems, novels, and interviews, as well as in Claude Lanzmann's epic documentary *Shoah* (1985), they show how testimony is actually a form of action, a speech act that releases the trauma from silence and repression into one of historical liberation. The testimony enacts history as a continual process of psychic and political negotiation about death, loss, and absences. They write, "through an exploration of the depth of history defined precisely as historical unspeakability, to a retrieval of the possibility of speaking and to a recovery and a return of the voice."[48] Testimonies, according to Felman and Laub, reclaim both life and history. People need to tell their stories of trauma in order to survive.[49] Such stories are not simply cognitive or logical events, as in the case of *Housing Problems*, but productive, performative acts.

Unlike commercial interview documentaries that extract factual evidence to prove deductive argumentative claims outside the subjects, the testimony itself is a form of process, a way of opening up the repressed trauma to enter history again and to complete "the process of survival after liberation."[50] Unlike the interview that accrues facts and experiences as evidence and therefore prohibits any moving through trauma, the testimony is defined by the act of witnessing, a dialogic relationship in which the listener learns "the imaginative capability of perceiving history—what is happening to others—in one's own body, with the power of sight (or insight) usually afforded only by one's own immediate physical involvement."[51] Unlike the filmmakers of *Housing Problems* or the network crews interviewing hurricane victims, the witness takes responsibility, according to Felman and Laub, for the speech act embodied in the testimony, for the history it rewrites, and for moving beyond the personal: "To testify is thus not merely to narrate but to commit oneself, and to commit the narrative, to others."[52]

The horrors, sorrows, and absences of war continue, penetrating and repeating, furrowing deep into victims of war and troubling those who listen to testimonies. Independent feminist documentaries that retell traumas of war through testimony, such as *Las Madres: The Mothers of Plaza de Mayo, Family Gathering, History and Memory,* and *Calling the Ghosts,* show that war is not only an image, but also an act of aggression against women, scarring bodies, psyches, family histories, memory. These films are not positioned outside the war, as in the case of military spectacles or news, but within it and its aftermath. These films speak from a gendered, racialized, and sexualized position that refutes the mechanistic patriarchal drive of war by testifying from a different place, one in which the film places the testimony into a world beyond the war.

These works present not victims but witnesses—an important distinction. As films of witnessing, they do not exclusively provide evidence or persuasion, although they pull these threads into their structure. Instead, their very act of speaking about various war crimes across the globe and across history dismantles their victimization by insisting on a dialogical process with both history and the viewer. These films take the repressions of the military junta in Argentina, the internment of Japanese Americans during World War II, and the rape of women in Bosnia and ask how testimonies can be enacted around absences to move beyond the war in order to critique it and reconnect the words to the image. These works do not narrate wars as military maneuvers or as images. Rather, they are films of testimony, where speaking is itself a rebuilding, a going beyond war's destruction of family and homes, the traumas of rape, the family silences. These films create imaginative spaces outside the boundaries of the nation where images, words, witnesses, and history can be resuscitated amid the rubble, the deaths, the silences. In these films, testimonies are not servants to logical proofs. Rather, the testimonies propel a process, a movement, between the past and the future.

In different ways, each of these films serves as a metacommunication on the relationship between witnessing and visuality as a historical trace. In *Las Madres*, the mothers of the Plaza de Mayo are interviewed surrounded by family photographs and demonstrate with images of their disappeared children hung around their necks. In *Family Gathering*, filmmaker Lise Yasui probes her family's step-printed and slowed-down home movies for visual evidence of her fantasy that she actually knew her grandfather, who was interned in the camps for Japanese Americans during the Second World War. In *History and Memory*, Rea Tajiri repeats a re-created image of her mother (played by an actress) filling a canteen with water in the desert, an image she says emerged out of the only story her mother told her about life in the camp. *Calling the Ghosts* interrogates the disjuncture between images and witnessing. In one scene, Nezreta, an attorney who was raped by Serbs, says she can no longer watch loud films because they evoke the screams of the concentration camp at Omarska, where she was incarcerated. In her description of how the Serbs captured her, Nezreta says, "I was in shock. Is such a thing still possible in this century? People taken to camps? I thought that was the past, something I used to watch in the movies."

Las Madres: The Mothers of Plaza de Mayo (Susana Muñoz and Lourdes Portillo, 1985) opens with a group of women crowding around a reporter. They exclaim, "Where are our babies, where are our children? . . . There is evidence for everything, the testimonies are at the Ministry of the Interior. All we want to know is where our children are, are they dead or alive?" The film thus begins by rejecting official, legal testimonies as insufficient for resolution of the disappeared and inadequate for history. The film exemplifies Felman and Laub's observation that testimonies liberate silence and repression by instigating a renewal of history and movement into the world: the film concludes with other mothers around the world, in El Salvador, Guatemala, Lebanon, Peru, and Chile, wearing white scarves and protesting the disappearances.

Las Madres figures the mothers' testimonies as the link between the painful past, where children were abducted and tortured, and the future, where their public demonstrations mobilize larger political actions. Rather than following the linear history of Argentina's military regimes and reigns of terror, the film moves from loss to speaking, to healing and hope, to political action in public, with the women's testimonies the fulcrum for each action. With each move, the military recedes more and more, its public pretense replaced by the women's speech and actions. Describing the first time she decided to walk with the other mothers, one woman admits, "I couldn't hold back. The first question they asked me was, 'Who do you have that's disappeared?' Then I felt that we were all the same person."

Las Madres layers three structures on top of each other to map this moving out of silence into history on the poetic, historical, and personal levels. One strand of the film chronicles the stories of four different mothers, their stories of their children's political involvements in social justice campaigns in Argentina and subsequent apprehension by the military, their own despair, and then their awakening to public political action and solidarity to demand justice. Only a very small portion of the film focuses on the actual incarceration of the children and the response of the parents; instead, the interviews enact the process of coming into testifying and demonstrating for information, thus defanging the victimization of the parents through a focus on the act of testimony itself as one of survival. Near the end of the film, one mother realizes, "We parents have understood this much too late. I learned from my children. It's been our best experience." The film ends with various parents explaining how their fight for information about the disappeared has changed them; thus their testimonies continue the political actions of their children, keeping their political struggles alive in spite of their own deaths.

The second strand woven between these testimonies is made up of the political and economic history of the military juntas in Argentina in the 1970s, their squashing of the opposition through state terrorism, and the insidious connection between U.S. foreign policy and the military regimes. The testimonies of the mothers reframe the public history of the nation-state as violent and antidemocratic, a reversal of many documentary strategies in which interviews inform and enliven national history. In *Las Madres,* the nation-state is figured as outside the people—in fact, it is named as an enemy. The testimonies of the mothers relocate the actions of the state from its military and security dimensions to the families it has so brutally torn apart.

A discourse on silence and absence constitutes the third layer forming *Las Madres.* As the stories of the mothers overpower and defuse the history of the military in Argentina, positioning it increasingly as the film progresses as a corrupt, terrorist state bent on brutalizing all dissidents, the moral and psychoanalytic issue of silence and silencing winds around both strands. The film explicitly shows how the state silences through the mothers' detailed testimonies about how the military came into their homes, or how they set out to round up university students engaged in political action campaigns. And each testimony not only chronicles how each mother came to

The Mothers of the Plaza de Mayo in Argentina stage a protest demonstration demanding information about their disappeared children in *Las Madres: The Mothers of Plaza de Mayo* (1985). Dir. Susana Muñoz and Lourdes Portillo. Photograph courtesy of Women Make Movies.

walk on the plaza, but how her statements and actions reconstruct history and, as Felman and Laub term it, "re-externalize the event."[53] The film visualizes this reexternalization by repeatedly intercutting the historical and archival sections as public history and the testimonies as private suffering with images of the mothers circling the plaza or chanting at large demonstrations. As a film of testimony, *Las Madres* does not merely chronicle the story of the mothers' losses, but moves beyond personal loss into a larger and more dialogical world: it absorbs spectators into the process of witnessing the act of survival through language transforming itself into action.

Family Gathering (Lise Yasui, 1988) sites testimony within an aesthetic geography different from that of *Las Madres*. Family silences about the Japanese American internments during World War II repeat in the third generation in the queries and fantasies filmmaker Lise Yasui summons about her own family history. The film works through silences, absences, and fantasies as an act of reclamation. In a letter from camp, Masuo, Lise's grandfather, writes, "There are many things I would like to tell you but I am not permitted to write any more."

Family Gathering operates as a new writing of World War II, an act of resistance to continue translating the war across generations in defiance of erasure. The film enacts the process of undoing what Felman and Laub call "the bondage of the secret" by rebuilding both the narrative of Yasui's grandfather's imprisonment as a "potentially dangerous enemy alien" and moving into and beyond the psychic textures of fear, repression, a family torn apart, suspicion, and detention.[54] The film braids together incomplete traces of suppression, racism, and resistance in sedimentary layers rather than in a causal or logical sequence, the space between their differences opening up a new zone where the psychic and political are no longer separated. *Family Gathering* is quite literally a gathering together of the residue of the trauma of World War II: family movies, snapshots, letters that Masuo Yasui wrote home from camp, interviews with relatives, government documents, absences.

The home movies of Lise as a young child and her parents are not presented as evocative evidence of family harmony. Instead, the home movies are positioned as a template to connect with testimony. The film opens with a photographic image of Yasui's grandfather that is then refigured as an absence: in voice-over, Yasui says she never met him—he was, in her mind, a creation from "images on my father's movie screen." As testimonies from various aunts, uncles, and her father pile on top of the idyllic images of children playing in a beautiful yard, these images shed their indexical and referential connection and emerge as fantasy constructions screening out loss, silence, and absence. As the film progresses, the home movies themselves gather and condense the psychic residue of World War II on the Yasui family: although the war is not visually presented, it is psychically present in the idyllic backyard settings that refuse to image the war that robbed them of their house. Through their insistence on landscape as a space to be freely inhabited, the postwar 1950s, the home movies—shot outside—negate Masuo's imprisonment visually. By the end of the film, when family history is exposed and testimony provides resolution, Yasui observes, "So now I watch these movies and everything looks a little different. This is a past not to be taken for granted. It's a past my family made for themselves, and a past they gave to me."

The act of filmmaking itself, where relatives are interviewed and home movies are scrutinized as visual mythologies, marks Yasui's repossession of the traumas of the camps in her own psychic construction as historical reckoning. The structure of the film itself inscribes the testimonial process; her aunts' and uncles' stories recounting government treatment of their father during the war emerge with much greater significance than simple family saga. The film is structured to follow the coming into voice of the entire Yasui family. Early in the film, when Lise returns to the Hood River Valley with a camera, attempting to trace her family's history as fruit growers and small businessmen, she interviews an uncle who is speaking with an old friend of her grandfather's in Japanese. From behind the camera, Lise says, "What'd I miss?" In voice-over, she moves from gathering information from the outside, across the country in Oregon, to the inside, to her own testimonial process within her own family in the East: "I felt frozen behind the camera. I kept expecting someone to mention the war, but it never came up. Then I realized I was avoiding it. I had inherited my father's protectiveness of the past. If I wanted to know what had happened, it was time to just head home and start asking."

The film doubles history with testimony. On one level, the film painstakingly reconstructs the story of how Masuo Yasui was interned, his correspondence with his children from the camps, his son's legal fight against the internment, and his trial. But on the meta-level, the film tracks the trajectory of testimony, of moving through crises toward integration of the past with the future. At the end of the film, Yasui describes in voice-over her father's revelation that her grandfather committed suicide before she was born, unable to live with the trauma of the camps and his own distrust of the U.S. government. "I cried because in that instant, my grandfather seemed more real to me than ever before," Yasui admits. The film concludes with a scene that traverses between the past and the future, between fantasized history and historicized fantasy. Slowed-down, step-printed images of Yasui's grandmother playing with her on a swing suggest a recognition of the small moments of hope and intimacy embedded in the past, a retrieval and rehabilitation of the visual for history. In voice-over, Yasui concludes, "And although my grandfather died before I had the chance to meet him, I'll always remember that one evening I stayed up late, listening to him talk into the night."

History and Memory: For Akiko and Takashige (Rea Tajiri, 1991) also excavates the relationship between image and testimony to enact the historical speakability of a Japanese American family's experience in the internment camps during World War II. Like *Family Gathering*, it mines questions of loss and silence, moving from absence to presence, from image to speech. However, *History and Memory* reverses the testimonial strategy of *Family Gathering*: rather than a procession that opens into speaking of trauma, the tape performs an act of coming into image making as the visual register of testimony.

Over excerpts of newsreels of the bombing of Pearl Harbor, clips from the Hollywood film *From Here to Eternity,* and a John Ford film made for the military, director Rea Tajiri comments on the task of visualizing testimony:

There are things that have happened in the world while cameras were watching, things we have images for. There are other things that have happened while there are no cameras watching, which we restaged in front of cameras to have images of. There are things which have happened for which the only images that exist are in the minds of the observers present at the time. While there are things which have happened for which there are no observers, except for the spirits of the dead.

Tajiri enters history through the image in its multiple discursive configurations as memory, as myth, as family record, as nationalist projection, as government cover-up, as fantasies of images that perhaps exist only in the mind. The texture and incompleteness of history, rather than its linear progression, are mapped in *History and Memory* by the image in its various locations and forms. The tape explores the location of the image in history, how its imprint bespeaks larger traumas condensed into its contours. Bill Nichols has discussed *History and Memory* as well as other films that reconstruct a self as a strategy of remembrance and resistance. He writes: "The politics of location, questions of magnitude, issues of embodiment, all address the filmmaker as well as those filmed. These politics, questions, issues stress the local over the global, the specific over the general, the concrete over the abstract. The experience of place and subjectivity is tactile, everyday, corporeal."[55] To extend Nichols's argument even further, *History and Memory* actually disentangles images from their location in the symbolic and recasts them as physical evidence, corporal embodiments of the remains of persistent memory.

History and Memory conducts its psychoanalytic work on racialized trauma through image fragments, which operate like small splinters erupting out of the past, holding much more psychic injury to a Japanese American family during wartime than words alone could name. In this tape, the traumas migrate into future generations, unfinished, repeating, shards unattached to history. Over a tracking shot of a building in the internment camp at Poston, Arizona, Tajiri says, "I began searching because I felt lost, ungrounded, somewhat like a ghost that floats over a terrain witnessing others living their lives yet not having one of its own." Images of a small carved bird, a reenactment of her mother filling a canteen at a faucet in the desert, a house, traveling shots of the desert outside Poston repeat, detonating the divide between family history and political history with each repetition. In some scenes, the images exceed memory: Tajiri comments that the only story she remembers her mother telling about the camp surfaces in the canteen image. In other scenes, the images resist official history: home movies of the camp shot with an 8mm camera smuggled in despite government regulations forbidding cameras counter the excerpts from the horren-

Rea Tajiri's grandparents posed in front of an American flag, from *History and Memory: For Akiko and Takashige* (1991). Dir. Rea Tajiri. Photograph courtesy of Women Make Movies.

dous U.S. government film justifying the internments, *Japanese Relocation,* as well the archival footage produced by the government of happy, productive Japanese American internees.

History and Memory repossesses images and words, remaking their links beyond description toward a reclamation of their dual capacity to close unfinished memories and open new histories. Felman and Laub explain that "repossessing one's life story through giving testimony is itself a form of action, of change, which has to actually pass through, in order to continue and complete the process of survival after liberation."[56] Tajiri's tape, then, functions as a passing through of images and testimonies to resituate them within survival.

This reclamation is visually imagined in the shots of the palm trees that the internees grew in the desert, which signify the process of passing through images to survival. Tajiri notes: "That was the thing about the Japanese, they took barren land and brought water to it. They bought up all the land no one wanted and made things grow on it." Similarly, the barren land of her mother's memory, where her mother forgets the stories of the internment at Poston, is irrigated by Tajiri's camera at the end of the film, panning the land around Poston that her mother never saw as she rode the train to the camp, effectively rerouting the image to the testimony from which it has been cleaved. In voice-over, Tajiri observes:

> I've been carrying around this picture with me for years. I hear my mother describing this simple action, her hands filling a canteen out in the middle of the desert. For years I've been living with this picture without the story, feeling a lot of pain, not knowing how they fit together. But now I feel I can connect the picture to the story, I could forgive my mother her loss of memory and could make this image for her.

More than half a century after World War II, the nationalist civil war in Bosnia has manufactured new traumas for the new world order to ignore and deny: genocide against Bosnians veiled by the euphemistic language of ethnic cleansing, mass rape, amputations, concentration camps, massacres, towns and villages leveled and pillaged, refugees in unprecedented numbers.[57] A Serbian media campaign to rewrite the history of multicultural Yugoslavia ensued, reviving folk history, presenting the Serbs as victims, and demonizing all non-Serbs to accelerate and heighten patriotic nationalism. Independent media in Serbia were strangled, leaving the official, Serb-nationalist television channel the nearly exclusive source for news.[58]

The multicultural city of Sarajevo, where Muslims, Serbs, Croatians, Bosnians, and Christians all lived together, has been leveled; its film and television studios and vast multilanguage library among the Serbs' first targets, an attempt to symbolically and physically annihilate difference, history, memory, the capacity to image and imagine, as shown in the powerful French documentary about the war, *Bosna!* (1994). As the Paper Tiger tape *Mythmaking: The Balkans* points out, the Western media frame the war in Bosnia as an impenetrable morass of ancient ethnic rivalries and deep religious antagonisms to repress unbridled Serbian nationalism. This formulation provides an easy way for the West to disregard the brutal war in Bosnia as far away, over there, never here, a black hole of incomprehensible politics never to be entered or crossed into, a phantasmagoric landscape. Former Yugoslavian writer Slavenka Drakulic writes about how the war seeps into the psyche, altering it: "The war devours us from the inside, eating away like acid, how it wrecks our lives, how it spawns evil within us, and how we tear the living flesh of those friends who do not feel the same as we do. It is not enough that death is everywhere around us. In the war death becomes a simple, acceptable fact. But life turns to hell."[59]

The war in Bosnia has been a war waged through women, who are reduced to symbols of the nation as family: Serbs have raped women to annihilate Bosnian history and its future. In her compelling book *Hatreds: Racialized and Sexualized Conflicts in the 21st Century,* Zillah Eisenstein, discussing the masculinist nationalism of the Serbs, argues: "Genocide is the attempt to destroy a people's identity. War rape is sexualized violence that seeks to terrorize, destroy, and humiliate a people through its women."[60] By some estimates, more than twenty thousand women have been raped. Uncountable numbers of women have been forcibly impregnated.[61]

In *Calling the Ghosts* (Mandy Jacobson and Karmen Jelincic, 1996), Jadranka, one of the two Bosnian Muslim women featured, declares: "The world watches coldly while everything passes through women's bodies. Destroying a woman is destroying the essence of a nation. They were killing and raping old women, killing and raping living history. They were raping young women, destroying future generations." For the first time in history, the International War Crimes Tribunal has declared rape a war crime.

On the most simple, literal, descriptive level, *Calling the Ghosts,* a compelling, haunting tape, follows two women attorneys from Prijedor who were incarcerated, raped, tortured, beaten, and degraded by Serbs in the Omarska concentration camp as they recount their experiences and their reentry into society as refugees in Croatia. One of the few films chronicling the horrifying civil war in Bosnia to examine rape as a war crime and to provide a feminist critique of the war in its gendered and sexualized dimensions, *Calling the Ghosts,* shot over three years in Bosnia and Croatia, won the Nestor Almendros Award at the 1996 Human Rights Festival.[62]

On a more epistemological and political level, *Calling the Ghosts* more deeply rejects victimization, isolation, individualism, and silence; these various subject positions reproduce Serb nationalism by destroying history and allowing the fantasy of the unified Serbian state to continue its wreckage of women. bell hooks, commenting on the space for speaking from the margins, has observed how the position of victim is always permissible: "We know that the forces that silence us because they never want us to speak, differ from the forces that say speak, tell me your story. Only do not speak in the voice of resistance. Only speak from that space in the margin that is a sign of deprivation, a wound, and unfulfilled longing. Only speak your pain."[63]

Calling the Ghosts refuses to only speak its pain. Only a small portion of the tape chronicles the women's experiences at Omarska, their recounting of the horrors of their imprisonment, the rapes, tortures, screams, lost homes, ethnic cleansing. Very little iconography from the camps is presented, underscoring the consummate importance of testimony and language and the culpability of the image to be encased in dispassionate voyeurism and fetishism. In *Calling the Ghosts,* the image is never ever enough. It is always a floating signifier. Responding to the request of a Western photojournalist who asked her to point out the "raped women" in her women's

Jadranka Cigelj gathering documentation of war crimes in a Bosnian refugee camp, August 1993, in a scene from *Calling the Ghosts* (1996). Dir. Mandy Jacobson and Karmen Jelincic. Photograph courtesy of Women Make Movies.

association in Croatia, Nusreta glares and says, "It bothers me when we are referred to as 'raped women'—find some other term—women victims of war . . . as if you had no other characteristic, as if that were your sole identity." *Calling the Ghosts,* in its invocation of women's voices, challenges women as simply and reductively symbolic, and places them instead as analysts and creators of history.

Instead, *Calling the Ghosts* speaks the problem of speaking itself as an act of survival, political resistance, and finally as feminist organizing on an international scale. Speaking, here, is not inscribed as some self-reflexive move to deconstruct interviews in documentary as a realist scam. Instead, to speak at all in war reinvents the documentary form itself as an act of witnessing; it summons the spectator to both listen and act, to move beyond the self as Jadranka and Nusreta move beyond the rapes. They relocate their own rapes into their legal and political efforts to ensure that the International War Crimes Tribunal functions to investigate the rapes.

The title of the tape indicates this process of witnessing despite great personal risk as the only way to avenge the deaths of other women in the camps. It is a call to action through words: calling the ghosts. It refuses death as a finality. Jadranka Cigelj and Nusreta Sivac dedicate their work in the film to five women who never left Omarska: Mugbila Besirevic,

Sadeta Medunjanin, Velida Mahmuljin, Edna Dautovic, and Hajra Hodzic. *Calling the Ghosts* thus transforms the finality of death into a future where women speak and justice is served on an international scale, where testimony connects to the larger world.

While in the camps, women put pieces of paper in a circle and lit a candle in the middle to summon the ghosts to maintain their spirits in order to survive. When the guards entered, demanding to know if they were calling the ghosts, one woman hid the burning pieces of paper and the candle in her skirt, which exploded into flames. *Calling the Ghosts,* then, is not merely a film about Jadranka and Nusreta, but about "invoking the past, to call the ghosts" to continue the identities and spirits of the dead women of Omarska in the present, refusing the deaths as a finality.[64]

The opening scene of the film visualizes this choice to speak or not to speak: Jadranka's face is superimposed over a burning field and then dissolves into an image of water—the antithesis of fire—a way to douse the flames, to heal, to reintegrate the torn parts of the self and the nation in which the body lives. She says: "In the beginning I had the reruns on my own film. There was a period of self-questioning before me. To stay silent or to speak. If I stay silent, how moral would that be? When I remember the night I was taken out my own broken bones start to hurt. If I speak, how good is that for me? I would actually have to expose myself." In this statement, the act of testimony and the act of representation—the filming of horror, the imaging of war—are set up as the central philosophical and political inquiries of the film. How and when to speak, and its relationship to morality, is questioned not only by Jadranka, but by the entire structure of the film, which is organized to move from and through personal trauma to political organizing, to gathering others in political solidarity, to testimony before the International War Crimes Tribunal. The film's structure, in fact, argues that to just express the trauma is to fetishize it and to create voyeurs; the testimony and the filmmaking must move beyond the self, into the social and political, but even more important, into the historical world of action that intervenes in the future.

Calling the Ghosts engages the rapes of the women only to disengage them from private suffering. The tape does not simply evidence the rapes in Bosnia, but imprints within its structure the form of witnessing itself. The largest amount of screen time is devoted to the issue of how to speak—not simply how to tell—the postcamp experience. The structure of the film reflects a constant, painstaking, excruciating building toward the future. Each testimony from Jadranka and Nusreta functions like a small brick in the road to the future, constructed piece by piece through descriptive detail: elaboration of feelings while in the camps and toward neighbors who became guards, analysis of the Serbs' actions and plans, growing awareness of the racism of the Serbs toward Muslims, introspection on the postcamp traumas of poor kidneys and inability to eat or be touched, political work, analysis of the witnessing of others. Both women recount how they came to speak of their experiences by breaking out of trauma. As she explains how she and her son finally told each other their experiences, Jadranka reflects, "You push into your subconscious and then you realize that it's no good to close yourself up." Nusreta admits that before she spoke, "I was so terribly burdened by the camp and I couldn't sleep."

Felman and Laub argue that "the literature of testimony" is thus not an art of leisure but an art of urgency: "It exists in time not just as a memorial but as an artistic promissory note, as an attempt to bring the 'backwardness' of consciousness to the level of precipitant events."[65] *Calling the Ghosts* is a practical work of urgency, one that positions testimony about the war in Bosnia and its crimes against women as a political promissory note. It drafts the aesthetics of editing, archival shots of the camps, close-ups of the women's faces in interview, live-action shots of their travel to the Hague to attend sessions of the War Crimes Tribunal, as pathways out of silence. Describing her work taking testimony from victims of the war, Jadranka asserts, "Our work must be a warning for the future. . . . slowly, the hatred I felt at the beginning began to subside and I started to listen to the testimonies in a new way. Now I am in the role of confessor."

Importantly for the political impact of the act of feminist interventions into witnessing, the tape rarely deploys images of Serbs fighting with guns, of Serb atrocities, of mass graves. It visually excises Serb atrocities, diminishing their importance as registers of the real by supplanting them and then obliterating them with the testimonies of the women. Words of women destroy male nationalist imagery and imaginaries. In the end, *Calling the Ghosts* disarms the Serbs by burying their images through testimony. Jadranka says, near the end of the film, "Without the live witness, one can only speculate about the crime. The crime has not been filmed by a camera; it is only recorded in the memory of the witness."

▶ ────────────────────────

Demobilizations: Anesthetics, Dreams, and Nightmares

However, verbal language and spoken testimonies do not hold exclusive rights to war traumas and the aftermath of war as it spreads through psyches and bodies, realigning them and disturbing them, reverberating into the future after the bombs have been dropped. Sounds and image traces do not retreat, but repeat in dreams and nightmares. They burrow deep, tun-

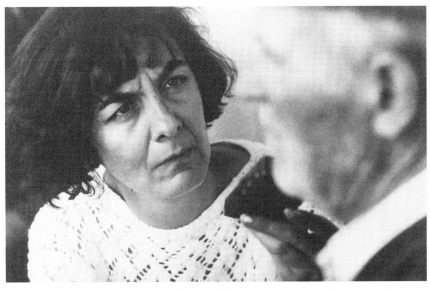

Jadranka Cigelj taking testimony from a refugee in August 1993 in a scene from
Calling the Ghosts (1996). Dir. Mandy Jacobson and Karmen Jelincic. Photograph
courtesy of Women Make Movies.

neling into the psyche, history, and archives. Wars leak into other languages besides speech; the image itself and its montage with other images
speak. As Felman and Laub observe, "The breakage of the verse enacts the
breakage of the world."[66]

There are many tapes and films about the aftermath of wars that draft
alternative, nonrealist-based formal practices to demobilize the aerial attacks of the war machine. If the war machine has swept the image up into
the air with sophisticated technology, these works skyjack various high
technologies, such as video image processing, computer effects, multichannel installations, and optical printing, to excise the image from its speed-
driven compulsion during war.

The archival and imagined visual remains of war are slowed down,
reduced, shredded, separated, multiplied in an attempt to resuscitate the
dulled senses and to establish new hybrid spaces between maker, the racialized others of war who had been figured as enemies, and a reimagined, re-
stored geographic terrain.

Surveying the poetics of documentary, Michael Renov has uncovered
a "repression of the formal or expressive domain."[67] He demonstrates,
however, that the expressive and aesthetic potential of documentary has
emerged in various historical works ranging from *Man with a Movie
Camera* (1929) to *Unsere Afrikareise* (1967). However, these works min-
ing the forgotten spaces after nations enact cease-fires do not only invoke

expressive, aesthetic strategies to summon emotional responses and desires in spectators—a textual strategy associated with the avant-garde. In these works, formal interventions decompose the realist image to assault the racialized process of "othering" that produces enemies. These technical strategies and complex montages, then, chip and pound and excavate at the process of racialization, of othering, of hatred itself, jarring and jabbing into its dichotomies, its binaries.

Historically, demobilizations of war imagery to recapture the senses from the immobilizations of the shock of war and combat have emerged almost exclusively in postwar independent productions, as aftershocks reverberating within the filmic text itself. However, it is important not to overstate the case for this sort of work, as this strategy of immersion in the senses is exceptional and unusual rather than typical. Although many of these works have employed archival footage as visual verification of the horrors of wars, their editing and argumentation reposition the images themselves as inadequate explanations for immoral acts like the Nazis' genocide of Jews or the bombing of Hiroshima and Nagasaki. Often described as works with high levels of formal interventions into a realist-bound documentary language infusing war with emotion and subjectivity, these works in fact move beyond form and emotion by opening up the catastrophic event, the event beyond comprehension, to the senses of smell, touch, taste, and pain.

For example, in *Listen to Britain* (1942), perhaps one of the most arresting and understated propaganda films of World War II, the sound of tanks and bombs is drowned out by classical music played by soldiers. In each shot, the war does not overwhelm daily life, but becomes part of it: a man carries a helmet to work, soldiers play classical music or sing in music halls, tanks enter a shot of children playing. The excesses of war—the loud noises of bombs, the militarizations of daily life—are drowned out by singing and concerts, signaling the fortitude of the British to carry on. The sound track and visual compositions do not simply displace the war, they provide a new space to hear and see outside the war.

In *Night and Fog* (Alain Resnais, 1955), the much-celebrated intercutting between black-and-white archival images of the Nazi concentration camps and color tracking shots of the postwar serene, parklike camps functions similarly, jarring each image out of spectacle. *Night and Fog* relentlessly annihilates the overdrawn spectacle of the camps and the Holocaust through a voice-over that reclaims imagination and resistance for those incarcerated in the camps and slaughtered. The voice-over supplies details and proximity rather than generalization or statistics, and this detail revives the sense of the internees: fingernails scratched on ceilings, hunger, fear, dolls and toys fabricated out of scraps.

Hiroshima-Nagasaki: August 1945 (Erik Barnouw, Barbara Van Dyke, Paul Ronder, and Akira Iwasaki, 1970) also recasts archival footage in order to move from the overwhelming scale of war into the body itself. Constructed from a Japanese cameraman's footage, which the U.S. government had suppressed for nearly twenty-five years—the film is structured as a series of visual contradictions between bombed-out buildings and the victims of the bomb: sequences of the destruction of buildings are followed by close-up shots of the victims in a pas de deux that moves the spectator from outside to inside, from space to bodies.[68]

Hiroshima-Nagasaki opens with a Japanese woman who survived the H-bombs describing her experience over shots of destroyed buildings, a landscape of near total destruction. The film thus begins not with the bomb, but with a survivor, marking her interior landscape as one that continues in spite of the annihilation of the exterior landscape. An atonal, avant-garde music track also propels this movement away from the visual spectacle of the images into a psychic space that reclaims the horror of the images.

Like *Night and Fog, Hiroshima-Nagasaki* emphasizes details that chart the senses, in an attempt to reposition the dropping of the bomb from the ground: images of permanent shadow inscribed into the wood, burned victims attended to in hospitals, kimono burns on a woman' body, hair coming out. The voice-over describes the sensory deprivation of the bombing: no one knew what had happened; fifty thousand people died; in the center, there was no sound. The film builds toward the body in pain; the voice-over describes how radiation sickness overtook the victims. Near the end of the film, the voice-over underscores the film's structure of contradictions between landscapes and people: "Vegetation grew wildly, stimulated by atomic radiation. . . . as people died, the city was covered in flowers." Like *Night and Fog,* in which the images of emaciated bodies bulldozed into piles is one of the last shots of the film, *Hiroshima-Nagasaki* also inverts the horror by ending with a shot of a nuclear explosion. In each piece, the most horrifying spectacle concludes the film, rather than opens it, an argumentative strategy in which the senses outlined earlier in each film infuse the image and consequently defuse its spectacle by positioning spectators within a new rubric of sensory attachment.

Susan Buck-Morss, in her breathtaking article "Aesthetics and Anesthetics: Walter Benjamin's Artwork Essay Reconsidered," demonstrates how modernity has recruited visuality to blunt all senses, to anesthetize the body from all that is social and, eventually, political, aestheticizing war and anesthetizing people in a movement that is ultimately fascistic. War, the shock of battle, the factory system, narcotizing drugs, anesthesia for surgery all "numb the organism" and "repress memory."[69] Buck-Morss says, "Benjamin claimed this battlefield experience of shock has become the norm in modern life." The multiple injuries to the human senses "paralyze the imagination."[70] To resist what she terms a cultural domestication, Buck-Morss invokes aesthetics to redeem the political from fascism:

> [Benjamin] is demanding of art a task far more difficult—that is, to undo the alienation of the corporeal sensorium, to restore the instinctual power of the human bodily senses for the sake of humanity's self-preservation, and to do this, not by avoiding new technologies, but by passing through them.[71]

Two tapes from the early 1980s, refusing the numbing shocks of civil war, embed this restoration of the bodily senses within their formal design as political action against the shock and numbing of war: *Meta Mayan* (Edin Velez, 1981), on the civil war in Guatemala, and *Smothering Dreams* (Daniel Reeves, 1981), on collective hallucinations propelled from war ideologies and psychic/physical wounds from Vietnam. These works use new technologies like video processing to redeem the senses, but also, beyond Buck-Morss, to reclaim racialized fragmentation of representations of war. The tapes create spaces outside, beyond, and after combat: *Meta Mayan* reclaims the landscape of Guatemala and the public communities of Indians, whereas *Smothering Dreams* recovers the psychic space of war indoctrination and combat wounds resulting from violent war ideologies and iconographies from a mass-mediated culture that inculcates violence and then genders it as masculinist.

Each tape initiates a withdrawal from war through performing reconstructive surgery on war images with high-end video imaging technologies. Here, the use of special effects technology to process the image (slow motion, reducing the images to letter-boxed shots like snapshots) removes the image from its indexical relationship to referents, where it stands in for Guatemalan insurgents or U.S. soldiers in Vietnam, and reconnects it like tissue to its nerve endings of sensory perceptions of sound, smell, texture, touch. In each of these pieces, the image is not simply manipulated or processed, as an archival document or as a visual fact; instead, the image is resuscitated as living tissue, an organism through which the senses beyond sight are summoned. In this way, these tapes do not merely revive the subjectivity of war; rather, they attempt to transport the spectator to, or envelop the spectator within, a world not defined by logocentrism, geopolitics, governments, nations, causality, a world that the spectator must move through by means of the senses. In Buck-Morss's words, these tapes "undo the alienation" of war, untying it from its mooring in logocentrism, nationalism, and spectacle, letting it float in more multifarious, complex waters, where a range of senses can seep in, loosening up the narcotizing of the image.

Meta Mayan reclaims the senses from the dulling effects of the news, figured here as words that float above the senses and landscapes of Guatemala's civil war. A haunting image of a woman staring directly into the camera, slowed down, opens the tape, a visual dare and insistence of everyday life. Steam fills the frame, then fire, then close-ups of faces in a market, signifying an initiation into sensations. A news report in voice-over describes how Spain has broken off diplomatic relations with Guatemala after leftist peasants barricaded the Spanish embassy. The report concludes with the information that Amnesty International claims two thousand Guatemalans were killed in the last year, accompanied by the image of the same woman from the earlier scene walking, suggesting the fierce continuation of life despite death and torture, despite a civil war, despite developed countries' news media figuring an entire nation as guerrillas.

Meta Mayan structurally decomposes objective news reports through the senses, filling the discursive space of war with the sensory, beyond words, experiences of the sounds of daily life. Images of a religious procession, men dressed in purple robes, swaying in and out of the frame, nearly floating, signify immersion in a world of textures and sounds. The tape deploys close-ups to resuscitate the senses, to move between the nerve synapses: in the marketplace, shots of cooking food, animals, clothes, hair, fabric, and the sound of voices not translated; outside a church, a woman swings incense, its smoke clouding over the screen. The tape moves between the marketplace and religious ceremonies, submerging the camera in the small moments of faces, cooking, walking in these public, collective events.

Composed of religious songs, drums, voices, and rainstorms, the multilayered sound track creates an open aural space that envelops spectators. With the extreme close-ups of people in the village and the rituals of everyday life, *Meta Mayan* does much more than insist on the transcendent daily lives of the Guatemalan people; it wraps spectators into its visual and aural folds, urging a way to stand beside, as Trinh T. Minh-ha explains it, through the senses.[72] A 360-degree pan of the mountains and valleys contrasts with the extreme close-ups of the tape, a pulling away but also an integration of the two landscapes, one of people, one of land. The pan is restorative as well: it visually maps an integration of the senses as one that both surrounds us from the outside and fills us from the inside in a double movement. The woman staring and walking, in slow motion, is the last shot of the tape, paralleling the circular pan with a circular structure emblematic of the integrative process of the tape. *Meta Mayan* salvages the senses that news images destroy through a reclamation of the sensory modalities of the image. In this tape, the war is displaced by the reciprocal landscapes of daily life and land, and the descriptive attributes of the image are displaced by senses.

"The senses maintain an uncivilized and uncivilizable trace, a core of resistance to cultural domestication," pronounces Susan Buck-Morss.[73] *Smothering Dreams* works through the relationships among masculinity, war, and combat wounds by anatomizing archival images, memory traces, and reconstructions to resist the domestication of Vietnam in postwar discourse and iconographies.[74] *Smothering Dreams* restages the entire war in Vietnam as a working through of political, psychic, visual, and physical wounds, blurring their distinctions to explain war.

On one level, the tape performs an inquiry into an ambush of Daniel Reeves's platoon by Vietnamese in 1969, in which he was brutally wounded, by asking how male culture that sanctions fighting for young boys develops into war between nations, a movement from self as socially constructed to wars between nations as projections of distorted selves. In voice-over, Reeves explains the issue propelling the film's visual explorations: "One of the biggest turning points in my life was when I was wounded and survived an ambush." In many ways, Reeves's aesthetic strategy is not simply to restage the ambush to explore the reason he was wounded, but to use the concept of ambush—quick surprise, overtaking others, juxtapositions—as an artistic strategy. *Smothering Dreams* ambushes images of Vietnam, both restaged memories and archival shots and narrative films, to unravel how they detour pain into male fantasies. *Smothering Dreams*, then, exorcises these images from their masculinist frameworks in order for Reeves to reclaim his physical pain as a combat veteran. It is through the wound that Reeves moves toward a recognition of how boyhood, violence, and nationalist wars conspire to destroy the senses. The tape tries to re-create the psychic space of combat pain for the spectator as well, not in the sense of having the spectator identify with Reeves, but in the sense of having the senses rewired to see war as destructive of the human psyche in a collective sense, a movement from the outside images of battle to the inside image-scapes of subjectivity. Near the end of the tape, Reeves clarifies this strategy: "I don't think the average person has any idea of what combat is like."

But *Smothering Dreams* also, like *Meta Mayan*, moves beyond the descriptive into the senses, materializing the dreams and nightmares of Vietnam, combat, and boyhood in images that can be not only repossessed, but reprocessed as traces of pain and distortion. The title of the tape suggests that the layering of these dreams of Hollywood action pictures, boyhood fights, masculinity constructs, and Vietnam combat smothers the self, suf-

Young boy actor reenacting childhood war games in *Smothering Dreams* (1981). Dir. Daniel Reeves. Photograph courtesy of Video Data Bank.

focating it and cutting it off from the senses that would reject war. Reeves says in voice-over, "Running from one movie dream to another . . . repeating a hand-me-down war story."

The tape performs a pathology report on the war in Vietnam as it is reconfigured and restaged repeatedly within Reeves, in both the physical and psychoanalytic articulations: it tears into the image constructions around Vietnam to decipher how violence is aestheticized by the U.S. government and by Hollywood, and burrows into Reeves's own psychic registers to reconnect his dreams and nightmares back to his senses. In *Smothering Dreams*, testimony winds back into the senses, juxtaposing different temporal planes. The images trace what has happened in boyhood and during the war, while the sound track compels the process of healing from all the wounds by expressing them through both written language and visual language, an excavation of the past to mobilize it and alter it in the present.

The disjunctive editing in *Smothering Dreams* refuses to elaborate a narrative of causality by explaining war as a result of masculinist associations of power with violence; instead, its editing strategy follows the "uncivilizable trace" that circulates between history and psychic formations, between Hollywood iconographies of masculinity typified in westerns or war movies and Reeves's memories of his own childhood playing war.

Combining different historical eras and fantasies about the war in Vietnam, ranging from Reeves's boyhood play at his Catholic school to archival images of bomber planes dropping napalm, to a reconstruction of the battle in Vietnam where Reeves was wounded, to shots of military toys, *Smothering Dreams*'s editing breaks open a space where causality is displaced by the visual and aural senses. Images of shattering glass punctuate the tape, a visual condensation of the psychic process of the tape itself, which shatters the smothering and numbing of war through shards of images that cut into emotional paralysis.

Another strategy to reconnect the senses to the image involves restaging and then inventing new zones between cultures as a space where the senses can be freed from their nationalized narcotization. By carving out new sensory landscapes within the works themselves, these works function as rituals of resistance. These works explore the problematic of how to visualize what cannot be represented—the senses, touch, feeling, taste, trauma—in order to fabricate an entirely different territory. On this aesthetic strategy that dislodges rather than confirms, Trinh T. Minh-ha has argued, "Strategies of displacement defy the world of compartmentalization and the system of dependence it engenders, while filling the shifting space with a passion named wonder."[75] For Trinh, displacement involves continual invention of multiple struggles, transversals, new subjectivities.[76]

This project of creating new spaces and landscapes outside of nations and between national borders resists geography; images and sounds displace locations and nations. The attempt here is to move the spectator into the senses but also beyond an individual subjectivity inscribed only within emotion and nation. These works fashion a collective subjectivity. Homi K. Bhabha has described this in-between space of displacement as a "third space": "The production of meaning requires that these two places be mobilized in the passage through a Third Space, which represents both the general conditions of language and the specific implication of the utterance in a performative and institutional strategy of which it cannot 'in itself' be conscious."[77] For Bhabha, hybridity articulates translation and negotiation between cultures. In film and video, this production of a third space is not simply a mixture of styles in the postmodern sense; its project exceeds aesthetic recombinations. It emerges as a newly forged and constantly developing political space where the traces of past wars mix with the contemporary moment to release new subjectivities and places for the senses. Hybridity, then, intensifies the senses because it is not linked exclusively to imagery or nation.

For example, Philip Mallory Jones's three-channel video installation

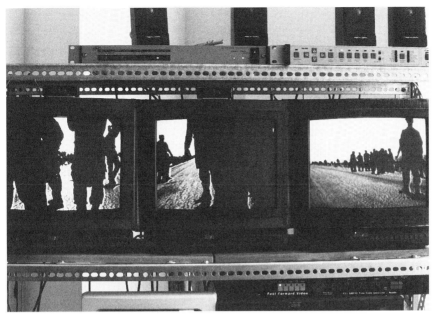

Photo documentation of *Dreamkeeper* (1989) installation, about the connection between Angola and black identity in the United States, with three monitors, decks, and speakers. Dir. Philip Mallory Jones. Photograph courtesy of the artist.

Dreamkeeper (1989) displaces the guerrilla war in Angola, Jones's own apartment in Baltimore, and the drumming and dancing of Africans in a village from their identification as stereotypical markers of armed struggle, artistic solitude, and tribal ritual through the sound of African drumming infusing the entire sound track. The traditional drumming, a form of communication between distanced African tribes, provides an aural metaphor for the political process of the tape, which attempts to visualize communication between tribes on different continents of the black diaspora by supplanting a language of words with a less nationalized language of sound and image.

The installation exemplifies the construction of a third space as that which defies representation. It recaptures the senses by manufacturing a new place for spectators to occupy that goes beyond the images themselves: each of these image categories moves across each of the three screens, literally jumping out of the televisual space and the confines of the composition. The tape begins with a close-up of an Angolan villager, a soldier walking, and the moon on each screen. In other sequences of the tape, images of drummers, dancers, soldiers, and a bare apartment repeat on each of the three screens, signaling how the visual can traverse multiple locations, defying geography. In other sequences, images move across each of the three monitors, playing with the location of the image itself.

In one section, for instance, soccer players kick the ball across all three screens, rejecting the space between monitors as a separation or a border. In another section, a figure of a Westernized black man, presumably the artist Jones, walks across all three screens as he moves through the private empty spaces of his apartment. This movement across all three monitors is paralleled throughout the installation, with dancers in silhouette, villagers, and children on a teeter-totter.

By processing all the images, changing their colors and their density and even their position on each of the three monitors, *Dreamkeeper* disconnects images from geographic and nationalized notations. In this installation, high technology in the form of advanced video imaging, multiple monitors, and African drumming heard through advanced audio systems demobilizes images and wars. It recuperates the senses in those in-between spaces that separate images, sound, monitors, compositions, and countries as effective, productive hallucinations of a new world forged beyond nationalism, beyond spectacle, beyond realism.

[**3**]   *Ground Wars and the Real of Bodies*

The official imaging of war travels through multiple altitudes. Its power is derived from its agility to move between and occupy different spaces, in the air and on the ground and all places in between. However, official documentaries nearly always deny the ground and bodies (or fictionalize them) because they are too anchored in the aerial, disembodied fantasy of nationalism. Therefore, an insurgent documentary practice must retake the ground, reposition bodies, deploy multiple technological formats, and engage in reconnaissance in order to devise new offensive positions.

▶

On the Ground

If bombs and images are bursting in air, what is happening on the ground, the place that aerial wars reduce to images, obliterating inhabitants with larger geographies? Cockburn and Cockburn's film *The War We Left Behind* (1991), a PBS *Frontline* documentary, investigates the devastation of Iraq from the ground level rather than from the point of view of a smart bomb or stealth bomber, rejecting the sanitized war without bodies as a fantasy manufactured by the U.S. government. The film reverses the visual and perceptual strategies of the post–Cold War military: it is on the ground, not in the air. It sides with bodies, the public health disasters precipitated by the destruction of Iraqi infrastructures, and the lack of medical supplies incurred from embargoes, not with high-tech imaging's manufacture of spectatorial distance and psychic splitting.

The ground is where the bodies are and where new documentary strategies can be imagined that promote different histories and new subjectivities that rewire the new world orders. The ground materializes the local as a site where cameras and bodies exchange both glances and politics.

Caren Kaplan has argued, for example, that the politics of location has emerged as a pivotal wedge in the deterritorialization of globalization. She contends, "The term 'local' signifies a more particularized aspect of location—deeply connected to the articulation of a specific time—and a potentially transformative social practice."[1] Thus the local grounds political iconography, simultaneously anchoring it within bodies, terrains, communities, vocalizations, struggles. It amputates surveillance.

Rather than crafting new psychic landscapes for the senses and third spaces beyond specific places by passing through technology, these works are in and of the landscape itself. They assert as a given that place, location, the local are where the threads of social and political life interweave and materialize. However, they do not depict some pastoral landscape without conflict or contradiction. Instead, they literally remap landscapes as places staging struggles for new territories, such as those of the Zapatistas in Mexico, of disabled persons, and of those dealing with racism and homelessness, struggles both outside and within our own borders where space is always under assault. In Chantal Mouffe's terms, these works engage new subjectivities and identities as they operate in the middle of conflict and contradictions.[2]

In the twentieth century, the nation-state has typically controlled the air war while the opposition has been tethered to the ground, defining itself as holding on to, redefining, and reclaiming territories. A classic example of radical filmmaking that prefigures this on-the-ground strategy is Joris Ivens's *The Spanish Earth* (1936), a film shot in the trenches with the Republican army fighting Franco and produced to raise funds for ambulances.[3] The camera is always positioned with the Republican army, shooting where they shoot, jostled by gunfire and bombs: it intensifies the point of view of the antifascists as it disavows any distinctions between cameras and guns. Both technologies are technologies of mobilization. Commenting on the production of *The Spanish Earth*, Joris Ivens said, "After informing and moving audiences, it [the militant documentary film] should agitate—mobilize them to become active in connection with the problems shown in the film."[4]

The story of Julian, a young man from the village who joins the Republican army, winds through the battle footage. *The Spanish Earth* never shows images of Franco or his army, only the devastation unleashed on Madrid, where people crowd the streets, looking for help amid the ruins. Emphasizing the press of daily living beyond the battle, a story of how a village built irrigation ducts is interwoven with the battle scenes. In his analysis of Ivens's mixture of different documentary visual styles of battle scenes, constructed mise-en-scène, and the village scenes, Thomas Waugh has described the film as "a cinematic hybrid in the uncontrollable laboratory of war and revolution."[5]

The Spanish Earth, then, does not figure resisting the fascists as nationalism, where the land and identification with it is of paramount importance; instead, it identifies the antifascists as those who revive the land rather than destroy it. The antifascists work with the land, but their identity is not forged on the land. Waugh sees the structure of alternating between battle and civilian scenes as fundamental to the political project of *The Spanish Earth*: "In countering images of victimization with images of resistance and revolution, *Spanish Earth* articulates a world view that sees people as agents of history, not its casualties."[6]

The ground functions as the site where territories are made more porous and where uncontested, national space is attacked and pluralized. Ground is seized inch by inch, fought over, strategized, never appropriated by decree. Governments and nation-states can command the air much more easily than others, guaranteed access to advanced technologies for imaging and destruction. If the nation controls the air, the ground war is fought by the new nations and new subjectivities emerging within, fighting for, and reorganizing space by occupying it and capturing the shifts with cameras.

In documentary history, the ground war within the nation has most frequently been located within films chronicling labor struggles. In the Workers' Film and Photo League films of the labor struggles of the Depression, the camera is always on the side of the demonstrators, jostled as the police move in, in the middle of the crowd, seeing the police from the point of view of the unemployed. This style of partisan filmmaking, where social struggles are staged on the ground from the disenfranchised side of the battle lines, is continued in the labor films of Barbara Kopple, *Harlan County, U.S.A.* (1976) and *American Dream* (1990), both of which cover brutally long and bitter strikes in a cinema verité style that positions the camera alongside the workers both on the line and at home. Although structured within the classical narrative arc of cinema verité, these films are remarkable for the complexity, nuances, and depth of their representation of working-class people. *Harlan County, U.S.A.* and *American Dream* depend upon capturing the emotions and thoughts of the participants in crisis during strikes against coal mines and meatpacking plants in order to produce an emotional and affective warrant for social justice, rather than an argument based exclusively on evidence. The ground war, as one of the localized sites for documentary, is not only fought on "foreign soil"; it is also fought within the nation itself, on the fronts of, for example, homelessness, disability, health care, AIDS, race, and labor, new territories and spaces not located on the land.

A distinguishing feature of war documentaries on the ground is the close connection between the event and the camera. Characters often address the camera directly, explaining actions or preparing the cameraperson for what is going to happen in a collaborative manner. In *Chiapas: The Fight for Land and Liberty* (1995), Jon Alpert breathes heavily from behind the camera as he trudges up a hill following Subcomandante Marcos, the leader of the Zapatistas, a political movement of indigenous Indians fighting for better living conditions in southern Mexico that launched several offensives after the passage of the North American Free Trade Agreement in January 1994. He asks Marcos if he ever found it hard to climb the hills, and how he survived in the mountainous terrain. His face concealed behind a woolen ski mask, Marcos explains that he found it very hard at first. Alpert and Marcos are engaged in the same activity, but from different geopolitical subject positions. In fact, Marcos's ski mask and Alpert's camera are both devices that cover their faces and obscure their identities, but both men, as signified in this early scene, are trudging up the same steep hill toward social justice.

The camera and the mask, then, can serve as disguises or, more politically, can reposition the self within a larger social and political struggle on the ground. These are not selves of individual identity, but selves that translate across borders, Marcos from the indigenous Indians to the Western press, Alpert from Chiapas to the North. Unlike the network news that focused almost exclusively on romanticized images of Subcomandante Marcos and his troops with ski masks and guns, Alpert quickly dispenses with the image of Marcos by having him talk, and then spends the rest of the twenty-seven-minute piece with the Chiapan people whose marginal existence demands betterment. Alpert speaks with them in their homes, in refugee camps, at state-manufactured rallies, in villages.

Alpert's enormous body of video work is often criticized for exploiting its subjects; Alpert's aggressive interactions from behind the camera are sometimes misread by some viewers as manipulation and condescension.[7] However, the charge of voyeurism and exploitation is difficult to defend given the visual construction of spatial relations within *Chiapas*. Throughout, Alpert talks with peasants in Chiapas in their homes, where they describe the lack of medical resources, their need for water, and their poor living conditions. He functions as translator, literally shifting between Spanish and English, and also as guest, recording their testimonies and building his argument, which debunks the "Third World guerrilla imagery" proffered by the mainstream news. The piece not only deconstructs the North's imagined representation of Zapatistas as masked men holding press conferences as a sort of Third World liberation performance art,

A peasant woman from Chiapas describes the lack of food, health care, and housing in *Chiapas: The Fight for Land and Liberty* (1995). Dir. Jon Alpert. Photograph courtesy of DCTV.

but works as a transcription and transversal across cultures and across the South to the North.

A range of documentaries embody this zone of claiming space on the ground, both literally and figuratively. However, they differ from what has been typically identified as guerrilla or activist work in quite clear ways, manifesting a significant historical change in the structure and design of oppositional media work from its roots in the 1970s to its practice in the 1990s.[8] These new works shift from a depiction of marginality and identity toward a capture of new spheres and spaces with transformative capacities. *Testing the Limits*, *Diana's Hair Ego: AIDS Info Up Front* (1990), *Access Denied* (1991), and the Pixelvision works of Sadie Benning are a few salient examples.

The relationship between filmmaking and subjects changes from a strategy of representation to a strategy of transaction, a moving across different spaces, domains, discourses, actions, politics, and subject positions. This tactic moves from images *of* to maneuvers *into*, a significant epistemological difference. It unsettles the very space of politics and views the space of the film and the space of the political as different registers organized around a site that is jointly shared. Rather than exclusively representing those subcultures and oppositional political voices marginalized by dominant culture in the modality of the visual, these on-the-ground works function within a different political agenda: they operate more as transcriptions across and through technologies of representation to inscribe political action and active spectator positions within the work itself.

Bill Nichols has termed this practice of working with subjects the interactive mode of documentary, a strategy he historically links to Dziga Vertov's project of opening up the relationships among filmmaker, subject, and spectator. He shows how interactive films "draw their social actors into a direct encounter with the filmmaker."[9] Filmmakers are not positioned as observers distant from the events they chronicle, but instead are full participants. Nichols identifies *Chronicle of a Summer, Poto and Cabengo, Sherman's March,* and Jon Alpert's *Hard Metals Disease* as interactive works "rooted in the moment of interaction."[10] Nichols sees great political potential in the interactive mode because it spotlights the "situated nature of documentary representation" as well as "the contingencies of the moment."[11]

In the 1990s, the interactive mode is more complexly figured within this spatialization. These more recent works urgently push representation into a different position, less as a metacritique of documentary form than as a repositioning of the documentary project as codeterminate with social actors from racialized and sexualized positions. If early interactive works from the 1970s and 1980s repressed sexual, gender, racial, and national differences within their performative qualities, these newer pieces create new social and political spaces by speaking through their differences. Paula Rabinowitz has also argued that documentaries that intervene in history operate differently, offering great potential to move beyond psychoanalytic or formalist concerns: "The historical documentary—the documentary that seeks to intervene in history—mobilizes a subject of agency."[12]

In these ground war films, the war is not in distant lands, but here, in the United States, a war for territories within, altering the dimensions and terrains of the documentary project. They are not simply about interactions, but about transactions, across different politics, constituencies, and spaces, aimed at impelling change, wherein the filmmaker, the filmmaking, and the social actors are all united in historical agency within a proxemic politics.

Michel Foucault has elaborated the power relations of proximity and distance. He claims that history depends on abstraction, purity, periodization from power and universalized forms, instituting distance as a constituent of discourse, enforcing dominance by effacing its own grounding. Genealogies, on the other hand, are sited at the body within dispersions and differences rather than abstract unities. Genealogies, then, as anti-essentialist discourses, map the complex fissures of proximity.[13] These works, then, which site their epistemologies on the ground, sustain a similar genealogy of combat. They operate within proxemics, eschewing distance, with the camera located at the body and within the dispersions and differences, contradictions, and battles.

Take Over: Heroes of the New American Depression (Peter Kinoy and Pamela Yates, 1991) materializes this on-the-ground tactic of proxemics in both subject choice and shooting strategy. The film chronicles eight different groups of homeless activists in cities across the country (New York, Detroit, Oakland, Chicago, Los Angeles, Minneapolis, Philadelphia) as they engage direct action by breaking the locks on HUD-owned housing. *Take Over* debunks the image of the homeless as helpless, immobilized victims by concentrating on how various homeless political groups organize to obtain affordable housing. The film does not simply make space for homeless persons to speak their difference as a way to counter their silencing by mainstream media as a form of melancholia and recuperation; instead, the participants' analysis of the government's housing policies and their strategy sessions literally take over cinematic space, staking out their discursive ground as they problematize the very construct of "giving voice." In direct contrast to a film like *Housing Problems,* where the problem/solution structure of the argument ends in resolution by the state, *Take Over* not only exposes the inadequacy of states' policies on housing but remedies the problem through joint direct action between the activists and the camera crews. In most scenes, the camera is side by side with the participants, breaking into buildings with them, marching in demonstrations, sitting around a table at an organizational meeting, thereby jettisoning the privileged position of observer and assuming the subject position of collaborator.

But interactivity, agency, and proxemics do not fully account for how dramatically these works diverge from a more historical mode of guerrilla filmmaking. Although historically congruent with oppositional independent work that carves out space on the margins, these works destabilize both the distant, aloof observational stance of direct cinema and an evidentiary structure that subordinates subjects to the argument of the film, which is outside lived relations and often abstract and universalized.

Writing about a newly imagined ethnographic process that would overcome the closed communications of rationalized science, Stephen Tyler has argued for a postmodern ethnographic practice that is dialogic, collaborative, participatory, polyphonic, and experiential.[14] For Tyler, a postmodern ethnography constructs a cognitive utopia comprising author, text, and

Ron Casanova and other homeless take over a building in New York City, May 1, 1990, in a scene from *Take Over* (1991). Dir. Peter Kinoy and Pamela Yates. Photograph by Mike Greenfield, courtesy of Skylight Pictures.

reader rather than the "impossible world" of scientific objectivity. A post-modern ethnography aims "to reintegrate the self in society and to restructure the conduct of everyday life."[15] Tyler's argument suggests that the space between ethics and writing constitutes one of the only positions to be occupied, a position of constant flux and fluidity.

In films on the ground, where the battles of the new world order as it is experienced within the United States are defined at local sites, the works implicitly reject a notion of the filmmaker's self as paramount, restructuring the self into multiple and diverse selves working across communities, as in the case of the multiracial homeless groups. Similarly, these works operate on the seams of this in-between space, where the ethics and politics of the actions depicted and the very writing of the action within the film or tape are constantly negotiated. For example, in *Take Over,* the major narrative organization of the film involves the taking of physical space by the homeless rather than the bestowing upon them of discursive space. *Take Over,* then, is not an argument about why homelessness exists; rather, it is an exposition of how the representational construct of "homeless" can be actively remade into a new subjectivity that is mobilized through and in collective action.

In these works, the filmmaking apparatus is alongside the subject, rather than outside it as an observer or chronicler. It is not so much simply partisan filmmaking, arguing from the same side and fighting the same wars, as it is media work that collapses the border between maker and subject as a false divide and depoliticized binary opposition. Thus on-the-ground filmmaking constitutes a political strategy that expands the notions of committed or guerrilla filmmaking into a joint effort between social actors and the action of image making. It refines, expands, and complicates the concepts of interactivity by changing the functions and sites of the camera itself.

On-the-ground documentaries mark a significant shift in the power structures of the apparatus, stripping it of its technological privileges. Rather than a machine of voyeurism, distance, representation, documentation, and appropriation, the camera in these various works is instead recast as a membrane, a permeable surface through which relations between and alongside maker and subject pass and commingle.[16] The camera does not provoke; rather, it is the site for a multilayered negotiation and exchange between subjects and makers, among aesthetics, camera positions, and politics. Maori documentary filmmaker Merata Mita has observed, for example, that her filmmaking is always "a negotiation with communities rather than a trespass into them."[17] When the camera performs as a membrane, the borders between maker and subject, active agents and representations, dissolve into a more fluid, permeable construct.

When Billy Broke His Head . . . and Other Tales of Wonder (Billy Golfus and David E. Simpson, 1995) is a compelling documentary in which Billy Golfus, a disc jockey who has suffered brain damage from an auto accident, moves immediately from his own isolation into the disability rights movement. Unlike many activist films that are structured to follow the course of consciousness-raising from solitude to political solidarity and liberation, *Billy* starts where most activist films end—with a militant act of civil disobedience in Chicago in front of a federal building, where disability rights activists literally crawl out of their wheelchairs and throw their bodies on the ground. The film does not ask us to understand disability and quietly accept differently abled bodies from a dispassionate yet empathic clinical distance. From the beginning, in an extremely radical move, *Billy* assumes we will see disability differently and participate with the characters, listening to them, demonstrating with them, our gaze quite literally thrown on the ground. Quadriplegics in wheelchairs yell at the police, enraged. The activists lying on the ground, the only place they could be, the place where they literally occupy space that excludes them, chant, "Health care is a right, not a privilege" and "Down with the nursing homes."

Billy explains in voice-over, "I thought disabled folks were supposed to act tragic but be brave and cute and inspirational. These folks weren't

Scene from a disability rights protest in Chicago where activists in wheelchairs and on crutches were arrested during an act of civil disobedience, from *When Billy Broke His Head* (1995). Dir. Billy Golfus and David E. Simpson. Photograph courtesy of Fanlight Productions.

sticking to the script." The issue of taking the ground is reinforced with the camera work in this opening scene. Slawomir Grunberg, the cinematographer, shoots the disabled activists from the ground, the camera always pinned at their point of view: the camera work itself does not suggest an able-bodied operator so much as an able-bodied operator who is able to cross into another subject position, side by side. In the melee with the police that follows, we see the police from the point of view of a paraplegic sprawled on the ground, a brilliant formal move that sets up the entire epistemological operation of the film: we are not moving into an empathy with these differently made bodies; we are, through this different architecture of cinematic space, immersed in their point of view and in the imaginary space of their bodies. The film thus deposits us on the ground with the activists.

Unlike *Roger & Me* (1989), the film to which journalists have most frequently compared *When Billy Broke His Head*, because of the two documentaries' similarities in employing a first-person expedition in cinema verité style, *Billy* is never about the narrator per se. Rather, *Billy* is about disabled people who organize and agitate for their rights. Billy never interviews the other people in the film; he talks with them, sitting beside them, asking how they manage and garnering their analyses, something that is missing from most films on disease or health. The film does not show pathetic victims, but empowered, analytic people. It features many characters with severe physical disabilities, such as paralysis, cerebral palsy, and ALS, talking to the camera, forcing the spectator to engage with them not as victims, but as analytic, strong, forceful presences that ask the spectator to move away from more comfortable distances. *When Billy Broke His Head* moves in reverse compared with most health-oriented documentaries, starting with the demonstration and ending with the family: Billy and his elderly father fish from a boat tied to a dock, his father ignoring his own hearing disability.

These seamless forms of camera and subject are often discounted within a postmodern-influenced documentary rubric and vocabulary where image fragmentation, montage, and recontextualizations of representation predominate. Often, these on-the-ground works are discussed for their content and use value for oppositional political organizing and consciousness-raising in struggles such as those concerning AIDS, reproductive rights, homelessness, and health care, sustaining counternarratives and counterarguments to mass-media images of victimization, corporatization, demonization, and privatization. Because they use a handheld style of camera work, employ interviews, and attempt to persuade spectators to action, the epistemological and aesthetic strategies of these works are frequently reduced to two maligned areas within film theory: cinema verité, critiqued for its opaque realism and transparent reproduction of power relations, and organizing film, often unfortunately ignored by critics and theorists because of its supposed aesthetic insufficiencies and emphasis on rhetorical modes of persuasion heavily reliant on evidence rather than on deconstruction or formal invention.

This critical tendency marks a repression of the new and multiple formations of political documentary, its different locations and sites in between different communities and struggles. Elevating textual hybridity above bodies in space, much of this criticism locates wars exclusively within identity issues that write the self. In contrast, another kind of documentary situates itself within social collectivities and power relations that can be changed, opening up the fissures between contradictions. Further, these on-the-ground works cannot be viewed simply as texts, cut off from their ever shifting and volatile political contexts where lives matter. They function within an entirely different institutional discourse and practice, as organisms that thrive as living membranes for social relations and political debates to pass through. They are conduits, not art objects.

These on-the-ground works are part of the artillery of political action groups organizing around reclaiming the body (groups concerned with homelessness, AIDS, disability rights, health care) within discourse and place, often circling within movements to catapult strategies, arguments, and actions. As AIDS video activist Gregg Bordowitz puts it, they are proactive.[18] Most of these works do not figure the psychic dimensions of the individual self as their main site; rather, they work through pluralized identities marshaled together for combat—most of these tapes and films present multiethnic, classed, gendered, and sexualized characters, rebuking a unified, psychologized individual identity to create shifting and fluid hybridized political entities. On-the-ground works form new battalions across identities within new spaces. Thus hybridity is not simply on the level of textual operations, but traverses across contexts, collectivities, subjectivities, spaces.

Frequently, this interactive mode of activist media is wrongly collapsed into cinema verité, a form of handheld camera documentary identified as provoking actions rather than observing them from a distance as in direct cinema.[19] Jean Rouch's *Chronicle d'un Ete* is frequently invoked. The Pacific Street Film Collective's *Red Squad* interrogates camera surveillance by New York City police of antiwar demonstrations protesting the Vietnam War by using its own cameras to provoke a reaction to expose the questionably legal intelligence-gathering teams. The camera impels action or reaction but not interaction as officers harass the filmmakers. *Red Squad*'s structure traces the panoptical relationship between camera and subjects where the camera is the center of knowledge. Conversely, in on-the-ground films, the camera is not the center of knowledge, but merely one of many dispersed centers of knowledge production. Confrontations in the more classical form of cinema verité are staged to serve both as narrative design and as exposé of repressed ideological or suppressed power structures, as in the revelations of police brutality against demonstrators in *Red Squad*.

Rather than political confrontations emanating out from the camera as the epicenter of action, a move that often privileges the camera and filmmaker as the unified site of knowledge, these works figure cameras and representations as social and political actors together with the subject, a veritable pluralization of identities, locations, politics, and strategies. The camera does not galvanize events that would not have happened without it, as in more historical articulations of cinema verité; rather, the camera is transformed beyond representation, working alongside politicized subjects.

They locate themselves on the fault lines of contradictions over power, control of space, and self-determination.

A common visual marker of this work is the view from the camera in the middle of the action. However, the camera is not directing the action, with the interactivity flowing from an encounter between camera and subject. Rather, subjects speak, often without prompting, directly into the camera, talking with rather than being interviewed by—a significant epistemological difference.

Alexandra Juhasz has argued that the only way to see AIDS television practice is within its institutional and movement contexts, where the use value of the tape to operate within a matrix of education, mobilization, persuasion, community building, and ongoing political actions privileges its institutional and use context over its aesthetics. This is not to say that aesthetic concerns are insignificant, however. Juhasz identifies how the AIDS epidemic has recast the role of alternative media in historic ways: education, public health, identity politics, interventions into drug policies, aesthetic strategies. The empowerment of persons with AIDS (PWAs) demands not only new institutions and a remaking of social relations, but rehabilitating media practice from a weak auxiliary of political action into one strand of a multipronged attack.[20] Gregg Bordowitz has argued along these same lines: "Video production is viewed as a collaborative effort. . . . AIDS activist video is produced in a dialogue with the social movement to end government inaction. The documentation of protests is one form of direct action; distribution of these tapes are demonstrations."[21]

These new political subjectivities permeate discourse as well as visual representation, formulating a new amalgamated spatial territory to be assembled ad hoc and locally as public spheres shrink. These spatial territories amalgamate the virtual and material in a way that differs from media guerrilla work of earlier periods. It is precisely the diffusion and democratization of low-cost camcorders and VCRs that opened up private spaces to recruitment as politicized spatial territories maneuvering between the virtual world of the video image and the material world of political organizing.[22] Thus these new historical subjects take ground by means of cameras and distribution technologies that can be grounded: representation and visuality materialize as reconfigured space. It is not simply the camcorder that produces these new meanings and locations, but the camcorder paired with the VCR, which miniaturizes production and disseminates it into privatized terrain such as homes, circulating video at public libraries and in living rooms in the context of health care battles that no longer can be confined to patient-doctor confidentiality.

Tapes on AIDS activism such as *Diana's Hair Ego, Testing the Limits,*

ACT UP protest again the Reagan administration's lack of response to the AIDS crisis, from *Testing the Limits* (1987). Dir. Testing the Limits Collective. Photograph courtesy of Video Data Bank.

and *Voices from the Front* exemplify this reformulation of cinema verité within changing historical conditions of political and representational crises, wars on the body and access to health, and distribution. These works share several structural similarities. As much public health education as political action, the tapes are not simply confrontational, where the alterations emanate from or ripple out from the camera. Instead, the tapes traverse back and forth between the camera and the subjects of the tape who argue against U.S. government AIDS policies, the ignorance of safe-sex techniques, and the power relations among the U.S. government, the FDA, PWAs, and spectators. The project of these tapes is not only to educate and mobilize around AIDS, but to imbricate spectators into what Chantal Mouffe has termed "the creation of new social subjects."[23]

For example, *Testing the Limits* (1987) was produced by the Testing the Limits Collective, which was formed to document the struggles around AIDS and to support people dealing with AIDS. The tape chronicles demonstrations to demand the release of new drugs, civil disobedience actions, and public education about condom usage and dental dams in a quick-paced montage style edited to energetic music. It vividly shows that AIDS is not a gay white men's disease, but a disease affecting women and communities of color. By combining these multiple communities and political actions within one tape, *Testing the Limits* does not simply pluralize AIDS activism but respatializes it as moving across communities. *Testing the Limits* not only reweaves camera-subject relations as collaborative, but contextualizes this relationship within the dynamic of health care urgencies on the ground: the tape invokes a spectator who joins the collaboration.

The Nation Erupts, a tape produced by the Not Channel Zero television collective in the aftermath of the verdicts in the Rodney King case and the subsequent Los Angeles rebellion, clearly demonstrates how this on-the-ground strategy exceeds the aesthetics and politics of classical cinema verité. The Not Channel Zero collective is a New York-based media group of African Americans and Latinos/Latinas who use hip-hop, sampling, scratch and mix techniques, and camcorders to record racialized urban life.[24] In the opening of this tape, television news crews' helicopter shots of looting and flames from South-Central L.A. are transformed by video processing into ghostlike distortions, visually exposing and signifying their political agendas to obfuscate the racialized instabilities the rebellion opened up.[25] These aerial images are immediately undercut by demonstrations on the ground photographed by camcorders. Lambasting the reduction of the Los Angeles rebellion into an isolated black-and-white riot, the tape contains camcorder footage from racialized rebellions against police brutality across the United States—Seattle; Baton Rouge; Las Vegas; Portland, Oregon; Boston; New York City; Philadelphia; Washington, D.C.; Minneapolis; Madison, Wisconsin.

Each of these segments shows a multiracial protest against police actions, effectively decomposing, in the literal sense of the term, the binary opposition of black versus white politics by integrating scenes of African American, Korean American, and Latino protesters across the country through structure and montage, rather than within each separate shot, refuting Los Angeles as the epicenter of racial violence. The tape also doubles this pluralization in its aesthetic strategies beyond camera work in the middle of the action. It includes montages of processed images of fires, TV news footage, and cops with music; historical sequences explicating race riots from 1917 to the present as a form of state terrorism against Native Americans, African Americans, and Latinos; and a section punning David Letterman titled "The Top 11 Reasons to Loot and Riot." *The Nation Erupts* recovers discursive, visual, and political ground from the hyper-reality of the Rodney King episode, ground that had been dominated by race-blinded conventional news reporting repressing its white semiotics by means of objective rationality.

The Nation Erupts, then, structurally shoots down the distant helicopter images of South-Central Los Angeles by repositioning multiply racialized confrontations with police within a larger historical and national context, implicitly demonstrating that racialization of power defines the nation. This decentering from Los Angeles occurs only in the televisual spaces of the tape, where different communities, histories, and strategies can be rearranged beyond the bondage of linearity and place. By gathering pieces produced by different political organizations and video groups across the United States, *The Nation Erupts* redefines the ground—it is not that land mass lying below the camera suspended in the helicopter, but communities of color in different physical locations united through editing and montage into a newly imagined televisual space that is simultaneously virtual and material.

Sick and Tired of Being Sick and Tired, a 1994 Deep Dish T.V. satellite project on the national health care crisis, demonstrates how this on-the-ground strategy differs significantly from the more classical formulations of cinema verité and interactive cinema, where the interaction is positioned within individuals rather than within complex racialized and sexualized communities. A twelve-part series on a range of topics spanning the spectrum of health issues (health care in Latino communities, the national health care debate, holistic health, addiction, health issues among lesbians, toxic waste, reproduction, disability), *Sick and Tired* is meant to provoke interaction not between camera and subject but among camera, subjects, and larger social and political contexts of health care as a human right.[26] Unlike purely interactive cinemas, in which spectatorial pleasure revolves like a Möbius strip between camera and audience, *Sick and Tired* widens out from an interaction that speaks to an individuated, psychically formed spectator into a series of social relations with communities of subjects and spectators. The satellite production and distribution of the series, then, were not simply a new means of dissemination and popularization, but facilitated an entirely new epistemology of collectivized spectatorship that occupies different airspace.

Producers for the series came from diverse geographic, gender, race, and class locations, from San Diego to the Bronx, and deployed a veritable lexicon of formal strategies, from realist documentary to interviews and exposés, from camcorder activism to experimental techniques. The various tapes in the series are united in their attack on the corporatization of American health systems, the denial of health care, and the media presentation of the health care debate as one between corporations. These multiple visual and structural strategies laced with pluralized identities indicate the range of forces that need to be mobilized in different ways at different junctures. As a whole, the tapes in *Sick and Tired* reclaim pluralized, different bodies within the U.S. health care system, shifting the very ground of debate from policy to human rights, from national and nationalized debate to localized politics of different regions, communities, and bodies.

Sick and Tired is significant because it employs an on-the-ground epistemological strategy to dismantle the national imaginary on health care. While each separate program assaults an issue neglected and marginalized in the more mass-mediated health care debates, the series creates a new social and political space by using satellites to uplink and downlink programs, creating solidarities across differences and regions. On-the-ground work, then, takes over territories that span the virtual, the material, the social, and the psychic, refuting their separations.

▶──

Reconnaissance

Wars often require more than cameras operating like membranes. They also necessitate reconnaissance, an exposition and explanation of enemy positions in order to map strategies and inaugurate assaults. Although the postmodernist emphasis on intertextuality produces mappings between representations, it often drains explanation from documentary form, thereby severing the reworked imagery from other historical discourses and ethical modalities. Documentaries that expose the enemy's position are viewed with a certain suspicion by critics: these works are categorized as realist texts because they rely too heavily on argumentation, information, persuasion, and exposé rather than critique the form of representation itself.

Films such as *The Panama Deception* (1992), *Ballot Measure 9* (1995), and programs produced by Paper Tiger Television and Deep Dish T.V. are often hailed for their fearless muckraking, whether concerning the U.S government invasion of Panama or the right-wing fundamentalist assault against homosexuals in Oregon.[27] However, despite their political revelations, these same works are often castigated as residual in formal terms because they eschew textual and formal complexity. They are the inheritors of the Edward R. Murrow/*See It Now* legacy of the self-indicting interview and the argument that shifts consciousness. Yet, in some ways, compared to works with complex editing strategies and effects, they seem like throwbacks to an out-of-date formal practice lacking a critique of representation and signification. Compared to more formally complex works that create new modes of experience for the spectator, these works address the spectator through argumentation, building up the case with evidence and working with strategies of persuasion.

Since the early 1980s, the expository ethic of commercial news organizations has dwindled as news has become fragmented, dispersed, and trivialized, heavily reliant on the image and on reporting that assiduously avoids confronting major structural issues as news organizations transform in the 1990s into transnational conglomerates.[28] The legacy of Murrow's *See It Now*, an acclaimed investigative news show that helped to topple Joe McCarthy through the reediting of news footage of his speeches, or *Harvest of Shame* (1960), an exposé on the deplorable working conditions of share-croppers, has migrated away from the sanitized, controversy-exempt cor-porate media sector into the much less visible, diffuse independent sector.

Many historical, psychic, and economic factors account for this shift: the concentration of transnational media conglomerates that control the news and also have interests in the military (General Electric, a major mili-tary contractor, for example, owns NBC), the end of the Fairness Doctrine, the high cost of corporate documentary production, and the increasingly cozy relationship between large media conglomerates and the government. Theorists Jean Baudrillard and MacKenzie Wark have argued that the news media have simply ripened into the hyperreal, recirculating images and de-liberately amputating them from the social and from referents. Elaborating simulation, Baudrillard writes: "No contemplation is possible. The images fragment perception into successive sequences, into stimuli toward which there can be only instantaneous response, yes or no—the limit of an abbre-viated reaction. Film no longer allows you to question. It questions you, and directly."[29] Increasingly, the investigative and expository tradition of documentary is the sole province of independent producers, whose work, in the Baudrillardian sense, interrogates and questions the ideological foun-dations of the spectator outside of binary responses. The more conglomer-ated mainstream news media, then, within this hyperreal matrix, have no room for a long form like documentary precisely because its multiple layers of interrogatives are antithetical to the very structure of the transnational media system, which requires streamlining.

Bill Nichols and Brian Winston have both written incisively on the ex-pository function of documentary as one of its defining characteristics, a trait that distinguishes it from fiction, which is more reliant on emotional and psychic suturing into the narrative by means of characters and identifi-cation. For these authors, the rhetorical mode is salient in documentary, a style of cinema that makes arguments about the world in order to change it and to mobilize spectators.[30] Nichols, for instance, writes: "Argument about the world, or representation in the sense of placing evidence before others in order to convey a particular viewpoint, forms the organizational backbone of documentary. This backbone constitutes a 'logic' or 'econo-my' of the text."[31]

Within the transnationalized media formation, the political relations of independent documentary have shifted from interrupting the dominant ideology through production of new discourses that were repressed toward the production of new social places for the distribution of any interrogative discourse at all. If textuality, content, argument, and mobilization were the old battlegrounds of independent documentary, the new battlegrounds are the places where any kind of interrogative work can be seen, in public, private, or hybrid public/private domains that are newly forming. In other words, while new technologies like camcorders have somewhat democratized access to production, the new economic formations of media and the demolition of arts funding have nearly foreclosed access to distribution and depleted public space.

Therefore, independent media are now engaged in reconnaissance not only on the level of the structure of texts, but on the level of surveying the enemy position so as to strategize new ways to take ground in order to, quite literally, make public places. It is not surprising, then, that many documentaries evoking reconnaissance, that track wars within the nation (culture wars, antigay agendas) and outside the nation (Rwanda, Bosnia, East Timor), have been produced by organizations that spend nearly equal amounts of effort on transforming the discursive relations of production and on developing the social and technological relations of distribution.

For example, *The Panama Deception* does not at first viewing look all that innovative, despite its penetrating exposé of the U.S. government's questionable intervention into Panama. Its central epistemological mode is evidentiary and logical. However, the innovative distribution by the Empowerment Project (the producer of the film) represented a major strategic shift to reclaim public space for documentary. The group devised an imaginative theatrical run that bypassed the major, highly concentrated, commercial film distributors and exhibitors. The Empowerment Project also took advantage of VCR and videotape, and sold copies of the film directly to viewers in order to secure the widest dissemination, thereby using home video as an organizing tool.

The Empowerment Project reached large audiences for its 1988 political documentary *Coverup: Behind the Iran Contra Affair* as well as for *The Panama Deception* through what the group has termed an "integrated distribution strategy" that includes theatrical, home video, educational, and television release organized by the filmmakers themselves.[32] The filmmakers organized with local political groups at each screening, remaking the public space of the theater into a community mobilization.

Perhaps no other organization has done more work in this area of documentary reconnaissance in the sense of discovering the nature of the enemy's resources and gaining information than Paper Tiger Television, which produces the Manhattan-based weekly public access show founded by DeeDee Halleck and dedicated to analyzing the information industry. Paper Tiger takes advantage of the Federal Communications Commission's provision that all cable television providers must supply public access channels in exchange for their right to monopoly ownership of cable connections and right-of-way in local communities.[33] Paper Tiger represents the convergence of the guerrilla media heritage with public access and camcorders. Since 1981, Paper Tiger in Manhattan as well as collectives in San Diego, San Francisco, Tucson, and other places have produced more than two hundred shows deconstructing various print media, such as *TV Guide*, the *Los Angeles Times, Pravda, Seventeen, Variety, Psychology Today*, the *National Enquirer*, and the *New York Times*, as well as searing analysis of contemporary politics, including such topics as Chiapas, Rwanda, Bosnia, cyberspace, AIDS, the new right, the FCC, Haiti, and East Timor.

Paper Tiger's half-hour shows depend on sophisticated yet accessible analysis by critics, scholars, activists, and journalists combined with a handmade, nontechnocratic look. The shows are produced by volunteers who work in a collective way, rather than as individual auteurs. Most shows are produced for under less than two hundred dollars, and they reveal their own means of production in their use of a multitude of Brechtian devices, ranging from direct address and performance art to signage and pirated film and video clips, to illustrate points. William Boddy has argued that Paper Tiger opens up a unique public space within the realm of commercial media; it was born and survived during the Reagan/Bush regimes, which chopped away at both Public Broadcasting and arts funding.[34]

Much has been written about the pithy analysis and funky look of Paper Tiger Television, particularly on the content of the shows and analysis provided by the various performers, especially in such hits as *Joan Does Dynasty, Twist Barbie*, and *Herb Schiller Reads the New York Times*. However, very little attention has been directed toward the simultaneous democratization of the means of production and the means of distribution that Paper Tiger sustains, the very modalities that establish its significance in the area of contemporary documentary. Amy Taubin, a critic for the *Village Voice*, has pointed out that Halleck's project with Paper Tiger has been focused less on specific programs and more on the issue of organizing around access, a further decentering of the text and authorship, rethreading production/distribution into new media ecologies that imagine radical democracies.[35]

Paper Tiger's signature look is low tech, handmade, quick production, and low budget, in direct contrast to independent long-form documentaries that often take five years to produce and require significantly larger bud-

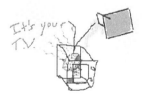

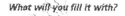

Screen grabs showing four homemade logos from Paper Tiger Television and Deep Dish T.V. Web site www.papertiger.org.

gets. Paper Tiger Television is certainly the grandchild of the Workers' Film and Photo League, which also attempted to make films for the people about people's struggles and to create new distribution venues. Paper Tiger programs deploy an array of experimental devices such as montages and manipulated footage, but the main focus is always on the argument, which integrates analysis with factual evidence in an attempt to debunk the objectivity myths encasing more commercial news and media.

The programs then become sites where small-format technologies such as camcorders shed their consumerist aura and are reimagined as instruments of democracy; it is through the camcorders, access studios, and handmade sets that the production and distribution relations of documentary are altered, in effect popularized, in the political sense of the term. Sherry Milner, a Paper Tiger producer, explains the importance of "cheap media": "One rich vein of much cheap media is the revelation of its own process, a process in which the homemade and the handmade are reconciled with technology."[36]

As an intervention into documentary theory, Paper Tiger offers a different view of political documentary, one that moves beyond the production of the text and textualities into the construction of new media ecologies that combine low-tech camcorders with high-tech cable and satellite systems to produce new social relations of reception as a form of reconnaissance. Linda Iannacone, a Paper Tiger producer, explains: "The freedom isn't in the technology, or even in the act of image making. It's all in the act of reception and how that reception has meaning or impact."[37] Joan Braderman, a cultural critic as well as a Paper Tiger presenter, has explained that Paper Tiger's political vision is "about building our own systems of public intervention and address."[38] Helen De Michel explains: "The brilliance of the Paper Tiger TV model is that it forgets the 'mass' part of media, and looks at video as a field of endeavor that can reach out to audiences in the most unlikely and untraditional places — from a cablecast to a museum, to a media center to a mall to a labor meeting to a community storefront on VHS to a satellite."[39]

Developed in 1986 as an outgrowth of Paper Tiger Television, Deep Dish T.V. is "the nation's only grass roots satellite network."[40] Describing its uplinking of camcorder activists, Linda Yablonskaya, writing in *High Performance* magazine, notes that Deep Dish marks "a subversive use of the sophisticated technology."[41] Deep Dish literally repositions advanced technology such as satellite as a means of production for a different distribution system, one that imagines and intersects with new, local communities as they are constantly forming, reforming, and realigning. As Halleck explains: "Deep Dish is a reconstructionist solution to the deconstruction of Paper Tiger. Paper Tiger tears apart the media, and Deep Dish presents the other side, or rather, other sides."[42]

Theoretically, the regional and local are rethreaded into a newly reconceived and refabricated national. In Deep Dish, production and distribution are no longer distinct processes; instead, distribution emerges as a new form of production that taps into shifting, fluid new communities on the ground, a reconnaissance for connecting disparate communities. DeeDee Halleck has commented on this relationship between technology and distribution: "If the camcorder can be seen as a retail item, then the satellite channel, or transponder, can perhaps be seen as a wholesale distributor. . . . The electronic technology of distribution on a wholesale level is now available for a relatively low price."[43] Tactical and mobile, Deep Dish is able to challenge the separation of regions, aesthetic strategies, and communities.

Deep Dish series have reflected this strategy of connecting across communities and forming new coalitions through technologies: *Will Be Televised* was a series of five one-hour programs curated by Shu Lea Chang from five regions of Asia (Korea, the Philippines, Taiwan, Hong Kong, China) documenting movements for press freedom and democracy using camcorders. The idea of the series was to "challenge the one-way flow of U.S. media and the export of 'the American Way' to the other side of the world; we provide another side of the communication highway; video from people's movements to the multinational media headquarters."[44] Other series have included *Behind Censorship: The Assault on Civil Liberties*, which analyzed arts funding and social control; *The International Women's Day Video Festival*, which showcased productions of women from around the world; *Green Screen: Grassroots Views of the Environmental Crisis*; and *Getting a Grip on Access*, which profiled public access shows produced by various ethnic, racial, socioeconomic, and geographic groups.

One of the most historically significant joint Paper Tiger/Deep Dish projects was the Gulf Crisis TV Project, a series of four twenty-eight-minute tapes produced in 1991 in response to the virtual media blackout on factual and analytic reporting on the Gulf War: *War, Oil and Power*; *Operation Dissidence*; *Getting Out of the Sand Trap*; and *Bring the Troops Home!* During the buildup to the war in the fall of 1990, Paper Tiger issued a call for tapes to local access producers across the country, a call that yielded tapes chronicling teach-ins, demonstrations, speak-outs, antimilitary activities, and conscientious objection in rural areas, small towns, and urban areas. Not only were the tapes aired via cable access and satellite, they were also used for teach-ins and screened for packed houses in movie theaters. Six more tapes were produced during the war in 1991: *Manufacturing the Enemy, News World Order, Lines in the Sand, Just Say No!, Global Dissent*, and *War on the Home Front*.

A handful of PBS stations, responding to community pressure during the war regarding the militarization of the news, broadcast the Gulf Crisis tapes: WYBE in Philadelphia, KCET in Los Angeles, and WNET in New York City. However, KQED in San Francisco refused to air the tapes, citing "technical problems." After pressure from Paper Tiger West, KQED programming staff admitted that the station didn't like the content.[45]

Despite the fact that the Gulf Crisis TV Project constituted one of the only televisual interventions to deviate from and aggressively critique the postmodern media blitz of the commercial networks that sanitized the war, very little attention has been devoted to historical analysis of this enormously significant project in the plethora of scholarly books that have emerged analyzing the postmodern conditions invoked by the Gulf War. The Gulf Crisis TV Project not only sustained a rational, evidentiary critique of the war that was missing from commercial media, which assumed a public sphere could be created, it also developed new distribution channels across different milieus, from public television to satellite and from VCRs to theaters to community groups. This strategy, then, applied postmodern pluralities to places, not simply to images, inventing zones of contention exactly as they were being annihilated and controlled.

Most of the writing on the Gulf War and media has been trained on the commercial media, where the density of the digitized imagery of the war merged with the evacuation of political meaning, geopolitical understanding, and referents. This body of work skillfully and brilliantly deconstructs the militarism, technofetishism, destruction of the public sphere, nihilistic postmodernism, and image manipulation that have invented the image banks of the new world order in the post–Cold War world. However, in its own textual fetishization, it reveals a latent pessimism about the new order, which indeed presents new possibilities through technology within differently formed political situations that are both hyperreal and real at the same time but in different ways. I use the term *hyperreal* here to refer to image culture disconnected from history and materiality. In his ringing critique of the poststructuralist interest in the Gulf War as the first war of simulacra, Christopher Norris has argued that the

> reason for engaging postmodernism in terms of the Gulf War "debate" is one that demands a much greater degree of argument critical resistance. That is to say, it brings home with particular force the depth of ideological *complicity* that exists between such forms of extreme anti-realist or irrationalist doctrine and the crisis of moral and political nerve among those whose voices should have been raised against the actions committed in their name.[46]

This Gulf War postmodernism, while identifying some of the central moves through which the national imaginary was marshaled by imagery, has focused on the consumption of images rather than on their production, distribution, and reception, committing a formalist fallacy of reducing historical and economic context to the hyperreal. In other words, this criticism has necessarily focused on the exchange value of the new technoimage empire, rather than on the incipient use values of these technologies to create new places for public discourse between the cracks in the information superhighway.

The Deep Dish satellite network is extremely important for the theorizing of political documentary because it attempts not only to multiply, pluralize, and propagate the visual representations of communities but also to unite them through the high technology of satellite networks usually deployed in more nationalized and militaristic wars. Deep Dish T.V. constitutes a new way to think through the relationship between the ground wars and air wars: the satellites here are not to be above, but are a means by which images from the ground can create different interconnections for different and newly emerging political struggles. Anyone with a satellite dish can receive Deep Dish programs. As Bill Stamets has observed, Deep Dish presumes nothing will be scrambled, therefore "poaching will be invited. . . . steal this signal."[47]

▶ ───

Healing through Images

All of these wars, inside and outside the nation, embedded within representation in labyrinthine ways, beg the question of peace and healing in the midst of all this destruction and hate. Daniel Reeves's *Obsessive Becoming* (1995), a nearly hour-long experimental documentary tour de force five years in the making, deploys an extraordinary range of digital and image-processing techniques and archival images to illuminate the psychic reverberations between family violence and nationalist wars in the twentieth century. The tape deconstructs masculinity in its patriarchal forms. It rewires the masculine subject position through images and words, a creative construct as obsessive becoming. In fact, the tape is dedicated to Suzanne Lucille Sticha Reeves, Daniel's mother.

To expunge these wars, *Obsessive Becoming* fuses and layers the testimony, aesthetics/anesthetics, on the ground, and reconnaissance modalities, transcribing each upon the other to create a rhetorical and visual density that forms a new public architecture for both the self and politics. In Reeves's own words, the piece is a "surreal autobiography" plumbing his own dysfunctional family, a wrenching tale—which Reeves designates a "compulsive desire" in the opening credits—of physical and sexual abuse, violence, bigamy, and missing relatives narrated by the women in his family, exposing the repetition fetish marked by family violence. In voice-over, Reeves observes, "What we failed to look for will come back, to sleep in the dreams of our children."

Many critics and curators have commented on the deeply personal, affective nature of *Obsessive Becoming*, often referring to its technical arabesques as "poetic exorcism."[48] However astute their writings are about how the tape formally triggers these emotional and psychic registers, they repress a major trajectory of the piece that unequivocally links these early traumas to the larger political issues of war and technology in the twentieth century. For example, repeated throughout is a digitized image of two young boys boxing, superimposed over an archival image, perhaps from World War II, of a wall falling down, presumably after an aerial bombing. This image condenses the connections between a warped patriarchal familialism and a warped patriarchal nationalism.

In *The Nervous System,* Michael Taussig describes how a Putamayo healer "explained to me that the healer passes on an image, the 'painting' as it is called there, to the sick person who, seeing it, gets better—all this accompanied by waves of nausea gathering fires of sensory storm, vomit, the cleansing pandemonium of purging."[49] For Taussig, the image holds possibilities beyond representation and iconicity; it can, under the right ritualized conditions, revive the magic that modernity suppresses, a magic that releases pain and moves toward something new that is never fixed. Taussig sees the image as curative and empowering, especially in montage, where hallucinatory juxtapositions flow, stopping and starting, "holding a history of nations."[50]

Obsessive Becoming epitomizes what Taussig describes as healing through images. Its visual density and layering between home movies and archival war films unhinges these images from fixity and repetition, unleashing their power by pushing them into a flow. Water imagery, suggesting baptism, cleansing, thirst that is quenched, dominates the visual design. Words that appear on the screen are processed to look like waves of flowing water. Family snapshots are digitized into a stream of images, with water behind them, shots repeated several times in the tape. Many war and family images are superimposed on water. In the middle of the tape, Reeves throws his father's gun into a pond. In the tape's coda, family snapshots are morphed into each other, with water imagery shimmering in the background. In voice-over Reeves observes, "If I raise my hand to the light, I see my dead mother in my palm . . . they move together in every moment like a garland of water, and like writing on water, they cannot be held, but are always becoming, forever moving, forever entwined."

Fluidity, then, psychoanalytically and politically loosens the fixity of psychic repetition and nationalistic borders. But it also invokes Zen teachings for peace. Thich Nhat Hanh, a Vietnamese Buddhist monk who contributes voice-over edited over a war sequence from Vietnam in *Obsessive Becoming,* has written, "That is why I use the image of water to talk about understanding. Knowledge is solid; it blocks the way of understanding. Water can flow, can penetrate."[51]

Digitally processed and layered image from home movies of Daniel Reeves, his brother, and his father, from *Obsessive Becoming* (1995). Dir. Daniel Reeves. Photograph courtesy of Video Data Bank.

Obsessive Becoming transforms testimony in war documentary at several altitudes. The first section of the tape is constructed of testimonies from relatives interrupted by home snapshots that float in space like flags or are superimposed on other images. Only the women in Reeves's family testify to his stepfather Milton's beatings and shootings on camera, and their testimony is shot in a conventional straight documentary style. They sometimes hold up old family photographs in their hands, next to their faces. Women, then, narrativize family trauma, displacing patriarchal history with a form of melodrama where family contradictions, pain, and conflicts between the public and private world are exposed.[52]

These interviews are intercut with onscreen historical information about the hoax marriage of Milton to Reeves's mother and Milton's beating of Daniel and his brother Thomas, where the text points to the silences in the family testimony. In another sequence, we hear an audiotape made when Reeves was a child, in which his mother interrogates him, asking him what animal he would be and where he goes to school, an example of the terrorization of children through enforced forms of testimony. Other images of silencing surface: a shot of a nun taping a young boy's mouth shut is repeated throughout the tape against a white cloudy background, suggesting Reeves's experience in Catholic school. Yet Reeves's narration functions shamanistically, analyzing the silences in his family and his attempt, through the video, to speak the trauma: "And all these whispered lies form an anvil heaving and corrupt from the blight of this denial and tied to the wings of our aspiration and wisdom. It pulls us ever downward if we do not choose to name them. I choose to name them."

Nearly halfway through the tape, Reeves pulls away from narrative and linear construction; he says, "I want to dive far beneath this story line to see all this neurosis and damage, all this brilliance and strength as the clear song of one whole life." At this halfway point, *Obsessive Becoming* shifts from family memory to a political history of wars, shaking off the anesthetic of war by using technology to pass through and reconnect the images to the senses and to a larger history of war itself. Images of science and technology are layered throughout the tape: nuclear power plants, subways, space flights, science experiments, moon walks, rockets, gun sights—referred to in Reeves's narration as "this machine world," a world of instrumentality and rationality that denies the magical transformative properties of the image by using it rather than moving through it.

A rebirth through the imaginary occurs; an image of a birth and then a baby crawling, evoking a new self born out of personal trauma and larger political trauma, is layered over war iconography spanning the twentieth century. However, *Obsessive Becoming* does not reject all technology, only that technology hijacked by violence. Indeed, *Obsessive Becoming* is in many ways an exorcism of analog and digital forms, using technologies to penetrate images, remake them, form new spaces, literally moving through the technology rather than reifying its capacities. An image of a sonogram suggests the possibilities of rerouting new technologies for life.

Obsessive Becoming visually argues that aerial wars can be won only on the ground. Images from Edward Curtis's *In the Land of the War Canoes*, suggesting the genocide of Native Americans, to the Nazi death camps, to the Warsaw ghetto, to Vietnam, to Martin Luther King, to aerial shots of bombings in Vietnam, to Hiroshima, to the Gulf War high-tech bombings, signify this shift from private trauma to political trauma, denoting how the very image of war is aerial, suspended. These archival images of the horrifying wars of the twentieth century are not allowed to be viewed as separate anomalies, but are visually transcribed through montage and layering to signal their connections to racialized genocide across the globe and across history. At the end of this sequence, images of rice fields, presumably in Vietnam in the postwar period, return to the ground, to growing, harvesting, living. Onscreen titles inform us, "Every day on this planet as many as forty thousand children die for lack of nutrition." With these images and words, Reeves broadens from his own abused childhood and devastations of war to the war on children, the young bodies on the ground, requiring nourishment, the war that must be fought now, in the present.

Obsessive Becoming undertakes reconnaissance as well, surveying the enemy in order to secure a position. The tape scopes out family trauma and war, explaining each through the other, folding back into itself, erasing borders. This analytic strategy to reject the false divides between the private and the public is not described but visualized throughout, where family images are layered into or within war iconography. However, to avoid the trap of the binary opposition between family and war, private and public, the tape presents a visualization of reconnaissance in its performative elements, which function as shamans on the images, floating over them, dancing. These images suggest that it is only through a reinvention of the self and a reimagining of all borders that healing and peace can be materialized, through becoming, creating. All of these performative images are shot against white backgrounds or are disconnected from any mise-en-scène at all, floating over other images, suggesting both their ritualistic function and their metacommunicative position over the archival images. An altar boy changes into an angelic figure, swirling over the images of war; a boy sitting in a chair with his face taped dissolves into white; a man in a bear costume dances over the images. Tom Waits sings over these final images, "You're innocent when you dream"—not so much a summation of the artistry of Reeves's hallucinogenic image making as a teaching about how to extricate pain and horror from the world.

Obsessive Becoming operates as a transfiguration of familial traumas and nationalist violence through imaging. It refutes the fragmentation bombs of history and the fragmented imagery of memory by conjuring every means possible—digital image processing, morphing, montage editing, digital layering of images, voice-over—to connect home movies, snapshots, archival footage, performance, and interviews into a spiritually renewed psychic zone that reclaims dreaming and reconnects fractured words and shanghaied images for peace. In this sense, *Obsessive Becoming* shows how the different threads of the central binary oppositions of war iconography—official versus unofficial, image versus blood, nation versus communities across borders—can be embroidered together to create a new space for imagining. This illuminated manuscript is suspended between the psyche and politics, between bombs in the air and fighting on the ground. *Obsessive Becoming* morphs more than simply archival images of Reeves's own family; it morphs the undergirding concepts circulating around and in between war imaging. *Obsessive Becoming* braids together the public space of war and the private terrors of family life with multiple technologies and their capacity to build new spaces as a form of video insurgency.

Ambushes

[4] *Female Body Ambushes*

▶

Seeing Body Battlegrounds

Technologies, discourses, and the imaginary of reproduction have ambushed the female body. Anita Hill, Murphy Brown, the Republican Party's attempt to deify family values, Zoë Baird, and the shooting of Dr. David Gunn at a Florida abortion clinic in March 1993 are all sites of newly fashioned feminist battlegrounds. The U.S. Supreme Court's 1993 decision in *Bray v. Alexandria Women's Health Clinic,* upholding the right of Operation Rescue to block entrances to abortion clinics, signaled a sharp retreat for women's reproductive rights and legitimated the antiabortion movement's strategy of direct assault and annihilation of women's bodies and right to choose.[1] But these battlegrounds are constructed differently from those of geopolitical wars, where combatants fight with guns, missiles, and media propaganda for geographically demarcated places defined by borders. These surprise attacks against the female body occupy much different locations, both real and virtual, imagined and material.

As film and video are gradually defunded and privatized as a way to stem the explosion of access made possible by state-supported funding initiatives of the 1970s and technological advances of the 1980s, the U.S. Supreme Court in the past decade has maintained the construct of *Roe v. Wade* but progressively deteriorated access by a range of women in a series of repressive rulings. The cumulative effect has been to privatize both media production and abortion, protecting them almost exclusively for the white middle class. Racial politics, particularly the rollback of affirmative action law, underpins both of these discursive and legal moves.

Amateur camcorders used by reproductive rights activists to document demonstrations at clinics reconfigure the public sphere around abortion politics and female bodies in the 1990s. It is in these spaces that the radical potential of low-end consumer imaging technologies can be scouted out. The new social relations of production offered by amateur video technologies shift discussion about what constitutes political oppositional media practice away from a more monologic, formal analysis of textuality and toward a more dialogic politics of community and active spectatorship.

I argue on two interwoven levels here: the level of the mass-mediated version and that of the oppositional video revisioning of reproductive rights. I theorize the significance and possibilities of amateur media to generate a feminist oppositional public sphere in light of a repressed and repressive political and media context that amputates the female body—in all its multiple forms—from representation. Second, I analyze specific tapes in terms of how they simultaneously negotiate reproductive rights activism with specific, multiple social formations of age, class, and race, terms not associated with reproductive rights in its earlier historical formations, and insist on the female body.

These tapes disintegrate arbitrary borders between text and context, art and politics, spectator and participant, with new amateur and low-end video technologies. This work functions as guerrilla raids on technology, creating feminist bodies constructed from conjoining flesh and visual machines. These tapes invent a new social space for women precisely because they ambush less gendered and less specified female body formations in representation.

Feminist body battlegrounds are not defined exclusively or explicitly by geography.[2] Their borders are amorphous in the material sense, smudging the lines that separate media representations, political agendas, the female body, technology, and place. They cannot be mapped—analytically, physically, philosophically, or critically—in quite the same way as geopolitical wars, most significantly because gender and sexuality operate within a much more fluid and infinitely contestable expanse.

Gender, sexuality, and reproductive rights in the 1990s are difficult to "see" and to "situate"—although they penetrate nearly every political discussion and media representation. Their polyvocal, heterogeneous, fluid, changing forms shatter borders between humans and machines and challenge the stasis of phallocentric systems of politics and representation.[3] In the case of the war over representation and reproductive rights, the feminist raid on technology to create new activist positions that entail action and the remaking of visualities provides access to these new places.

This argument concerning heterogeneous identities must be hewn carefully, however, so that it does not totally launch feminist media political strategy into the potentially unproductive construct of utopian cyber-

Activist leading a chant at a reproductive rights rally, from *Access Denied* (1991).
Dir. ReproVision. Photograph courtesy of Women Make Movies.

space unhinged from concrete social relations. The realpolitik dimensions
of gender, sexuality, and reproductive rights located in the courts, the law,
public policy, health care, and the real lives of women remain vital to any
feminist media agenda. The difference that I am trying to argue for here is
that although realpolitik is necessary, it is no longer sufficient to produce
social change precisely because the web of social relations within which
women live is also a compilation or assemblage of technology and representation. This imagining of a collaboration between women as body and
machine as visuality, then, proposes not to jettison the "real," but actually
to expand it, complicate it, demonstrate its multivocal, multilayered construction that breaks down distinctions, borders, and domination.[4]

These feminist battles over reproductive rights track the disturbances
provoked by women in a differently ordered and constructed public sphere
that has transformed politics in the 1990s. The most horrific concrete example of this collapse of the borders between representation and the "real"
is the 1993 assassination of Dr. David Gunn, an abortion provider in
Florida, by Michael Griffin, a pro-life supporter. Although the shooting of
Dr. Gunn marked the first death of an abortion provider and therefore signified the escalation of the civil war against women to deadly heights, it
also occurred within the context of increasing clinic violence during the

preceding several years (bombings, arson, toxic chemicals injected into Planned Parenthood clinics, assaults against clinic personnel, vandalism, trespass, and physical confrontation of abortion providers). The pro-life shift from ideological to physical warfare diffused to multiple clinics across the country and explicitly centered on assaulting the pregnant female body has unfolded for the past ten years, unimpeded by any intervention from the Justice Department to protect the civil rights of women or their access to health care.[5]

However, the pro-life political strategy has itself not been confined only to physical and legal realms. It, too, has obscured the boundaries separating female bodies, representation, politics, and reproductive rights. Operation Rescue chapters have instituted a campaign called "No Place to Hide." The campaign features "wanted" posters with pictures of doctors who perform abortions and their telephone numbers. Dr. Gunn was the subject of one of these posters. It would not be accurate to view the use of these "wanted" posters as provocateurs of abortion violence, as that kind of analysis suggests an antiquated, hypodermic model in which media directly impel politics. Rather, these posters, the killing of Dr. Gunn, the Planned Parenthood media campaign afterward, and the embattled pregnant female body demonstrate quite forcibly that a new construct smearing the lines dividing media, technology, and politics has emerged that requires careful examination if a new feminist media politics of counterambushing is to be forged.

The pro-life movement is not defined on only one, unified, monologic, level anymore; rather, it is both national and local, both ideological and physical, both for "babies" and against women, both invoking 1960s civil rights strategies and engaging more postmodern technological frames of telephones, faxes, and video documentaries. In the case of Dr. Gunn, the attack against pregnant female bodies inscribed by choice was rendered physical by the killing of a male abortion provider, who himself traveled between clinics in Alabama and Florida. Thus the pregnant female body was both absent and present simultaneously. Therefore, a feminist media strategy must not only reinsert the female body, but reinvent visual representations, media technologies, and politics as multivocal, heterogeneous constructions that travel over different discourses and terrains.

All of these feminist battlegrounds and sites suggest the emergence of a new political territory, a region marked off not so much by material space or location as by a shifting, constantly realigning set of interconnecting relationships among the female body, new technologies, mass communications, political rights, and visual encodings of different female bodies within representation. These new territories, where the borders between media and politics or discourse and representation or the body and technology disintegrate, require a rethreading of what constitutes feminist media theory and practice and a reimagining of its political possibilities for intervention to change the discursive and material conditions of women's lives.

▶ ───

Blurring the Body of Documentary

Reproductive rights, then, emerge as a specific gendered site of enormous importance to an investigation of the multiple dimensions of these realignments between media and politics, gender and representation, sexuality and visual imaginaries, the maternal and the pregnant body, the female body and the nation-state. I argue that this collapsing of media and politics into a new configuration of power needs to be considered dialectically. On the one hand, this merging reveals a strategy for containing feminist articulations of reproductive rights within mass forms of communications dependent on capitulation to the discursive dominance of textuality. On the other hand, the blurring between media and politics offers a strategy for feminist intervention that installs the oppositional female body with new technologies like low-end video camcorders to build a new social and representational space that imagines new contexts and different material conditions. Constance Penley and Andrew Ross, along these same lines, have argued for the emancipatory potential of new technologies and for a revision of the definition of radical politics: "Activism today is no longer a case of putting bodies on the line; increasingly, it requires and involves bodies-with-cameras."[6]

Rather than pitting alternative media against dominant network or print media in a David and Goliath scenario of scarcity and heart versus abundance and manipulation—a common strategy of radical media politics in the 1970s and 1980s—I want to play with the notion that all of these multiple registers, from the dominant media of commercials and news stories to right-to-life videos to activist video to experimental art video, trace the contours of the multiple battlegrounds in the fight for reproductive rights. This range of media discourses registers particular multiple typographies of the female body: maternal, pregnant, militant, oppositional, imaging apparatus. These typographies are not distinct, and they often overlap. On a theoretical level, the political urgency of media on reproductive rights hinges not on representation alone, but on these media's organization of the female body within these multiple zones to critique patriarchal nationalism.

If we junk these oppositions between dominant media and alternative media and concentrate instead on how the social, representational, and discursive dimensions of feminist reproductive rights converge, then we must revise the definition of political documentary—if not abandon it altogether as a false construct separating media practice from politics by locating them within a seesaw dependency. Politics stokes the necessity of media intervention; media intervention transforms politics and consciousness. If we begin with the supposition that these distinctions are no longer viable, both because of new technologies and because of the problematization of gender and sexuality in the new world order, then we need to revamp our notion of political media entirely by pushing it through the grids of gender and sexuality.

Political documentary theorists and critics (with a few exceptions, such as Julia Lesage, Julianne Burton, and E. Ann Kaplan)[7] have often been blind to gender, sexuality, and emerging low-end technologies like camcorders. They have in many ways been codependent on textual analysis of formal strategies or argumentation, locked into a Griersonian or neo-Marxist or religious conception of documentary redeeming the nation and the spectator through good works and good intentions, like a missionary to the masses of the uninformed. Whether these documentary works depend on realist conventions of expository documentary or more deconstructive, interrogative, and self-reflexive forms is inconsequential: their relationship to spectators remains identical.[8] They pose as redemptive. They rescue the spectator from ignorance or passivity. They repair the nation.

As interconnected modalities rather than parallel tracks, gender, sexuality, and new technologies such as camcorder video and digital imaging systems have the potential to revamp our theorization of political documentary. False theoretical oppositions between media texts and historical and political contexts must be destroyed if women are to survive. If both Donna Haraway, as a feminist, and Ross Perot, as a renegade multimillionaire capitalist, can redefine politics as the convergence of the body with the technological—where distinct borders between the aesthetic and the social, the private and the public, media and political identities fuse—then documentary theory also needs rehabilitation from its 1960s rhetoric of agitation and its fetishization of texts themselves as central to activating politics. Documentary needs to assume a feminist guerrilla approach that raids technologies for their ability to produce new image spaces, going to the streets with amateur video cameras just like the Buffalo Media Coalition for Reproductive Rights or Reprovision in New York City. But it needs to reimagine these streets in a less linear and more fluid way, with multiple voices and multiple political nodal points. While the fight for reproductive rights is increasingly bifurcated between the legal system as interpreter of the law and the clinics as enactments of it, a feminist documentary strategy for reproductive rights must interweave these two strands.

▶

Graphing Feminist Public Spheres

But how do we justify why oppositions between textuality and contextuality in political documentary need to be jettisoned along with our old bell-bottoms and granny dresses? Why is a feminist public sphere where art and politics, the private and public sphere, amalgamate via video an urgent necessity during the war on the female body? I would like to graph out two different trajectories on abortion—one representational, textual, and symbolic, the other discursive and legal—to show how both, although different, share reactionary structural similarities in their relationship to the visual terrain of reproduction and the production of the national imaginary.

During the 1980s, feminists not only lost ground on the legal front for reproductive rights, but also experienced a retrenchment on the visual front as the antiabortion movement marshaled the visual representation of the fetus as its main artillery. As Margaret Cooper noted in a 1986 *Cineaste* article titled "The Abortion Film Wars," since the dissemination of the antiabortion film *The Silent Scream* in 1986, the abortion debate has engaged both right-to-lifers and feminist media producers in combat over representation.[9]

In her decoding of the complicated relationship between media spectacle and clinical experience in *The Silent Scream* and imaging technologies such as ultrasound, Rosalind Petchesky has argued that not only has the pregnant body been effaced or peripheralized or absented, but the fetus itself has been represented as "primary and autonomous." Petchesky notes: "The strategy of anti-abortionists to make fetal personhood a self-fulfilling prophecy by making the fetus a public presence addresses a visually oriented culture. Meanwhile, finding 'positive' images and symbols of abortion hard to imagine, feminists and other pro-choice advocates have all too readily ceded the visual terrain."[10]

Discussing a wide range of reproductive discourse in the 1980s from newspapers, magazines, and television shows, Valerie Hartouni argues that the decade can be characterized by the mass media's obsession with women and fetuses. She notes that an entire range of political debates about the family, the military, gays, careerism, hedonism, affirmative action, civil rights, and welfare, for example, had reproduction as their subtext. The imaging of the fetus deployed science to institute visual identification and bonding, to reintegrate women with an essentialist maternalism. Hartouni advances that although the decade of the 1980s left feminists in a defensive and somewhat narrow position concerning reproductive rights, the context of these technologies, techniques, and representations is unstable and vulnerable. She claims:

> Contained in the disruption of conventional meanings and identities and their particular vulnerability to contestation are numerous possible political openings—multiple points of resistance as well as projects of reconstruction. Naming and seizing these possibilities, however, require imagination, a new political idiom, as well as a certain courage—to eschew a lingering attachment to things 'natural' and 'foundational,' and to jettison the essentialism clung to by all extant participants and opponents of the repro-tech drama.[11]

All these writers acknowledge that the battle for reproductive rights has shifted to visual representation and practice, partially displacing exclusively discursive formations. Although Cooper sees hope in alternative documentaries that tell different stories about abortion, she does not theorize how these films could work to restructure the relationships among politics, media, and the female body. Although Petchesky and Hartouni concur that the antiabortion movement has virtually seized the visual front, they do not propose concrete counterstrategies for feminists to regain visual culture and to imagine a concrete counterambush that places the female body within social and historical relations in order to claim space currently occupied by antiabortion discourses and practices.

Ultimately, representation alone is insufficient, vulnerable to endless recodings and recontextualizations. Signification without social relations and the female body is an impotent salvo in the face of the attack on reproductive rights. An activist, feminist oppositional media practice around abortion is vitally urgent. As both longtime reproductive rights activists and feminist cultural theorists know, our opponents in the culture wars and the female body wars can conjure up easily digestible, romanticized, and maternalized visual codes and conventions in imaging fetuses and children. They can marshal discursive homologies equating abortion to the Holocaust or slavery to invoke civil rights within a rhetoric dependent upon metaphor and emotion unhinged from historical specificity.

Conversely, the pro-choice side has traditionally banked on cognitive and political arguments regarding a woman's right to choose and analysis of the problematic of women's differences from men within the U.S. health care system.[12] Although valid, necessary, and compelling, these positions do not easily lend themselves to visual representation where the object itself could be reproduced, because the object—abortion rights—is a discursive construct with multiple dimensions and forms. Therefore, there is no simple, seemingly straight documentary, unmediated, one-to-one correspondence between object and image. A radical intervention into representation, then, must, by necessity, assemble different layers of images, discourses, bodies, and politics together to combat the wholeness of the image of the fetus as consummate.

These arguments are abstract and not easy to represent within Hollywood cinematic narrative conventions invoking desire or narrative affective excess. In the 1990s, textual, contextual, representational, political, and argumentative modes have congealed into a new kind of social formation that is neither distinctly media nor distinctly political. Therefore, a feminist radical media practice requires decomposition of these arbitrary borders. I deliberately deploy the term *practice* here, following Foucault in *The Archaeology of Knowledge*, as a way to suggest the disintegration of boundaries between the political and the representational, yet to avoid postmodernism's blurring of everything into a pluralist simulacrum disavowing power.[13]

During the 1992–93 television season, the Arthur S. DeMoss Foundation aired commercials on the major networks in selected markets and on CNN depicting a multiculturally correct group of about thirty smiling six-year-olds exiting a clean, suburban school. The DeMoss Foundation, located in Philadelphia, is a rather curious organization, founded nearly forty years ago by Nancy DeMoss, wife of Arthur S. DeMoss, president of the National Liberty Corporation in Valley Forge, Pennsylvania. Upon Arthur's death in 1979, Nancy committed herself to celebrating what she terms "Life." Nonprofit and expressly committed to producing educational publications and media presentations on what the foundation statement terms "major concerns within our society," the DeMoss Foundation accepts no contributions. Instead, it asks that potential contributors donate money to one of the pro-life organizations whose addresses are reprinted in a thirty-two-page glossy brochure that is mailed to anyone inquiring about the organization.[14] The television ads are part of an elaborate media campaign. In its own statement, the foundation proclaims: "This campaign celebrates life. It deals with family values and treats a delicate subject in a kind and gentle way. It seeks to change minds, not laws, by getting people to think about a difficult subject in a new light. These spots simply ask the question: What could be more important than the right of someone to be born?"[15] The foundation refuses to disclose the names of the producers and will not circulate the tapes.[16]

In the cable television ad, the voice-over proclaims that the mothers of the children onscreen chose life for them, and that is why we can "see" them now. The DeMoss Foundation ran this series of pro-life, pro-family spots for more than a year during prime time. Other notorious spots feature happy, white parents doting over a child on a playground, with a syrupy, concerned male voice-over explaining that the couple had considered terminating the pregnancy because they weren't sure they could afford a child.

With their perfect composition, soft lighting, pastel costuming, and bourgeois mise-en-scène, these slick commercials merge the commodity fetishism of advertising with the psychoanalytic overlays and conventions of Hollywood melodrama. These ads elaborate an emotional brocade of the family romance. Here, both the production and representation of children collapse into each other: the 35mm image of the happy, yet voiceless, child is reproducible on the level of representation precisely because biological reproduction on the level of the woman's body was not tampered with by "unnatural" forces such as abortion. These DeMoss ads invert classical melodramatic modes: rather than contradiction between sexuality and convention, between woman's independence and her place within the confines of the home, between repression and expression (tropes that form the resistant, oppositional potential of all melodrama), the ads present us with upscale versions of happy home movies in which all contention is deleted.[17]

This evening-out of contradictions facilitates an affective response on only one register—emotion. The subtext of the ads is that no other analysis—feminist, analytic, legal, social, political—is legitimate, because no available single image could overpower that of the beatific child. The child, then, as in Holocaust and civil rights imagery, is figured as a survivor and the moral imperative to continue to be vigilant. This strategy does not differ significantly from most television commercials, where the fetishization of commodities—in this case, children—depends on addressing affective desire through the excessive opulence of the image design.

But most important, the DeMoss ad pictures the child without the mother as parent, as an independent, autonomous being almost outside of familial relations. Woman's body and mothering are invisible, not simply erased, which would suggest an active deletion. Carole Stabile has noted a similar move in mass-media representations of fetuses: "The maternal space has, in effect, disappeared and what has emerged in its place is an environment that the fetus alone occupies."[18] Numerous close-ups amplify the child's identity, subjectivity, and presence, whereas the mother is reduced to a verbal construct with no visual valence or power. In other words, the maternal space is jettisoned to the outside of the image as a sort of distant satellite, still transmitting, but on the "outside," secondary to the needs or the image of the child.

E. Ann Kaplan, in her book *Motherhood and Representation*, describes this fusion of the mother and child to submit to the rule of the father as the maternal sacrifice paradigm. This paradigm establishes women's relationship to their children as one typified by loss of self, identity, and differentiation between the women and their children.[19] Extending this paradigm to the elision of abortion in the DeMoss ad, women sacrifice choice and autonomy from the nuclear family to live in a world where the rule of the father is inscribed on three different registers. First, a disembodied male voice-over asserts patriarchal authority. Second, 35mm commercial film production affirms technological authority. Third, access to prime-time markets on cable in the realm of distribution and diffusion confirms economic authority. Following most pro-life imagery, the child (and in other media representations, such as magazine photographs, the fetus) is positioned as the glorified subject of the family romance, its subjectivity overpowering, engulfing, and annihilating the mother. The DeMoss commercials merge the fetus and the child; each invokes and winds back on the other, inseparable in practice and discourse.

My second example of the complex, dense discursive topography of abortion is none other than President Bill Clinton's reversal of five rulings on abortion on the twentieth anniversary of *Roe v. Wade* on January 22, 1993, only two days after he took office. Women's groups pressured the Clinton administration to initiate some significant interventions on abortion on this important historical day to show the symbolic end to twelve years of Republican and Supreme Court chiseling away at *Roe v. Wade*. To summarize, the rulings reversed the prohibition on the counseling of women regarding abortion in federally funded clinics (the gag rule), permitted military hospitals to perform abortions if the woman pays, reassessed the ban on RU486, opened the way to provide money to international groups that provide abortions, and allowed research on fetal tissue to proceed.[20]

On the discursive and political level, Clinton's actions on abortion signaled his debt to women, who helped him win the presidential election in the first place. This was true even though he equivocated on abortion: he stated that it should be safe and legal, but rare. Although his position on abortion is minimal, this statement "speaks" abortion yet silences feminism. It should also be noted that during the transition, Clinton railed against women as "bean counters" for demanding more women appointees to cabinet positions in his administration. What has emerged in the Clinton administration's discursive construct around women is a splitting of the subject of women into multiple parts, each of which can be handled in specific ways to curb potential destabilization of neoliberal pluralism by a radical multiplicity. For example, abortion is severed from the discourse of equality and access, women appointees to cabinet positions are positioned as women and not as women interested in women's issues. Hillary Rodham Clinton is remodeled into perfect mother, supportive mate, glamorous fashion plate, and health care policy wonk. Thus the Clinton administration disarticulates any political complexity of women and feminism. This more singular, unified media image of women modifies women's political power and reduces the political volatility of women's issues.

The Clinton reversals on abortion should not be so easily read and acclaimed as remedies to the legal setbacks of the 1980s. These reversals are both similar to and different from the U.S. Supreme Court decisions of the 1980s and early 1990s such as *H. L. v. Matheson* in 1983, *Webster v. Reproductive Health Services* in 1989, *Hodgson v. Minnesota* and *Ohio v. Akron Center for Reproductive Health* in 1990, *Planned Parenthood v. Casey* in 1992, and *Bray v. Alexandria Women's Health Clinic* in 1993. All of these Court decisions limited access to abortion, yet kept the formal/legal status of abortion intact. Clinton's reversals actually only inverted what the Court had advocated: the right to abortion remains, but equal access to abortion is severely diminished, with the rulings covering only very specific areas such as the military, scientific research, and disbursement of funds internationally. However, the Clinton rulings also differed from the Supreme Court decisions because they opened up new discourse on abortion, typified in the lifting of the gag rule. Thus the Clinton reversals severed practice from discourse: the practice of abortion remains locked within the regressive Supreme Court rulings, while the discourse on abortion is released from legal bondage.

However, despite what was on the level of policy a breath of liberal— but be apprised, certainly not radical—fresh air after the virulently anti-woman regimes of the preceding decade, on the level of visual representation and narrative structure, the *New York Times* coverage of the Clinton reversals structurally duplicated the DeMoss Foundation's ads.[21] The news coverage of this event deleted women, feminism, and reproductive rights visually and discursively. Out of twenty-four paragraphs in the *New York Times* story, only one featured a response from a pro-choice leader, Kate Michelman of the National Abortion Rights Action League. That sole sentence was located on the jump page, a visual and ideological displacement of women.

The bulk of the article covered various pro-lifers, from the archbishop of Los Angeles to Senator Jesse Helms to the seventy-five thousand pro-life protesters outside the White House. This discursive erasure of "women" and silencing of "feminism" was doubled in the two news photographs illustrating the story: on the front page, a group shot of about seven pro-life men with picket signs; on the jump page, a shot of a large crowd of pro-life demonstrators with the phallic Washington Monument centering the composition. This double move of silencing feminism and representing women has emerged as a strategy of the Clinton administration in the example of Hillary Clinton's carefully orchestrated, yet mostly mute, press image. When Clinton announced that Hillary would head the task force on health care reform, she did not speak. Yet the press coverage of Hillary, in biographies and anecdotes, constantly affirms her strong voice in policy.[22] So her visual representation itself splits the symbolic, the real, the hyperreal, and the virtual.

One could argue that these images of antiabortion protest are merely ideological capitulations to the inherent use of binary opposition in news coverage to establish a narrative conflict between large, overpowering forces such as the government and an angry mass movement. Yet on a more visual and visceral level, they underscore the repression of women as a class and the maternal as a complex multiplicity by the "law." Within the news coverage of the reversals, the "law" is figured in multiple forms that are not split apart discursively. The "law" is government, yet it symbolizes Clinton's authority to intervene and change government policy. The "law" in this media representation is caught between social debates, yet also operates psychoanalytically as the rule of the father and language. If the entire context of the news during this period is read as a Hollywood melodrama script with various roles and subplots, repression and contradiction erupt, signifying narrative excess and radical ruptures with patriarchy. As Clinton signed the reversals, "nannygate" erupted on Capitol Hill in the case of Zoë Baird's nomination to attorney general and questions regarding her hiring of illegal aliens for child care.[23] Here, the contradictions that emanated from the Baird nomination emulated the classic ingredients of 1950s melodrama: woman as mother challenges woman as worker; the private and the public realms, which constitute "woman," crash into one another. In the case of the attorney general nomination, Baird's position as a rich, elite professional superseded the gender issues of mothering in the discourse surrounding her employment of illegal aliens, yet the confirmation hearings vacillated between her qualifications as a legal professional and her disqualification as a mother who performed an illegal act. Further, the private realm of Baird's mothering and child care detoured the public realm of her ability to serve as attorney general. In this case, gender issues around mothering underscored class privilege as a "problem" for government service. It is only in the figure of nonmothers like Janet Reno, then, that woman can participate in the Clinton presidency.

Maternalizing Narrative

I would like to detour from unraveling the gender, class, ethnicity, colonial relations, and corporate collaborations trajectories of the Baird case and move the focus to the narrative structure of the maternal in news coverage from the period of January 21 to January 24, 1993. During this time, three breaking news stories mapped maternalized space: the Clinton reversals on abortion, the Baird case, and the installation of Hillary Clinton in the West Wing of the White House. If we can reimagine this period not as news, but as an imaginary 1957 Douglas Sirk melodrama called, perhaps, *All That the Law Allows,* then we can more easily see the rule of the father in Clinton's discursive legal reversals, his malevolence toward women in the offering up of Zoë Baird as the female replacement of the very same "law" for the position of attorney general, and his admission of women to some truncated, silent form of power in Hillary's appointment. Following the narrative patterns of classic melodrama, the phallic mother — the non-nurturing, sadistic, controlling mother — is in evidence in the Baird story. The mother who chooses to live in both the maternal realm of the private sphere and the social world of the public sphere is punished, silenced, and exiled from the narrative, or, in this case, the Department of Justice. Despite the Clinton abortion reversals, the social annihilation of the phallic mother on the symbolic level and the political destruction of the "materiality" of mothering on the level of the real continued at a ferocious, almost pathological, pitch, further maternalizing the narrative functions of the state.

How do these two separate but interconnected media trajectories — one rabidly antiabortion, the other a passive aggressive neoliberalism — relate to amateur video and the formation of a feminist oppositional public sphere supporting reproductive rights? Both examples are inflected with similar articulations of a subplot or subtext on sacrificial mothering as proper behavior for women, eradication of women's bodies and voice, and suppression of abortion rights discourse. In this way, the DeMoss ads and the news coverage of the Clinton legal reversals demonstrate some of the very complicated congruencies between conservative and neoliberal politics, especially when sifted through representation of the female body and the shifting needs of the post-1989 nation-state. Both positions depend on disentangling women from mothering, mothering from social relations, social relations from visual representation, and representation from the female body. Both positions demonstrate an inability, or perhaps refusal, to situate women within a more complex, multiple formation either inside or outside the nation.

It could be argued that Bill Clinton, not Ronald Reagan, is actually the first truly postmodern president. I define *postmodernism* here as the separation of the signifier from the signified through the simulacrum available from new technology and as the annihilation of history and agency through a concentration on representation. Clinton's particular inflection of postmodernism is not so simply a play of media surfaces: it is much more insidious. It revitalizes traditional liberal rhetoric of participation and social welfare, but eviscerates subjects, social space, and history. Linda Hutcheon has argued that much postmodern art disposes of conventional history, interrogating instead the construction and ideological underpinnings of historical explanation: "In a very real sense, postmodernism reveals a desire to understand present culture as the product of previous representations. The representation of history becomes the history of representations."[24]

In the case of Clinton, it is important to make a distinction between postmodernism as a descriptive, covering term charting major alterations in the social order and postmodernism as an artistic strategy that revamps the relationship between representation and referents to create new meanings. Although both clearly overlap and inform each other, Clinton's media construction of himself borrows its strategy from radical postmodern art, pastiching representations and history, yet denuding the reassemblage of radical critique. Barry Smart has identified postmodernism with a fundamental transformation in politics, technology, and capitalism from one based on justice to one based on performativity: "Associated with this process is the principle of legitimation of knowledge, away from the narratives of speculative self-legitimation and emancipation and liberty, that is from predominantly philosophical and political forms, towards the invocation of performativity, or techno-economic forms of legitimation."[25]

In the political sense, Clinton performs liberalism rather than engages it intellectually. For example, Clinton's penchant for the talk-show format as a way to get in touch with "the people" to push his programs relies on his performing the role of open host, when, in fact, the participants are carefully screened ahead of time. In an aesthetic sense, Clinton's particular inflection of the postmodern presents a representation of democracy as it diminishes its material, social relations that would provide access to participation in democracy, a move expressed in the Clinton abortion reversals.

Clinton understands the power of new media technologies such as cable, satellite, and e-mail that glibly perform and evoke nineteenth-century formulations of small-town, rural democracy (the electronic town hall), yet completely guts them of any emancipatory possibilities of forming a public sphere in the Habermasian sense of establishing truth through dialogue entered into equally by all. Mediated relations, then, dismiss the social and the material, suggesting access, but explicitly not ensuring it for everyone.

A feminist oppositional political and media practice must disentangle all of these intertwined levels of visual representation, politics, media, technology, and the female body, and must be multistrategic. The DeMoss ads and the Clinton reversals are both locked within conventions of home movies, commercials, state mandates, and melodrama that smooth over sexual and racial difference, struggle across common political interests, the historical position of women's bodies, and collective struggle of multiple sites. These two media representations systematically eradicate women's struggle and bodies by means of both the low and high-end commercial media production. The low and high-end media blur together as though viewed through a stereoscope.

▶ ────────────────────────────────────

Media Blackouts/Body Wipeouts

Because media blackouts and restrictions have curtailed access to the public sphere for reproductive rights activists, small-format video provides them with a means to create multiple oppositional public spheres where art and politics converge as though on a DNA strand. I would like to outline some of the contours of this media blackout on abortion to establish the urgency of these activist videos. As Nina Leibman has noted, it was not until 1956, when the Production Code was altered, that Hollywood features could mention abortion. And even afterward, the few films that dealt with abortion constructed both sex and abortion as sordid.[26]

Steven Dubin, in his book *Arresting Images*, has outlined how the networks and the right have effectively eliminated abortion discourse and representation from the public sphere: characters in mainstream television series rarely mention the word *abortion*. Network television has vehemently shied away from abortion since a character on a 1972 episode of *Maude* had an abortion and sent advertisers fleeing. An episode of *China Beach* that featured an abortion was not included in the program's rerun schedule. Right-wing and antiabortion groups have also censured more avant-garde art that deals with abortion. The Heritage Foundation, a right-wing think tank recently notorious for its attacks on public television, attacked feminist artist Shawn Eichman's installation piece *Alchemy Cabinet*, a piece incorporating the remains of her own aborted fetus.[27]

The NBC television movie *Roe vs. Wade* epitomizes the instability that abortion poses and the way in which radical discourse on women's reproductive rights is contained. This 1989 docudrama (which is currently available for rental at video stores) was subject to extensive rewriting and network scrutiny to avoid bias. The network made every attempt to present an unbiased, balanced show that would not favor either side in order to avoid charges of political advocacy. Although Holly Hunter, an actress identified with reproductive rights politics, performed the role of Ellen Russell, the character standing in for real-life "Jane Roe" Norma McCorvey, the network inhibited her granting interviews about the film. Amy Madigan, an actress whose star image is one of a tough, uncompromising woman, played Sarah Weddington, the attorney for "Jane Roe." The script went through many rewrites in an attempt to maintain balance, and during shooting the producers used a different title to stave off protesters.

The movie is structured in almost a ping-pong style, with scenes alternating between Russell's life and Weddington's legal struggles juxtaposed against the work of the district attorney's team as they fashion opposing arguments. However, despite this "balance" between scenes, the emotional valence and spectator identification of the film reside with the two women, most particularly because the melodramatic genre of women's difficult lives as they traverse among home, work, and the body overpowers the more sterile legal arguments of the opposing side. In addition, the casting of Madigan and Hunter, both stars associated with commercial film rather than television, further situates *Roe vs. Wade* within the history and conventions of the woman's picture and legitimates abortion as a woman's right to control her life, a fundamental tension of classical melodrama. Although "Jane Roe" wins the case, the entire plot of the film revolves around the difficulties of Russell's working-class life, and even includes the birth of the child she sought to abort. This narrative structure focuses the film on the victimization of Russell by social and legal systems, a trope identified with the position of women in classical film melodramas. *Roe vs. Wade* aired the week after the Supreme Court heard arguments in *Webster v. Reproductive Health Services*, which further increased its political volatility. Some advertising executives argued that *Roe vs. Wade* was simply good television; its controversial and topical slant would secure good ratings and generate ad revenues. However, the Reverend Donald Wildmon and the American Family Association endlessly harassed network sponsors to withdraw their advertising. Many advertisers did back off, claiming that the subject matter was too provocative. However, the advertisers who bought airtime, at a significantly reduced rate, were clearly focused on attracting the women's market, the typical audience for made-for-TV movies: Murphy's Oil Soap and General Foods.[28]

Both CBS's *Murphy Brown* and ABC's *Sisters* have featured main characters mulling over abortion, but then choosing to have a baby, in a capitulation to the pro-life bias of the networks, according to a study by Fairness and Accuracy in Reporting (FAIR). Another study conducted by FAIR shows that most abortion reporting relies on a rhetoric of compromise and common ground in the abortion debate, as well as presentation of extremists and angry rhetoric.[29] Dan Quayle's condemnation of *Murphy Brown,* then, was flawed: she represents not the single mother rejecting the family, but the single woman locked into patriarchal and statist agendas on abortion. His conflation between mother and woman was off target. He should have applauded Murphy Brown for following the script and having the baby, instead of blaming the Los Angeles riots on her decision to become a single parent without a man. Finally, the minimal coverage of the April 5, 1992, Reproductive Rights March on Washington—considered the largest political demonstration in U.S. history—by the *New York Times* and other major news outlets underscores the thoroughness of this media blackout. With the *Casey* decision gutting *Roe v. Wade* in June 1992, more commercial and "public" media effectively detoured from any discussion of reproductive rights, as evidenced by the 1992 presidential elections. Family values and the economy diverted discussion about reproductive rights and "real' family politics out of what emerged as a newly defined, circumscribed, noncritical public sphere of CNN and talk shows.

But what about independent film and video in these struggles over visual representation and reproductive rights, two formations that could be used interchangeably in the context of this argument? Of course, some significant independent films were produced about abortion in the 1970s and 1980s, such as *Holy Terror, Abortion: Stories from North and South,* and *With a Vengeance.* However, compared to the amount of work produced on AIDS, there has been a relative dearth of independent work on reproductive rights. The gendered context of production was highlighted for me when I served on a New York State Council on the Arts film panel in 1990—one of the largest funders of film and video in the country. Out of more than three hundred proposals, not one was for a project on abortion, and more than 75 percent, by my estimate, were for narrative films about personal issues by a variety of producers. B. Ruby Rich has railed against the gendered confines of independent film and video, noting that independents in the 1980s unconsciously subsumed the right's agenda to disembowel controversy in government-funded media by moving into narrative feature film. Because women have been traditionally positioned as outsiders in media production, Rich claims that the independent media scene witnessed a gendered division of labor in the 1980s in the face of severe budget cutbacks (totaling a 50 percent reduction of funds over a twelve-year period): men produce narrative film, whereas women, she argues, have moved into video, a cheaper and more accessible format that is not so reliant on huge production budgets and can be produced more quickly.[30] In the case of reproductive rights media, a survey of current film and video rental catalogs reveals that the amount of work produced on video far exceeds the amount produced on film.

▶

Low-End Difference

What possibilities does video, especially low-end video, offer in this age of defunding and privatization of the Corporation for Public Broadcasting (CPB), the Public Broadcasting Service (PBS), and federal and state grants?[31] What sort of interventions do new technologies like amateur video provoke in an era of increasing concentration and centralization of all media industries? First, the 1992 attacks against public television by Laurence Jarvik, the Heritage Foundation, the Family Research Council, and Senator Jesse Helms were not new salvos against the so-called perverse, postmodern, antifigurative, artistic left. After more than twelve years of allegations that arts agencies and public television liberal biases left no room for conservative viewpoints, this new round of attacks could only be seen as part of a much longer historical trajectory.[32]

Conservatives invoked the Fairness Doctrine, modernist notions of objectivity, and a return to traditional art forms to save media production from the terrors of postmodernist decentering of white male hegemony and linearity. They mounted a three-pronged attack: first, invocation of a reinterpretation of the law that narrowed its scope; second, philosophical rejection of postmodernism through reconstruction of a modernist and scientific truth claim; and third, reinstitution of the boundary line between the high culture of form and the low culture of emotion and rage. Their terror of this threat of instability—both political and aesthetic—was epitomized in the outcry raised by Pat Buchanan and some conservative groups against local public television stations for airing Marlon Riggs's black gay anthem, *Tongues Untied*. It was not just sexuality that threatened the status quo in this case, as some radical cultural critics have claimed, but a proliferation of multiple sexualities and the situating of this difference within historical specificity. Let us not forget that the latest cycle of PBS and CPB bashing was blamed on two women, none other than Anita Hill and Nina

Totenberg—Hill for her accusations against Clarence Thomas and Totenberg for breaking Hill's story. Some conservative congressmen cited the exposure of the Anita Hill sexual harassment as a misuse of public funds and senators' privileged access to testimony. Ironically following the plotline of the Hollywood film *Basic Instinct,* women with linguistic power—a journalist and a lawyer—were the root cause of social and aesthetic decline and the enervation of powerful white men.[33]

The defunding of PBS has been systematic and steady during the culture wars of the past two decades. For example, in 1980, 27 percent of PBS funds were derived from federal sources, whereas in 1990 only 16 percent were, representing a reduction of more than 50 percent, while corporate funding increased from 10 percent to 16 percent.[34] These figures illustrate what has amounted to—on the theoretical and political level—the gradual erosion of a publicly funded, publicly protected, mediated public sphere quite different from what Habermas imagined, yet following his contours. Thus this napalm attack against the arts and public television occurred on two fronts. First, the economic base, according to conservatives, needed to be liberated from the state and privatized with free enterprise market relations—an argument that has been used to reinvent mass communications along capitalist lines in the former Eastern bloc. Second, the superstructure, which had exploded with a kind of uncontrolled postmodernist ecstasy of racial, sexual, gender, and regional difference and deconstructive historical strategies, needed to recenter traditional art forms and white male patriarchy. However, these refutations of postmodernized discourses covered up the real psychic/political horror posed by the material difference of women and people of color producing any media at all. In the work of Jean-François Lyotard, Jacques Derrida, and Jean Baudrillard, decentering is located within language and difference. These new media practices take decentering one step further: they materialize difference with new gendered and racialized producers. Not only were different media images created, but the images marked their difference, thereby altering the political relations of production and reproduction, the working landscape of media production and distribution.

However, the underpinnings of this debate regarding the funding and program priorities of Public Television and the National Endowment for the Arts are even more complicated when we focus on women, feminism, and reproductive rights. The 1980s witnessed two potentially contradictory movements: on the one side, the conglomerization of media and drastic reductions in network public affairs programming; on the other side, the dissemination of such new technologies as amateur camcorders and satellite communication that decentralize and democratize media production and distribution.[35] This democratization and dissemination of access facilitated what I would like to call the explosion of *difference through diffusion*, a phrase I utilize to denote the convergence of representation, politics, and technology within more radicalized, offensive oppositional media formations. In this context, media groups like Paper Tiger Television and Deep Dish T.V., AIDS activist groups such as ACT UP, and reproductive rights media groups such as the Buffalo Media Coalition for Reproductive Rights have linked low-end, low-tech technologies with deconstructive argumentative and visual strategies. The amateur camcorder could be retrieved from the privatized confines of the traditional bourgeois nuclear family — the gulag where all amateur media technologies have been condemned to stunt their democratic potential. This retrieval process pivots on two political moves: (1) access to media production to alter the social relations of production and (2) discursive and textual realignments of history, present, and future in the analysis of reproductive rights and tapes to arrest erosion of the public sphere.

The parallels between democratic access to media as potentially subversive of dominant media and unrestricted access to abortion as a woman's civil right are almost uncanny in both discourse and practice: both protect differences of voices and bodies, in particular female ones, whose specificity poses unique interventions. A true democratization of both media and abortion depends on the practice and protection of access and not just on a commitment to equality and plurality. The issue of access, then, emerges as the fulcrum upon which "rights" can be imagined as articulations of multiple differences of voices on the level of discourse and multiple bodies on the level of practice.

Most significantly, the conservative attack on public television and the arts has cited as precedent the abortion ruling on the gag rule in *Rust v. Sullivan* to argue for limitations of free speech and access to information when government funding is provided for the arts. Richard O. Curry has argued that the issues of abortion and freedom of expression are joined in *Webster v. Reproductive Health Services* (1989) and *Rust v. Sullivan* (1991). The *Webster* decision upheld a Missouri law that prohibited the spending of public funds to counsel a woman on abortion. The American Library Association filed an amicus brief with the Court, asking the Court to consider the effect of the ruling on intellectual freedom and dissemination of material about sexuality in libraries. In *Rust v. Sullivan,* the Court ruled that guidelines for federally funded family planning clinics that prohibited personnel from providing information on abortion were constitutional.[36]

According to the American Civil Liberties Union (ACLU), conservative arts watchdog groups, especially the American Family Research Council and the Heritage Foundation, have initiated a series of court injunctions against certain forms of art by citing *Rust v. Sullivan* as precedent for limitations on free speech.

The ACLU has argued that "the Rust decision fueled arguments that the government may likewise prohibit 'indecency' in NEA-funded projects, or may deny arts grants for ideological reasons. *Rust* was undoubtedly a blow to freedom of speech, but it is far from clear that the Supreme Court will extend its reasoning to the arts funding context."[37] The ACLU advances three arguments against the importation of *Rust* as a precedent for arts censorship: first, *Rust* focused exclusively on medical services and delineated that content restrictions in areas expressly dedicated to speech activity were not included; second, private patient-doctor communication, the focus of the *Rust* decision, differs in scope from arts contexts and funding, which have "impact beyond the actual dollars spent"; and third, arts funding permeates an entire institution or work project and is not as containable as abortion counseling.[38] These debates on freedom of speech and recent Supreme Court abortion rulings demonstrate quite forcefully how distinctions among arts production, the law, women's rights, abortion, and access have congealed.

Sean Cubitt, in his book *Timeshift,* argues that the proliferation of video technologies multiplies the number of sites for cultural struggle. These technologies fragment a coherent market of consensus broadcasting with diffuse and intensely localized practices. He writes: "We have to think of the term 'technology' as a centrifugal net of interacting discourses, and as a function of them: educational, legal, aesthetic socio-cultural, scientific. . . . The first break is to rid ourselves of the prescriptive power of definition, and to think instead in terms of process and relations."[39] Cubitt's notion of inscribing technology within process and relations and removing it from static definitions evokes this idea of the raiding of imaging technologies in order to reform vision; the videomaker, then, emerges as a sort of traveler between discourses and practices, a weaver of fractured social and aesthetic spaces and creator of new public frontiers. Along this same line of excavating the radical potential of new technologies, particularly consumer technologies like camcorders, DeeDee Halleck has observed: "The challenge is to develop Mumford's insights into emancipated uses of technology in a decentralized and genuinely democratic way. . . . In fact, it is evident that pockets of resistance have arisen that have the potential to evolve into more highly organized and autonomous centers of democratic communications."[40]

These discussions of the radical potential of consumer technology concentrate not on their dissemination and control by major corporations, but on their ability to increase access to production and to diffuse the sites where media intervention can occur.[41] Systematic exclusion of independent political voices can be challenged by inclusions of multiple voices via access to technology and a commitment to rephrasing the normative modes of production offered by commercial media. Rather than a technological nihilism that views all technology as reactionary and co-optive, Cubitt and Halleck argue that video technology presents possibilities for altering social relations that did not exist within previous media forms. The arguments of both authors stress the context and usage of the technologies rather than their inherent properties. As the antiabortion crusade relocates to clinics, video has become increasingly important as part of the artillery that feminist groups can use to destroy ideology with visual evidence.[42]

The case of the Buffalo, New York, Media Coalition for Reproductive Rights (MCRR) exemplifies this move. The coalition uses low-end amateur camcorders to combat Operation Rescue clinic blockades. Its tape *Spring of Lies* (1992) chronicles the attacks in May 1992 against several abortion clinics in Buffalo, New York. The tape places the videomakers in the middle of the action through handheld camera work. The videographers themselves frequently speak to the right-to-life protesters. MCRR's tapes are distributed to anyone for fifteen dollars, roughly the cost of a hard-cover book. They are often used as courtroom evidence to document illegal barrier of entry to clinics by Operation Rescue. The MCRR tapes circulate in a sphere that is different from that of more traditional oppositional films of the 1970s, exploiting the proliferation of VCRs to form underground feminist networks. Although their videography is often shaky and out of focus, the tapes' confrontational style overrides formal coherence with the feverish pitch of on-the-ground war photography.

MCRR's tapes are shot in the 1960s style of aggressive cinema verité, with the camera provoking action from either antiabortion or reproductive rights activists. They document the extent of Operation Rescue's interference by placing the spectator in the subject position of a pregnant woman going to the clinic. These tapes put the woman's body—excised and exiled by the U.S. Supreme Court and mass-media representations—back into abortion confrontations. They compare media representations of the attacks, which even out the conflict with the immediate and visceral ambiance of their own cinematography, where the camera, and by extension visual representation, is often physically in the center of the struggle and debate. These tapes do not simply serve as alternatives to network coverage, as research on anti-Vietnam War media has hypothesized the dialectic and binary opposition between alternative and dominant media formations. Rather, they provoke a new social usage of technology and a new social configuration of spectatorship as resistant, active, and social. The tapes function as feminist space-productions-through-visuality, the video technology provoking slippage between technology and woman's body.

US Bans Abortion (1990), produced by Paper Tiger Television in New York City, also inserts the female body into the health care system surrounding abortion through low-end video technology. This thirty-minute tape discusses the Bush administration's restrictions on Title X, which provides funding for health care clinics for poor women. The restrictions prohibited health care providers in federally funded clinics from providing information on abortion as an option to deal with pregnancy. The tape alternates between four feminist health care activists, as they analyze the impact of Title X restrictions on poor women's health, and footage of a Women's Health Action and Mobilization (WHAM!) demonstration at the New York City Department of Health, shot from the point of view of the participants.

The interview sequences with the four activists demonstrate how media representation, public policy on health care, and specifying the female body coagulate in both discourse and practice. These interviews are threaded in between the demonstration footage, providing analysis of the media blackout on Title X and analysis of its impact on poor women and women of color. The activists speak directly to the camera and argue that Title X restrictions could be potentially more devastating than the *Webster* decision, affecting more than five million women and four thousand clinics.

Marianne Staniszewski, a member of WHAM! and a cultural critic from the Rhode Island School of Design, explains that the media create our social landscape and collective memory; she claims that the lack of mainstream news coverage on the restrictions can be directly related to the fact that they would affect marginalized groups of women: teenagers, people of color, poor women. Later in the tape, Staniszewski shows how the language of Title X redefines life as beginning at conception; she quotes from Title X: "The health care worker must promote the interests of the unborn child."

Tracy Morgan, a health educator who works in a clinic, narrates an example of what her work life would be like under Title X restrictions. Currently, if a pregnant teenager came to her clinic, she would explain three options: prenatal care if the teenager decided to carry the baby to term, adoption, and abortion if she chose to terminate the pregnancy.

However, Morgan explains, under Title X, abortion would remain legal, but she would be prohibited from mentioning it to clinic patients as an option. A young man in the group explains that although *Roe v. Wade* in 1973 made abortion legal, the strategy of the federal government has been to attempt to cut off women's access to abortion through measures like the Hyde Amendment, which revoked Medicare funding for abortion. He then describes his failed attempts to garner media coverage of the WHAM! demonstration; he reasons that funding issues are not perceived by the mass media as a matter of rights.

A WHAM! activist concludes the tape by arguing that all of the attempts to curtail abortion constitute "retaliation against the massive gains" made by women; she asserts, "We never achieved reproductive freedom. We have to incorporate all women from all classes, races, and ethnic backgrounds." These interviews provide two lines of analysis. First, they establish the necessity for direct-action demonstrations because of a virtual media blackout. Second, they provide a historical and analytic context for the more heated footage of the demonstration. The interviews, then, anchor our reading of the demonstration footage within the larger issue of health care as a right for all women. By delivering a political analysis of the regressive impact of Title X on women's health care, these interviews, although all with white activists, discursively position the spectator in the subject position of a pregnant teenager of color by mapping how that specific body would be denied its rights.

Mirroring the camcorder strategy of *Spring of Lies,* the demonstration footage in *US Bans Abortion* is shot with low-end, handheld video. The camera does not maintain an objectified, ethnographic distance from the demonstrators; rather, the camera itself emerges as a participant in the direct action. The camera records the march down a New York City street by WHAM! activists from inside the demonstration, not outside on the sidewalks. Marchers speak directly to the camera in extreme close-up, explaining the reasoning behind their chant "Abortion is health care, health care is a right." When the women enter the Department of Health to plaster the office with red tape to symbolize the effect of Title X restrictions, a young women speaks directly to the camera about why she is performing this kind of civil disobedience. The WHAM! activists wear surgical masks with Xs to connote the consequences of Title X.

Although coverage of demonstrations from the point of view of demonstrators has a long tradition in political documentary film, extending as far back as the Workers' Film and Photo League's coverage of demonstrations during the Depression and continuing through cinema verité of the 1960s in the work of the Newsreel collectives, this camcorder footage offers a slightly different intervention. Rather than simply documenting the demonstration, the camera is at the eye level of the demonstrators, walking with them, stringing red tape on office walls, talking with them. The arbitrary border between videographer as omniscient and omnipresent and the subject as distant and pacified is abandoned.

This strategy is not merely a participatory form of media production to stimulate active spectatorship; rather, it situates the video camera and its operator within the sexualized and gendered subject position of woman-plus-imaging-machine opposing government policy and fighting back for reproductive rights. Instead, the video technology of the camcorder and the body of the videographer are transposed into a gendered, moving, resistant panopticon whose project is equally the making of representation and the execution of political action.

In a move similar to *Spring of Lies, US Bans Abortion* uses camcorder video both to reinsert and reassert the pregnant female body. Whereas the camera work in *Spring of Lies* positions the pregnant female body under virtual physical and psychic attack, the camera in *US Bans Abortion* imagines a pregnant, raced, and classed female body of the future that bureaucracy and politics try to mute and restrain, but that, in the end, refuses to be silenced or immobilized. Although many film theorists have interrogated the multiple subject positions constituting female spectatorship, this radical confederation of the camcorder, reproductive rights politics, and the sexualized female body proposes a different twist on psychoanalytic identification and more ethnographic reception theory: not only is the female body made visible and vocal, it is empowered and powerful through video technology, which facilitates a militant subjectivity and a collective participation in the making of public space.

Another example of feminist oppositional public sphere video is a tape by the activist group ReproVision, part of Women's Health Action and Mobilization, called *Access Denied* (1991). In comparison to *Spring of Lies,* this tape works more on an explanatory than a visceral level, yet it also obscures the line between spectator and participant, the law and the body. While showing street demonstrations, the tape elaborates the multiple contexts of restrictions on abortion across race, age, and sexual orientation lines, effectively deconstructing the complaint heard in the 1960s and 1970s that abortion rights politics evidences white, middle-class, single-issue feminism. Constructed in segments outlining reproductive rights issues within a larger context of race, health care, and teenagers, the tape interweaves demonstration footage with interviews, marking each segment historically with a short montage of archival footage deifying babies or mothers. The tape begins with clinic defense against Operation Rescue

Screen grab of image collage depicting assault on abortion rights at the state level, from *Access Denied* (1991). Dir. ReproVision. Photograph courtesy of Women Make Movies.

and interviews with WHAM! volunteers and escorts. It then moves from the streets to the legal plane, where it discusses the Supreme Court *Webster* decision restrictions on abortion. An African American woman activist relates how *Webster* affects women of color, citing evidence that prior to 1973, 80 percent of illegal abortions were performed on women of color. Another black woman describes her friend's hemorrhaging from an illegal botched abortion. Moving to a discussion of the gag rule, a black male proclaims, "You can't cut information."

Other segments of the tape refuse to position abortion as a single issue of privacy, focusing instead on the relationships between AIDS research and fetal tissue research, between prohibitions concerning sexual preference and the issue of women's right to health care, and between a description of a menstrual extraction and teenagers protesting parental consent restrictions. On the argumentative and visual levels, *Access Denied* explicates the multiple geographies of abortion politics. The tape ends with the direct address to viewers, "Come join us." *Access Denied* depends on constantly circulating between the private and the public, between the law and the clinics, between health care and sexuality, itself forming a new location somewhere between these polarities. It constructs a discursive multiplicity that implicitly argues for reimagining the larger political context of abortion, one beyond proper, white, middle-class unified discourse.

Although it does not utilize handheld camcorder videography, Kathy High's remarkable tape *Underexposed: Temple of the Fetus* (1992) also centers on the women's clinic as the space where the female body, reproductive technologies, and politics converge. The clinical space outlined in this tape is not that of the abortion provider, but rather a clinic of the future that retrieves embryos and implants them in women desperate to have children. High deciphers the clinical space within which women's bodies have been and will be suspended and how new reproductive technologies continue the discursive move of separating women from their wombs, turning the womb into what one character in the tape calls "a fetal environment." The tape later visualizes this discursive amputation with images of wombs that resemble spaceships. This clinical space entails a kind of feminist nightmare of male doctors controlling women's bodies through technology. One doctor asserts, for example, that in vitro fertilization (IVF) "is therapeutic for these women, the best way for some women to resume useful lives." The clinic of the future, as imagined by *Underexposed*, is one where women are reduced to wombs.

Like *Access Denied*, *Underexposed* weaves together multiple discursive and explanatory modes to define the space within which reproductive politics operates.[43] It layers together several different genres to investigate the politics of new reproductive technologies, specifically in vitro fertilization: historical archival footage of pregnancy and birth; a fictional, docudramalike story about a newscaster covering her friend's in-vitro fertilization; straight documentary interviews with international feminists who study reproductive politics; and a science fiction narrative about the future control of IVF by male doctors and corporations. Deploying these multiple textual strategies to unpack the position of new reproductive technologies within a feminist health politics, *Underexposed* locates the pregnant and desiring-to-be-pregnant female body within a network of politics, practices, discourses, science, and imaginings about the future.

The historical site of the female body is discovered through archival shots of C-sections, deliveries, and newborns. Because these old medical training films are juxtaposed with the fictionalized story of the news reporter covering the story of her friend's in vitro fertilization, their evidentiary and scientific claims are defused and their historical discourse, which positions the female body as a passive receptacle of technology, is underscored.

Underexposed insists that scientific exploration of new reproductive technologies is inextricably linked to the state. In an interview in the tape's imagined future, the head of the newly formed Department of New Reproductive Technologies proclaims, "This is not just a baby, it is a national

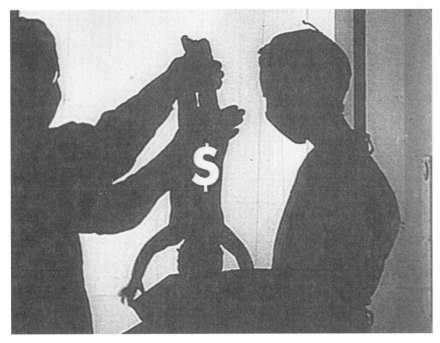

A high-tech baby is born in a scene from *Underexposed: Temple of the Fetus* (1992). Dir. Kathy High. Photograph courtesy of Kathy High.

issue." By utilizing the conventions of network news interviews, the narrative sequences with doctors practicing IVF and with a woman patient expose how scientific intervention into reproduction and pro-natalist ideologies can be reframed as commonsensical solutions and miracle cures for the complicated biological and social issue of infertility. The utopian possibilities of in vitro fertilization are undercut by the narrative of the tape, however: the woman who was implanted lost her baby at twenty-two weeks. In one fictional interview, a woman proclaims that the doctor at the clinic "was looking at my stomach and seeing dollar signs." The narrative of one woman's quest for a child, now that her career is under way, is located within two registers: the family melodrama of the impregnation and its subsequent failure told from the point of view of the woman patient, and rational, instrumental muckraking of the in vitro business by her best friend, an aggressive news reporter.

Thus, the "story" of in vitro fertilization in this tape is multitiered, simultaneously narrated from the emotional and personal point of view of the female patient and, logically, publicly exposed by a female news reporter. Both routes arrive at the same conclusion, a condemnation of the trivialization of women's reproductive autonomy. Both routes are positioned in this tape as equally important, equally urgent politically, functioning in a pas de deux with each other. Most important, the constant interplay between these two positions suggests that only a political strategy that can account for multiple and complex explanations at different levels simultaneously is viable.

In addition, the tape suggests the sexual orientation, class, and race dimensions of reproductive technologies. The female reporter interviews a pregnant lesbian couple who contend that the Department of Reproductive Ethics and Procedures, a government agency, restricts sperm to protect the unborn from AIDS. The couple explain that they procured sperm from "two Harvard guys" and argue that they, too, constitute a nuclear family. In a later fictional interview, an African American woman doctor exposes that in vitro fertilization is reserved only for middle-class whites. Consequently, *Underexposed* offers a critique of male-controlled reproductive utopias by rerouting its narrative trajectory into a failed pregnancy that then produces consciousness about how these technologies serve the nexus of science, the state, and capitalism rather than women.

Underexposed establishes that historical images of birth and reproduction, scientific training films, and narratives concerning the utopian future prospects for reproductive technologies all concoct imaginary fictions regarding the female body that rob it of autonomy, activity, and specificity. This fictionalizing of disparate materials and sources demonstrates the pacification of the maternal and pregnant body in discourse, practice, and image making. Actual documentary interviews with feminists from around the world who study the social consequences of new reproductive technologies are counterposed against these fantasy constructions of the female body that neutralize and confine the body within science.

Not only do these interviews provide a larger context and more analysis of the social and political ramifications of new reproductive technologies, they critique the truth claims of a scientific practice positioned as gender-neutral. In one interview, Gena Corea, author of *The Mother Machine*, describes scientists who work with new reproductive technologies as "exploring something like galaxy 38" and says that they use "woman-obliterating sentences." Joyanta Gupta, a sociologist, explains that these technologies operate within an ideology that sees women as useful only as mothers, marginalizing women and giving them less and less say over their own bodies. Christine Ewing, a biologist, argues that the success rate for in vitro fertilization is actually less than 10 percent and advances the notion that these technologies are actually a form of imperialism. Malina Karkal points out that medical researchers in India focus on infertility, despite high infant mortality rates. A surrogate mother describes how wealthy couples will use the court system to their advantage to counteract the birth mother's claims to the child. Through social and political analysis, these interviews mark off "truth" from a feminist perspective, demonstrating the multiple ways in which the real, lived positions of women and their bodies are excised from discussion and actual practices of new reproductive technologies.

In some ways, these interviews function as guides through the fictional and archival material, locating the spectator within feminist deconstruction rather than melodramatic identification or passive awe of the spectacle of strange medical training films. Although these interviews are shot in exactly the same style as the fictionalized interviews of the science fiction part of the tape, their veracity is discernible because they work in opposition to the utopianism of the other narrative. These interviews interrupt the futuristic narrative and historical imagery by continually reinserting women's needs into the discourse. They focus on women, not science.

As *Underexposed* alerts us, reproductive politics reconstructs temporality along less linear, phallocratic lines: these include historical formations that remove woman from the womb; new technologies that reconfigure the race, class, and imperial relations of reproduction; and male fantasies of a technological utopia where woman's individual control over her body aids patriarchal agendas for reproduction.

S'Aline's Solution (1991), a short experimental video by Aline Mare, utilizes technological and representational strategies similar to those used in the more activist tapes discussed above, but formally manipulates the images to specify further the point of view of the aborted and voiced pregnant female body. The very title of the tape suggests the merging of the medical/technological and the specified female subject: as saline solution is used in one method of abortion, *S'Aline's Solution* is one particular, historical woman's solution to an unwanted pregnancy. Thus the title of the tape not only functions as a pun on abortion, but demonstrates that the convergence of medicine and subjectivity constitutes the radicalized site of abortion.

This compelling and evocative tape in many ways performs an ideological exorcism on abortion, wresting it from the limiting discursive domain of the law and public policy and sheathing it within not only the female body but the speaking female subject and medicalized, imaged female organs. The tape specifies not only the female body but the site of abortion through medical imaging technology that allows for close-up views inside the body and its organs. *S'Aline's Solution* traverses three different political registers: the social/medical organization of the female body; the imaginary, emancipated female body of a specific woman who chooses; and the aborted, pregnant speaking subject. The female body, then, is split into three parts corresponding to each of these intersecting registers: medical images inside the reproductive organs of the female body; close-ups of a woman's mouth and images of a woman swimming; and lyrical voice-over that fuses assertion of personal choice, loss, science, and autonomy. Subjectivity here is redefined along multiple trajectories rather than linear unities.

The social/medical organization of the female body engaged in reproduction is presented through the use of slow-motion scientific imaging of female reproductive organs, sperm, ovum, and embryos. The tape opens with a traveling shot through the vagina into the womb, achieved by the use of some sort of high-tech, miniaturized video camera, accompanied by slow, eerie electronic music suggesting science fiction movies. This particular image presents a gendered intervention into the semiotics of the "traveling shot" of classical Hollywood cinema. Rather than moving through public space, this traveling shot literally invades the private and invisible space of the interior of the female. Access to the interior and interiority of the female is literally visualized as entry through the vagina. Various slow-motion medicalized, high-tech images of sperm, ovum, and embryos floating in space unanchored to the female body emerge, evoking science, medicine, and the activity of the womb's mysterious melodramas and spectacles. The torpid and tedious speed of these images reduces them to abstractions and highlights how this medical imaging technology generalizes, etherealizes, and isolates reproduction from any social/political context.

On the level of representation and politics, the lethargy of these images removes these sperm, ovum, and embryos from the antiabortion ideological construct that they are "live" by showing that they are actually only representations. This visual strategy employs a pun on reproduction: although the images are severed from the referent of biological reproduction, they operate as an interrogation of visual reproduction and a deconstruction of antiabortion ideological constructs that life begins at conception.

In *S'Aline's Solution*, a woman's life begins when she chooses. Indeed, to underscore the physical and scientific difference between fertilized eggs and babies, the tape concludes with a birth scene, where a baby's head emerges from a woman's vagina. Although on first viewing this birth scene may appear to be out of place, the construction of the tape actually changes the signification of the birth. It simultaneously confirms on the level of representation the biological difference between fertilized eggs and babies and affirms on the level of feminist politics that in choosing, a woman gives birth to herself.

The tape also employs live-action footage of a specific woman to counterpose a specific woman's body and identity to medicalized representations of an idealized and sanitized construction of Woman's organs. The

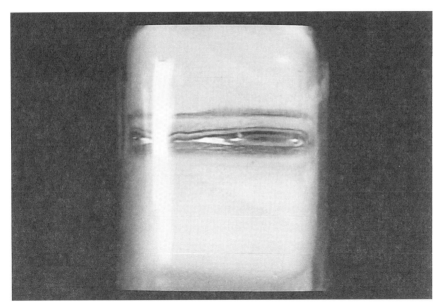

Video-processed image of interior of a woman's body, from *S'Aline's Solution*
(1991). Dir. Aline Mare. Photograph courtesy of Scott MacDonald.

extreme close-ups of a woman's mouth and of a woman swimming com-
pose another part of this splitting of the female body. These images also
evoke a dreamlike quality through slow motion and some distortion from
wide-angle videography, suggesting that subjectivity is tied to physicality.
Whereas the medical imagery dislocates female body parts with a scientific,
fragmenting gaze, these image-manipulated close-ups and long shots of a
specific woman relocate the right to choose abortion within the female
body. The repeated use of close-ups of a woman's mouth link identity with
speech.

S'Aline's Solution also crafts the aborted, female body as a speaking
subject and an active participant in the abortion. The speaking, pregnant
body counters medicalized images of female body parts as planets in some
outer galaxy waiting to be explored. The sound track is composed of a
somber, incantatory woman's voice-over intoning the words, "I choose, I
chose, I have chosen," which then progresses into the formula for saline solution and a poetic description outlining the feeling of abortion: "Flesh of
my flesh, you will never be flesh. Bye-bye baby, bye-bye. Animal, Vegetable,
Mineral. Dissolve. Disintegrate. Dismember." The voice-over concludes
with an affirmation that abortion is located not within the abstract and
ideological, but within the material, social relations of the gendered and
sexualized female body.

Feminist Technoambushes

In all of the tapes described in this chapter, video technology reinvents the political project of abortion rights through an emancipatory ambush of technology and women's bodies.[44] If the Supreme Court decisions have detached women from abortion, these tapes produce and reproduce women's bodies, restoring specificity to this war on the female body. The resistant, biological woman suspended within multiple discourses and identities is reinvigorated via the video camera, physically inserted into the action, her voice, body, and spectatorship central rather than erased as in the DeMoss Foundation ads or Clinton's press conference or mass-media narratives or the Supreme Court's *Bray* decision.

Rather than melodrama, these tapes function as combat videography, mapping the location of the gendered body and voice in politics. Rather than texts or discourses, these tapes function as physical intersections of the body, abortion politics, and technology. To discuss them solely on the level of formal innovation as avant-garde texts or on the level of argumentative structure to elaborate political context is to miss their political agenda entirely.

A day after Clinton signed the reversals, pro-life activists exclaimed that they would now take their struggle to the streets, suggesting that the war over control of female bodies is not simply discursive but physical, located within a specific time and location at clinics. However, the right-to-life invocation of sixties-style yippie politics remains hopelessly outdated, because the street as a political location, although clearly still important for all kinds of activism in the 1990s and on into the twenty-first century, is insufficient for the struggle over reproductive rights and the gendered, sexualized body.

The days when political organizers put all or most of their energy into various street actions are long gone, and such demonstrations look more and more like a hand-painted Volkswagen bus without an engine. The paralysis and inertia of what remained of the so-called left to confront the mass-mediated phantasmagoria of the Gulf War in any substantial public way beyond analyzing technoimages verify that activist politics urgently requires a vehicle better adapted to the techno-media-political landscapes of the twenty-first century, one with more power and agility to maneuver over multiple material, discursive, technological, and visual representational terrains simultaneously.

We must not only recapture pleasure and desire in our consumption of various images and imaginaries, we must ambush new tools such as camcorders, VCRs, and digital technologies for production of an entirely more mobilizing set of images and imaginaries. Picket signs alone are not enough, as they will be cast within residual modes and rendered ineffective and impotent, quaint signposts from another era demanding a different kind of intervention. One unified, linear line of defense is inadequate, whether on the level of explanation, visual representation, or political struggle. The low-end and high-end reproductive rights videos discussed here declare that we can fight this war on women only by reimagining woman's body within the construct of feminist public spheres, transitory and provisional places where the imaginary and technology morph together into something new. These videos not only certify that women's bodies are the battlegrounds, to paraphrase Barbara Kruger's famous image, they physically manifest that this new guerrilla construct of women's bodies armed with imaging technologies constitutes the fetal tissue of an emerging feminist public sphere.

Pirates, Not Plagiarists

In the gloomy cloud of intensive transnational media conglomeration, aggressive privatization of all public resources, and catastrophic arts defunding, hope for independent documentary beckons, a shred of blue on the stormy horizon. Although endangered and precarious, independent documentary can redirect tactics to widen the cracks for different kinds of democracies. Always the outlaw, independent documentary must mutate into something dexterously ingenious to change the new world orders of the new millennium. It can remake itself as a pirate. Independent documentary can surf and raid the global image flows to build new constructions and new spaces to counter the transnationalization of Hollywood. The promise of digitality and affordable new technologies, the high noon of copyright and fair use, and the pervasiveness of deterritorialization allow for new imaginings and new ambushes to materialize.

The word *piracy* rouses many different forms, fictions, and fantasies. In this chapter, I use the term *piracy* as itself a hybrid of history, fact, fiction, and fantasy, a practice that defines itself in rewriting borders and fantasizing new futures. I recuperate the term and decriminalize it. Media pirates, those who recycle images from other sources, are distinguished from plagiarists in two ways: first, the plagiarist uses images or words in their entirety, whereas the pirate decontextualizes images and words in order to recontextualize them; second, the plagiarist renders the copying process invisible and seamless, whereas the pirate foregrounds the process of snatching as a disruptive act and intervention, a rerouting of media tributaries. For example, a pirate editorial titled "So You Want to Be a Pirate?" explains, "So what's a pirate? A pirate is somebody who believes that information belongs to the people. Just as a book can be zeroxed or placed in a library to be shared, pirates provide a type of library service."[1]

The post-1989 economic and technological realignments have precipitated a variety of new formations of piracy. The conflicts among the countries of the North and South and West and East have transformed from militarization to mediazation. State power has been realigned along economic lines more than ever before, shifting the location of culture from a state prerogative for national history building to a narrative of transnational consumption of stateless, globalized commodities dependent on the circulation of image culture. As the CIA tracked weapons and nuclear capacity during the Cold War, the Motion Picture Association of America (MPAA) now pursues illegal pirating of Hollywood films to force nations to adopt stricter copyright legislation. The newly emerging democracies of Eastern Europe and China have spawned commercial pirates in droves; they copy and sell everything from *Forrest Gump* to Windows 95, Madonna CDs, and downlinked satellite broadcasts of *Friends*. As Gordon Graham noted in *Publishers Weekly* in 1990, "Piracy, as we know it today, is an eruption of the world post-colonial era."[2]

If the commercial pirate copies for profit, the media pirate copies for the pleasure of profaning the dominant commercial media discourse and turning it against itself. The commercial pirate operates in the realm of exchange value, trading money for a material commodity, whereas the media pirate functions outside and in between exchange relations, forging new ideas by cutting apart and twisting the old parts into something new that exchanges ideas in a circulatory system rather than products.

If the commercial pirate is a counterfeiter, the media pirate is a counter-discourser. The former produces an object; the latter produces new subjects. Media pirates conduct subversive art maneuvers that alter the material of the image by fragmenting it, whereas criminal pirates basically reproduce films, CDs, and software without any alteration of the material object or representational mode. Pirate media are the ultimate form of recycling in the transnational era: they salvage corporatized images for compost to grow something new out of the old.

Subcomandante Marcos, the leader of the Zapatista insurrection in Chiapas, Mexico, exemplifies this new piracy strategy. He commenced his offensive on the day the North American Free Trade Agreement (NAFTA) was signed, giving equal importance to media tactics and war strategy. Guillermo Gómez-Peña has dubbed Marcos "a consummate performancero" who "utilized performance and media strategies to enter in the political 'wrestling arena' of contemporary Mexico."[3] In an address broadcast via satellite to the "Freeing the Media" teach-in held in New York City on

January 31, 1997, Subcomandante Marcos remarked: "Independent media tries to save history: the present history—saving it and trying to share it, so it will not disappear, moreover to distribute it to other places, so that this history is not limited to one country, to one region, to one city or social group."[4]

Guillermo Gómez-Peña, also responding to the NAFTA provision that allows capital but not labor to move freely across the borders that separate the United States from Canada and Mexico, has also written about how expropriation of media and cultural elements is necessary in the new world orders to create more open and fluid systems, with art spaces creating what he calls "demilitarized zones." Describing the new hybridized cultural worker, he says: "S/he performs multiple roles in multiple contexts. At times, s/he can operate as a cross-cultural diplomat, as an intellectual coyote (smuggler of ideas), or a media pirate. At other times, s/he assumes the role of nomadic chronicler, intercultural translator, or political trickster."[5]

John Fiske, in a 1989 essay titled "Popular News," anticipated Marcos and Gómez-Peña. In contradistinction to the homogenizing and narcotizing structure of commercial news, he imagined a formally open, participatory news boiling over with contradictions that provoke public discussions and minimize distinctions among author, text, and reader.[6] Media piracy, as a form of popular news, deploys digitality and new technologies to open up previously closed and encoded formal systems, going beyond Fiske by materializing his ideas. Yet it also, in a crucial distinction from the postmodern inflection, collapses the frontier between author and consumer, between writer and reader. The media pirate, then, rejects the exchange value of the image and rescues its use value for new uses.

A 1992 Paper Tiger program called *Low Power Empowerment,* for example, chronicles low-power radio produced by women in Galway, Ireland, and by Black Liberation Radio in Springfield, Illinois, with inexpensive audio technology that creates community-based talk around significant issues such as women's work and housing. However, the tape is not simply a celebration of the appropriation of low-end consumer technologies for clandestine radio broadcasts; it also functions as a how-to primer on pirate radio: it provides viewers with tips on where to shop for components and instructions on how to rig a system.

Pirate radio operations around the globe foreground the confrontations among diffusion of new technologies, the surveillance of the nation-state, and democracy. The case of Radio Free Berkeley illustrates these points of rupture. In 1996, the Federal Communications Commission (FCC) fined pirate radio producer Steven Dunifer twenty thousand dollars for broadcasting without a license. Dunifer contends that the FCC investigated him after he shipped transmitter parts for low-power radio stations to villages in Mexico, Guatemala, El Salvador, Chiapas, and Haiti. The FCC countered that Radio Free Berkeley posed a threat to VHF emergency frequencies, aircraft navigation, civil defense, and law enforcement communications. In a *New York Times* story outlining the case, Dunifer explained, "You really can't have true democracy until there's equal access to all means of communication."[7]

In *The Complete Manual of Pirate Radio,* a technical how-to book on constructing a low-power transmitter, Zeke Teflon extends this analysis of democratic agendas and their inhibition by the growth of media concentration and corporate power. He says: "In theory, freedom of the press exists in this country. (Freedom of the airwaves doesn't even exist in theory.) In practice, only those individuals and groups with very large amounts of money can use print media effectively."[8] In his introductory chapter, he argues that all forms of media, from commercial to public television, to cable access, to print, require large amounts of capital and time investment, therefore making the means of communication completely inaccessible to most citizens. Teflon sees hope, however, in the diffusion of low-end technologies, which destroy the barriers to entry erected by more corporate media.

Media piracy, then, is a high-stakes affair of global proportions, manufacturing sanctuaries from the privatization of public culture by democratizing the means of production, now refashioned as a mode of information and image making. It is not the same thing as postmodernism, although they share some formal strategies. If postmodernist documentary appropriates images for deconstruction, pirate media appropriate both images and technologies, infiltrating old spaces and producing new spaces, consuming and producing, deconstructing and reconstructing. It moves between history and the future in a double move, as exemplified by pirate radio broadcasts.

In *Media Virus!* Douglas Rushkoff discusses media pranks by environmentalist organizations such as Earth First! and AIDS activist groups like ACT UP as metamedia in the dadaist tradition, a form of symbolic warfare that has the ability to penetrate dominant media systems.[9] Piracy, then, is not exactly new, but a great-granddaughter of dada, Soviet constructivism, and the anti-Nazi photomontagist, John Heartfield, all movements that sought "a provocative dismembering of reality" through the recycling of media images married with a distribution system that infiltrated mass media.[10] In this sense, then, images are not just reappropriated and analyzed; in their new formations, they infiltrate dominant media systems, produce space, and make histories.

The BLO Nightly News (1994), produced by the Barbie Liberation Organization, is itself a media prank that hijacks network news. The tape discloses how activists switched the voice boxes on three hundred Barbie dolls and G.I. Joes in forty-three states in the fall of 1993 to "culture jam" gender stereotyping in children's toys. G.I. Joes say, "Let's go shopping," and Barbie dolls speak of war tactics. The dolls were altered by BLO operatives, then returned to stores in what the BLO calls "shopgiving." Parents unknowingly bought the dolls as Christmas gifts for their surprised children. Local and network news covered the story of the dolls, themselves pulled into the web of the ingenious media prank to expose how toy manufacturers produce gender bias. The BLO even sent press releases to news organizations and ran a toll-free telephone number in a parody of public relations spin efforts.

The BLO Nightly News sabotages the objectivity of network news in a variety of ways. It reuses the conventional news coverage from NBC and CNN as clips, thereby turning the corporate commercial media into producers for the activists' agenda. It fabricates a fake television newscast replete with a sports announcer describing the advance of the altered Barbies over archival sports footage and a science reporter investigating the "corrective surgery" techniques employed in the transgendered alterations. At one point, a stolen image of President Clinton is keyed behind the fake news anchor.

The BLO Nightly News, then, instigates a two-way dialogue between the activists and the corporate media by means of the prank: the activists gain access to dominant media through gender bending and then reuse those news stories in their own tape. The dominant media are recast as penetrable to raids, and usable. The division between producer and consumer is blurred. The mass-media coverage of the pranks opened up a small discussion on sexism in children's toys through humor at a particularly heated time of the year for toy purchases. At the same time, the tape itself apes the slickness of corporate news visual models, but bends them with a transvestite weatherperson, montage editing that exposes the corporate media agenda, and a style of news reporting that highlights the performative pose of corporate media reporters.

The tape does not stop at documenting the Barbie and G.I. Joe voice box surgery, however; it also serves as an instruction manual on how to change the dolls. Through these multiple moves, the tape turns all consumption into production of ideologies, deconstructions, practices, or subject positions. Even the viewing of the tape itself changes spectatorship, assuming that the how-to aspect of the Barbie caper is as crucial as the why. The BLO Nightly News presumes that all technologies are infinitely mal-

A surgically altered Barbie doll gives instructions in how to perform gender-bending voice box operations on Barbie and G.I. Joe dolls in *The BLO Nightly News* (1994). Dir. Igor Vamos and Melinda Stone. Photograph courtesy of Video Data Bank.

leable, from toll-free telephone numbers to computer chip voice boxes in dolls, to television, to videotape, to satellite feeds, to the mail, to surveillance cameras, to ChromaKey technology.

To survive these new nearly debilitating structural realignments in public culture, democratic media strategy needs to deterritorialize, to adopt a more mobile, more multiple, more clever performance that is a productive relation on spatiality. It needs to embrace hybridity, rejecting the essentialism of identity politics, but also rebuffing formal purity, combining tools—from film to video to digitality—styles, and distribution systems. It needs to dispose of such concepts as guerrilla or alternative filmmaking, hangovers from older periods with quite different political debates and historical contexts. A theory of piracy and pirates offers a sailing ship with which to navigate the new world orders with new epistemological structures and political tactics.

In the 1970s, it was fashionable to refer to radical media practice as *guerrilla filmmaking,* a concept borrowed from Third World liberation struggles that sought to overthrow the colonization of territories. The guerrilla media maker operated outside, marooned in the margins, fighting for territory in an underground way. The term *guerrilla* suggests that media practice was itself militarized, armed, ready to bomb out the opposition, seeking discursive and geographic territory. A signifier condensing this strategy resides in the logo of the Newsreel collective: quick flashes of the name Newsreel with bursts of machine-gun sounds.

In the transnational era of mobile capital, fluidity, global communication flows, digitality, and diaspora, any concept of radical media practice that is lashed to binary oppositions between demonized corporate media and sanctified pure independent media is bound to fail at creating more democratic spaces. A more complex, constantly shape-shifting hybridity of strategies, technologies, and textual interventions is urgently necessary if there is to be any struggle for independent media at all.

As David Cordingly has argued in *Under the Black Flag,* the construct of the pirate has intertwined fact and fiction: in the seventeenth and eighteenth centuries, many pirates were criminal outcasts who chose to reject the naval operations of the nation-state for economic gain, but not all; in literature and Hollywood film, many pirates have been romanticized as dazzlingly handsome action-adventure heroes who lived a life of sailing, but not all.[11] Nearly a century before the French Revolution, pirate ships were democracies dedicated to liberty, equality, and brotherhood.[12]

In her novel *The Holder of the World,* a feminist novel about the transnational movement of a young woman in the seventeenth century who moves from the American colonies to England and then to India, novelist Bharati Mukherjee summons the image of the pirate ship. In narrativizing and reimagining the pirate ship, Mukherjee casts away its criminality, refashioning it as a mobile boat of resistance to capitalist companies, the state, colonization, and slavery. In *The Holder of the World,* pirates freed the slaves in Madagascar. In contemporary practice, media pirates free the media from its transnational corporate location.

Piracy is identified with an earlier period of mercantilism, when capital was in a similar era of change and growth internationally. Always on a boat, on water, moving in and out to raid and steal, the pirates were not moored to one nation. Pirate ships, as Mukherjee imagines them, had crews composed of many nationalities; they were ships of deterritorialized bodies, moving in and out of ports.

The information age, with its global flows in the vast ocean of cyberspace and its infinite reproduction of images, marks another era of great economic shifts. If piracy can be theorized as a media form that is fluid, mobile, and hybrid, then it can perhaps provide a way to rethink this new period of exploration and capital growth not as something huge, impenetrable, dominating, and depressing, but as an archive to be raided, its contents borrowed, mutated, digitized. Jacques Derrida has noted the indeterminacy and openness of the archive, its endless productive capacities in the period of digitality: "The archivist produces more archive, and that is why the archive is never closed. It opens out of the future."[13]

If piracy can be conceptualized as a new media strategy, it then becomes an insignia for difference(s), multiple layers of critique(s), intervention(s), and space(s). Theorizing piracy means disengaging from territories, deconstructing the binary opposition fueling most of a quarter of a century of independent media, and entering the global flows not as consumers, but as producers-in-dialogue. A notion of piracy refuses to recognize images as property, but instead collectivizes the images in the global image flows, severing them from ownership by the transnationals.

In rejecting the binary opposition between Afrocentrist essentialism and black nationalist pluralism, Paul Gilroy has also summoned the image of the ship as a central metaphor for hybridity, displacement, border crossing, circulatory systems, transformation, and reinscription. In his conception of the "Black Atlantic," he explains how sailors moved between nations on ships that were "microsystems of linguistic and political hybridity."[14] Gilroy's emphasis on movement, border crossing, plurality of forms, and open textuality as modalities of resistant cultural practice is materialized in the dubbing, scratching, and remixing of digitally sampled hip-hop music, a form of black music that ransacks other musical forms in order to refashion them into a new musical language.[15]

Media piracy, which reinscribes racializing and engendering discourses on dominant media that privilege whiteness and maleness, similarly refutes the binary oppositions between dominant and radical media by creating a hybrid structure that graphs together old media and new forms, a sampling and remixing of culture. Gilroy deploys the term *antiphony* to describe the democratic model emerging in African American call-and-response musical forms, a term that collapses the binary oppositions between producer and consumer, author and reader, into intersubjectivity and interaction.[16] Media piracy, then, can be theorized as an antiphonic relation, rather than as simply a marginal or resistant position. The former implies motion, whereas the latter suggests stasis.

Pirate antiphony, however, is not simply a productive relation, but a virtuoso invention of new social spaces designed with recuperated imagery and tactical practices. In *The Practice of Everyday Life*, Michel de Certeau theorizes space and its relation to poaching, a tactic of the dispossessed to change the register of totalitarian regimes by concocting a creative utopia through wit, trickery, and art, reversing the power relations. An example of this poaching emerges in folktales and legends, where the story enunciates this inversion: the disempowered trick giants and other ogres, signifying impregnable power and triumph, a pedagogy of utopianism and hope.[17] For de Certeau, space differs from place in that it is "composed of intersections of mobile elements," whereas place is bounded, fixed, located.[18] These notions of space and tactics rather than place and strategies are central to rethinking how to deal with the post–Cold War new world communication orders, which have simultaneously centralized (with mergers across industries) and decentralized (diffusion of new technologies such as camcorders and computers). Media piracy, then, produces mobile space through tactics in which, as de Certeau has said, "order is tricked by an art."[19]

▶

Transnationalizing Hollywood Images

Hollywood films are juicy targets for pirates. Hollywood, as an ideological fantasy and economic giant, condenses three phases that have fueled piracy: first, its images are hegemonic and globalized; second, its homogenization of narrative form and ideology has accelerated; and third, it has contributed to the intensification in the patrolling of the reproduction and circulation of images. Both commercial and media pirates prey on Hollywood.

In his short tape *Día de la Independencia* (1997), video artist Alex Rivera deflects the image of the alien spaceship descending over the White House and the advertising campaign from the blockbuster 1996 hit *Independence Day* to suggest that alien movies are really anti-immigration, racist narratives. In effect, he recodes and Spanglishizes the trailer from *Independence Day* through computer-generated animation techniques. Rivera executes a visual double entendre by exchanging a sombrero for an alien spaceship. The sombrero hovers over the White House, visualizing the anti-Mexican ideologies of the current popular discourse on immigration and space aliens.

In *Día de la Independencia*, Rivera engages digital imaging to racialize the Hollywood blockbuster. Borrowing from the short form of movie trailers, which create interest through anticipation, Rivera pirates the form of *Independence Day* to show that the Hollywood film subtextually propagates fear of racialized aliens across the border, disguised as space aliens. The tape perfectly mimics the slick editing, visual perfection, and tone of Hollywood studio summer blockbuster trailers, but completely subverts the content by assuming a Spanish-speaking audience rather than an English-speaking one and warning Anglos of the impending invasion.

Digitally produced sombreros invade Washington, D.C., from outer space in *Día de la Independencia* (1997). Dir. Alex Rivera. Photograph courtesy of Video Data Bank.

The tape concludes with the sombrero blowing up the White House in a visualization of racialized fantasies. In effect, Rivera recuperates digitality in order to reracialize special effects, to bring to the forefront that which they repress, a sort of psychoanalytic and political exorcism.

Piracy is perhaps the most significant issue for transnational media in the post–Cold War era. This economic context of more and more globalized and expensive media and expansion into new markets around the world surrounds and fuels artistic media piracy. As the gap widens between those who have access to media technology and those who do not, tactics for participation change. Since 1989, piracy and copyright violations have emerged as central international trade issues for the United States as it deals with the newly democratized countries of the former Soviet Union, Eastern Europe, and China, areas where illegal piracy has exploded exponentially as demand for Western entertainment has increased and such high-tech consumer goods as VCRs have become more available.

These regions represent some of the largest emerging markets for the media transnationals, and are thus heavily policed through threats, trade barriers, and trade sanctions by the U.S. government that are designed to ensure that transnational media products are purchased rather than copied.

The U.S. government as well as trade organizations for Hollywood, such as the MPAA, have become allies of the media transnationals, bolstering them by providing international policing of intellectual property rights. In Asia and the Third World, copyright piracy has continued to increase. On the other side, intellectual property—ranging from films, books, and computer programs to musical recordings—has become the third-largest U.S. export, after aerospace and agriculture. China, for example, has been found to account for nearly one-tenth of all losses from piracy, a particular threat to the transnational media sector because China is the largest and fastest-growing telecommunications market in Asia.[20]

The conflicting legal systems, histories, and cultural norms between the nation-state and the transnational era are typified in the cases of China, Poland, and Russia, where Western legal definitions of copyright are alien concepts. For example, as Derek Elley has explained in *Variety,* different cultural values on replication of material exist in Hong Kong cinema, "a film industry where plagiarism isn't a dirty word, where genres play themselves out at a furious rate in only a matter of years, and where audience happily applaud replication as much as complete originality."[21]

Since the revolutions of 1989, democracy has been equated with the market economy, and computer software, videos, and CDs have emerged as important components of international trade. The explosion of new technologies, the very technologies that have facilitated unprecedented global growth in the communications/entertainment/information sector, has simultaneously opened up the possibility of endless illegal reproductions by pirates in these countries who are copying entertainment goods for profit.

As argued in a 1995 UNESCO report on international cultural diversity, the concentration of media ownership worldwide has greatly accelerated since 1989, producing an enormous gap between those with access to media and those who do not have access.[22] Richard J. Barnet and John Cavanaugh have shown how the concentration and globalization of media have catapulted entertainment into the third-largest surplus product of the United States. They describe the postindustrial corporation shedding its manufacturing divisions and moving increasingly into information processing, communications, and marketing. For example, they document how the music industry has globalized, with MTV and CDs sold around the world, as music is a commodity that easily crosses language barriers.[23] The information/communications/entertainment industry conglomerated in the 1980s and then globalized in the 1990s, forming transnational webs of interlocking companies with high levels of concentration.[24]

These economic changes have had significant impacts on the form, structure, and design of Hollywood narratives. Herbert Schiller has noted that Hollywood in the 1990s has relied increasingly on visual and technical virtuosity produced through computer imaging techniques that rely on gut reactions from viewers rather than on cognition, creating new perceptual grids.[25] Janet Wasko has also recognized that as these transnationalized studios commandeer more and more new forms of distribution technologies, such as cable, CD-ROM, satellites, and the Internet, not only does competition decrease as barriers to entry are raised, but independent producers are squeezed out of the marketplace almost entirely.[26]

During the 1980s, Hollywood developed what is called "high concept" filmmaking, a blockbuster genre that depends almost entirely on marketability, star power, fashionableness, simplicity of plot, music tie-ins, and merchandising. According to Justin Wyatt, as studios conglomerated in the 1980s, the parent corporations elected to minimize risks and to integrate production, marketing, and advertising. Films such as *Flashdance, American Gigolo, Jaws*, and *Top Gun* exemplify this trend. The blockbuster era integrated filmmaking with marketing and advertising, consequently strangling narrative diversity in filmmaking and contributing to the decline of the small picture.[27] For example, Jon Lewis has shown how auteurist director Francis Ford Coppola's directing and producing career—which was identified with high-quality, actor-centric art films—plummeted during the 1980s as studios conglomerated.[28]

As a result of the infusion of marketing and advertising into Hollywood film, during the 1980s and 1990s, the studios became more and more dedicated to product tie-ins and merchandising, activities that hinged on patents, copyright, and licensing arrangements that yielded highly profitable returns by controlling the circulation of images. For instance, almost one-third of screen time in a Hollywood narrative is now occupied with product placement shots.[29] Perhaps the company most identified with inordinately successful merchandising, copyright control, and licensing agreements is the Disney Corporation, known as one of the most "synergistic" corporations because of its cross-fertilization among films, merchandising, rerelease patterns, and theme parks, which produce the most profit.[30]

As a result of this move toward product merchandising and control over the home video market, which has generated more profit for Hollywood releases than theatrical box office since the late 1980s, as well as the globalization of the exhibition and distribution of Hollywood product, the studios have been quite aggressive in the international policing of copyright infringement and in antipiracy campaigns. The transnational media companies consider piracy the major problem for film distribution abroad, exacerbated by the penetration of VCRs in developing countries since 1989, the lack of unified, enforceable copyright laws on a global scale, and lack of media diversity in certain regions, such as the Middle East.[31]

Within this context, the Hollywood film industry has changed dramatically, particularly in its relation to producing visual imagery and linear narratives. As Janet Wasko has argued, the media/entertainment sector has grown considerably during the 1980s and 1990s, with most studios now transnational conglomerates that are transindustrial, multilinked entities combining film, television, music, and publishing and utilizing new technologies such as cable, satellite, and VCRs for control over distribution. Although the studio system was divested by the 1948 Paramount decision, the studios have in fact reintegrated themselves vertically in the 1980s and 1990s. They have also globalized, earning more than 43 percent of their profit from foreign distribution.

As a result, copyright and piracy have emerged as major areas of concern: the Hollywood studios have become some of the fiercest advocates for free trade, especially for the General Agreement on Tariffs and Trade (GATT), which greases the wheels for the globalization of Hollywood products by lowering trade barriers.[32] A major plank of GATT is the protection of intellectual property rights such as copyrights and patents.[33] Ronald Bettig has observed that the signing of GATT "signalled the consolidation of control over intellectual and artistic creativity in the hands of transnational corporations in rich countries."[34]

Within this context of increasing regulation and policing of transnationally mobile images and archives, media piracy of a different register has materialized that reclaims these images as fragments of psychic imaginaries, public histories, new formations of subjectivities. This work rejects the privatization of the world's image banks by recuperating these narratives and images as a malleable, reproducible, infinitely mutable part of public culture, memory, and history. These acts of media piracy capsize the subject-object relations of the image: their tactic is to refuse the border between public and private by navigating the zone in between.

Rock Hudson's Home Movies (1992), by Mark Rappaport, is a direct assault against the transnationalized and purified image archive. Actor Eric Faar impersonates Rock Hudson, describing in first-person voice-over his sex life as a gay man in Hollywood, his studio marriage, his thoughts as he was represented as the epitome of 1950s heterosexual masculinity, his battle with AIDS. This imaginary gay narrative "voiced" by Rock Hudson rereads the Hollywood film clips from various Douglas Sirk films he starred in, simultaneously detaching the films from their patriarchal familialism and queering the straight sexuality of these films' representation of masculinity.

The archival trace of Hudson in Hollywood, then, is transposed into evidence of the blurred frontiers between public image and private life, straight sexuality and queerness, narrative representation and subjectivity, documentary and fiction. Faar impersonates the imagined documentary truth of Hudson's sexuality, diving beneath the tabloid hysteria surrounding Hudson's battle with AIDS to reveal an actor who adopted the role of trickster of sexual norms, while the Hollywood narratives, shorn from their context, are transcribed into documentary evidence of Hudson's skill at acting out the part of a straight male matinee idol. At one point in the film, the voice-over describes how Rock kissed and does subversive readings in which gay sexuality bubbles just beneath the narrative representation in a series of stolen looks, glances, touches. *Rock Hudson's Home Movies,* then, deconstructs Hollywood narratives and reconstructs gay male sexuality, elucidating Hollywood as a site for the consumption, reproduction, and distortion of sexual fantasy.

In *Joan Sees Stars* (1993), Joan Braderman performs a similar tactic of sexualizing and rereading the Hollywood archive through a reinscription of suppressed subjectivity and physicality by investigating how Hollywood celebrities permeate our psyches, our beds, and our dreams. The beginning sequence of the tape features a montage of various warnings about copyright infringement lifted from the front of rented videotapes, its excess and repetition signaling the futility of copyright enforcement.

The tape interweaves two stories of aging and illness: Joan's own serious, debilitating illness, which puts her in bed for months, and her friend Leland's deterioration from AIDS. With Joan in the East and Leland in the West, they communicate via phone, discussing the videotapes they rent from video stores to pass the time while they are bedridden. The Hollywood films, featuring various movie stars such as Elizabeth Taylor, function as talismans for hallucinations of physical perfection and beauty, fantasies that transport Joan's own psychic space from her sick bed and body to the realm of the imaginary, which she interprets as a useful distraction from her physical pain.

Joan describes devouring biographies on the stars, reading their images in the films as hallucinations of femininity, merging with them as celluloid goddesses. *Joan Sees Stars* explores the identification process inscribed in the new form of cinematic spectatorship, the home VCR, which, in privatizing and isolating the viewing experience, also opens Hollywood films up to a new kind of psychic recycling. As they are endlessly replayed, stopped, and fast-forwarded on Joan's VCR, the Hollywood films function more as ritualized obsessions, love objects, and repetition fantasies than as narratives. The space of the video screen, then, becomes the site of recuperation, both from illness and from corporate images.

Joan Braderman blue screens herself over copyright warnings as she pirates images from classic Hollywood films on videotape in *Joan Sees Stars* (1993). Dir. Joan Braderman. Photograph courtesy of the artist.

Gringo in Mananaland (1995), DeeDee Halleck's epic compilation restructuring of the "story" of the U.S. relationship with Latin America through reedited pirated clips from Hollywood films, newsreels, educational films, and industrials, also performs reconstructive surgery on commercial presentation, demonstrating that these Hollywood and newsreel images populate a public landscape. Twelve years in production, *Gringo in Mananaland* juxtaposes film clips to retell the story of U.S.-Latin American relations as one of rampant cultural imperialism, where a rich and exotic land is discovered by Anglos, where natives toil in the fields, where bandits threaten, and everyone desires U.S. aid. The producers compiled a database of more than seven hundred films from more than one hundred archival sources, ranging from the U.S. National Archives to the U.S. Marine Archives, the University of California, Los Angeles, the University of Southern California, the National Archives of Guatemala, and the Cuban Film Institute.[35] In the tape, clips from Hollywood films such as *The Cuban Love Song* (1931, MGM), *South of the Border* (1939, Republic Pictures), *Tropic Zone* (1953, Paramount), and *Fun in Acapulco* (1963, Paramount) are rearranged, shaved down, and rethreaded to reveal that nearly all the representations of Latin America, whether in newsreels, industrial films, or narrative films, serve as a fantasy of the U.S. national imaginary, projecting Latin America as a land of bounty, pliant natives, and bandits.

Halleck fashions a new narrative out of the old films, one that unpacks the racialization and class exploitation the commercial films repress, in effect, editing to expose the seams in the seamless representations. *Gringo in Mananaland,* then, historicizes narrative by showing that all narratives, whatever modality or genre, have an international trade context. Drawing on films spanning an Edison film about the Spanish-American War from 1900 to a 1963 Elvis Presley musical, the tape creates a new historiography of representation, one that rejects linearity and opts for an archaeology of the psychic and economic relations between United States and Latin America. For example, the films are not edited together in chronological order, but are interwoven in sequences announced through superimposed headline intertitles, the progression of which itself narrativizes imperialism: "arrival," "the past," "paradise," "problem #1," "bandits," "technology," "cooperation." Structurally, *Gringo in Mananaland* demonstrates that the fictionalized cinematic representations in Hollywood films enact the psychic fantasies of the political economies of imperialism, while the documentary footage from newsreels, educational films, and industrials enacts a projection of national and international fictions.

For example, near the middle of the tape, a sequence on banana production disembowels fictional and nonfictional representations as fantastic projections of labor. In a scene from the 1953 Hollywood film *Tropic Zone,* a woman tells her husband that her family founded their plantation to provide more and better employment for the laborers. This scene is then cut with a United Fruit Company film about "bananaland." The sequence that follows intercuts a dance sequence from a Fred Astaire film in which he pulls veils off of a Latin American woman, a Carmen Miranda dance number in which women sport huge bananas on their heads, and various newsreels and industrials that illustrate banana production and shipping.

In this editing, Halleck demonstrates that both Hollywood dance numbers and black-and-white newsreels fantasize labor and race, spectaclizing both to show subservience to the interests of capital. bell hooks has described the enjoyment of racial difference as "the commodification of otherness." For instance, a black-and-white newsreel image of a worker carrying bananas on his head is intercut with a similarly framed shot of Carmen Miranda with an enormous pile of bananas flowing out of her head, nearly five times larger than her own body. This cut crystalizes Halleck's political tactics: the real is fantastic, the fantastic is real, both speak the power of a racialized, sexualized economy of signs and products.[36]

▶ ───

The Crisis of Copyright in the Era of New Technologies

Copyright debates pit the diffusion of new computer and satellite technologies against regulation by large transnational corporations, public interests against private capital, information against property, the information have-nots against the information haves: but all of these oppositions are suspended in the fluid frontier of new technologies such as computers and satellites, which blur borders. Hayden Gregory, chief counsel for the House Judiciary Subcommittee on Intellectual Property, for example, has noted, "You can sum up copyright concerns in one word: digital."[37]

As Ronald Bettig has argued, "Copyright is monopolistic."[38] Copyright, which developed in the sixteenth century with the dawn of capitalism and the printing press, transforms culture into property. In effect, it materializes ideas, objectifying that which suggests interactivity and installing stasis into that which depends on movement. Copyright grants monopolies of knowledge to individuals and corporations instead of to communities, enforcing what Jane Gaines has termed the romantic idea of uniqueness, singularity, and authorship.[39] If folktales, songs, and stories were passed on and altered in communities as living, changing, communal, authorless works, copyright, in rewarding individuality, commodifies culture, information, and knowledge, transforming it into private property to be policed and sold rather than shared.[40] However, as Bettig and Gaines have both underscored, copyright, because it facilitates enormous regulation and surveillance of the image and information, can conflict with issues of access, freedom, creativity, and critique.[41] In other words, copyright operates as a privatizer of public spaces constructed out of discourses, images, stories. In a literal sense, copyright incorporates ideas into the corporate environs.

The development of new communications technologies, whether the printing press, photography, cinema, VCRs, satellites, or computers, has always threatened the monopoly control of copyright and ownership of images. As technologies are diffused, they have the potential to democraticize access to information and communications, a potentially destabilizing force requiring constant system adjustment in the laws, in national culture, and in economic structures.[42] Martha Buskirk writes, "The initial establishment and the subsequent development of copyright principles should be understood as a series of responses to the potential for disruption inherent in various new forms of technology."[43]

The first attempt to revise the world's copyright laws for the digital age occurred in 1989, a pivotal year in the new world order, at the World Intellectual Property Organization (WIPO).[44] WIPO members recognized copyright as a fundamental ingredient of the globalized economy. By 1996, the WIPO Diplomatic Conference in Geneva met to review the challenges digitization poses to the Berne Convention, the international treaty on copyright. The conference foregrounded the heated political debates between those who want to ensure greater enforcement of copyright to extend monopoly control and those who want to protect access to information.[45]

The Clinton administration and the film and recording industries were strong supporters of more aggressive copyright enforcement and an expansion of its reach, whereas the American Library Association, the Association of Computing Machinery, artists, universities, civil liberties groups, and computer manufacturers worried that the new proposals would limit public availability of information.[46] The Clinton and Hollywood positions would have wiped out any fair use provisions, which operate as a balance to monopoly by protecting access to material for educational and critical ends, in effect, supporting users rather than highly protectionist copyright industries. On the other side, a coalition of African, Asian, and Latin American countries lobbied against enlargement of copyright domains and stalled the copyright maximalizing position. As Pamela Samuelson has noted, "The battle shaping up in the digital era pits media conglomerates against users as never before."[47] This international copyright debate condenses the layered destabilizations that cyberspace opens up, especially concerning the distinctions between public and private, boundaries that become much more difficult to chart in the digital era and that contribute to the gnarly discourse enveloping all forms of piracy.[48] From the side of capital interests, for example, Howard C. Lincoln remarked in the *Wall Street Journal*: "Piracy has always been a threat to international trade, but it is especially so now. Thanks to technology's miracles, the products of the postindustrial age—like computer driven games and information services—are susceptible to piracy in ways that manufactured producers never were."[49] Jim McCue in the *Spectator* expanded this point even more: "Copyright law is falling into disrepute as technology makes it both unenforceable and irrelevant."[50]

With digitization, images and words can be endlessly mutated, copied, revised, manipulated, and distributed, eradicating the differences among producers, creators, artists, users, and spectators. Whereas this elaboration of a fluid space of change and exchange has provoked the legal/economic strata to rein in and colonize this new frontier, it has encouraged artists and activists confronting the end of arts funding to develop new formations that are perhaps less institutionally bounded and that manufacture new spaces. Commenting on the new possibilities that cyberspace and digital technologies offer to artists, Margot Lovejoy has said, "The potential of the new technologies is toward interaction and communication, a kind of inclusivity which encourages global exchange through which fresh insights can evolve through experimentation with diversity and difference."[51]

Yet these possibilities for new environments, which by their inscription of and immersion within intertextual structures refute the very notion of single authorship, defy the property presumptions of traditional copyright. Transmission of words and images is not only instantaneous, but subject to endless manipulations, transformations, and morphings that challenge the very notion of stability in any form or articulation. John Perry Barlow, a former songwriter for the Grateful Dead who has become a major voice for democracy in cyberspace, has noted, "Digital technology is also erasing the legal jurisdictions of the physical world, and replacing them with the unbounded and perhaps permanenetly lawless seas of cyberspace."[52]

Digital space, then, is not a bounded place, but an endlessly shifting context, where the differentiations between context and text are collapsed as each folds into the other. Much theorization of this digital zone has invoked the metaphor of ecology, a signification of how this interdependent, rhizomelike system operates as a living organism, where texts sprout from other texts, contexts die off yet fertilize new texts, and open, mutating systems link to other metamorphosing systems where there is always new growth. Recognizing digitality as a contradictory formation incorporating both the masculinist, privatized logic of the capitalist market and newly emerging possibilities for social collectivity, Bill Nichols has also summoned the language of environmentalism and ecology, arguing for a transgression of its capitalist delimitations through the new social formations and new visions digitality itself produces.[53] Consequently, because digitality arranges a more collective event and environment, it displaces the individuality inscribed within intellectual property laws. Pierre Levy, for example, in theorizing how digitality precipitates new artistic epistemologies and spaces, notes that it places users "in a living environment in which we are always already co-authors."[54]

This ecological modality of digitality, then, is built upon circulation rather than exchange, fluidity rather than static objects, a recontextualization of piracy itself as a democratizing practice that ensures environmental health. Umberto Eco has extended the public interconnectivity of this ecological framework, arguing against the privatization of computers themselves by formulating the idea of a public multimedia arcade, with public access to computers, giant communal screens for the posting of Web sites, and a public, social environment—the Mediterranean *osteria*—where people consume food, ideas, and each other.[55]

Norman Cowie's three-minute, explosively edited tape *The Third Wave* (1995) condenses and compacts these ideas of digitality as oscillating between a marketization repressing its own racialization and a social ecology of images to be reused, pirated, altered, forming a kind of compressed library of digital iconography and ideology. A voice-over in which Newt Gingrich explains the transition from agriculture to manufacturing to information opens the tape, mixed over archival shots of farming, factory work, and computers intercut with iconographic fragments of imagery from the Gulf War, black power demonstrations, police interventions, and surveillance. This opening sequence deploys montage to reconnect archival images of work with their racialized context of state power, illustrating how industrial images of labor, whether in factories or on computers, operate within a larger context of racial and international war. *The Third Wave* not only references but ransacks popular commercial forms of musical montage found on MTV, using the song "Let's Go Surfing" over images of computer screens and home shopping networks, but politicizes its form by inserting an overload of visual content. In the final sequence of the tape, the classic 1960s rock and roll song "Wipe Out" is laid over wordplay on the term *information* in large headline letters: the word *information* remains centered on the screen while other words appear below it in quick succession—*revolution, infrastructure, superhighway, business, security, overload, exchange, public, private, warfare, addiction, pirates, power, rich, poor, gaps, pleasures, paranoics*. This sequence performs a pedagogical function, reconnecting all of the linguistic structures forming the digital and information economy into a new ecology of information language that maps power.

Thus, as it pirates computer images and digital languages, *The Third Wave* both critiques the marketization of the digital and revives its circulatory functions, recuperating the possibilities of digitality through a montage of disparate elements. It creates, in effect, a sort of visual/aural library on the scope, range, and contradictions of digitality.

This amalgamation of circulation and intervention, market and critique, appropriation and reappropriation figures in much discussion of new technologies. In her semiotic and political analysis of hip-hop style as an Afro-diasporic form identified with the margins of the postindustrial, transnationalized order, Tricia Rose argues that new technologies such as digital samplers sustain an aesthetic defined by flow, layering, and rupture, where commercial culture is remade into an alternative naming of oppression and racism. Rose sees political potential in rap's cultural recyclings

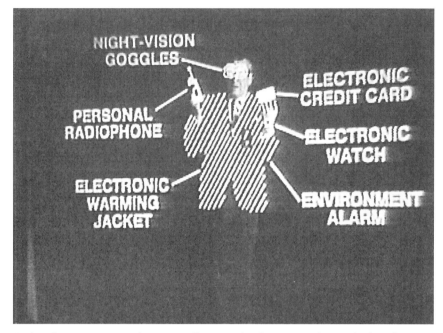

Archival image mapping how surveillance technologies remake our bodies, from *The Third Wave* (1995). Dir. Norman Cowie. Photograph courtesy of the artist.

and reclamations: "A style that has the reflexivity to create counterdominant narratives against a mobile and shifting enemy—may be one of the most effective ways to fortify communities of resistance and simultaneously reserve the right to communal pleasure."[56]

Following Rose, who traces the popularization of digitality in the form of samplers and consequently decenters the primacy of the computer itself as a fetish object, computers are not the only machines operating in this new technological environment to challenge copyright by establishing new social communities. Satellite technologies, which use outer space to transmit images and sounds across the globe in seconds, are also a central part of this new ecology. Satellites exhibit homologies to the social and economic contradictions of computers that need to be pirated and reinvested with communal pleasures as well.

Neither Ted Turner's CNN nor Rupert Murdoch's Star TV could be imagined without satellites. Satellite technology allows CNN to broadcast to more than two hundred countries and ensures that industrialized countries will control global news as nations deregulate and privatize broadcasting. However, the miniaturization of home satellite receivers, their dissemination to countries around the globe, and their drop in price constitute threats to this transnational control of news.[57] Because satellites leave a wide "footprint" that crosses national borders, anyone with a home satellite dish can downlink material, increasing the likelihood of piracy. The diffusion of satellite dishes around the world has contributed to the rise of piracy via satellite in Asia, the Middle East, and Latin America, which has been accelerating since the mid-1980s.[58]

Recently, pirate media productions have emerged that exploit the democratic possibilities of satellite technology to create new communal spaces and to imagine a world without distinctions between public and private and without nationalist borders. These productions repudiate the separation between the analog and the digital, the historical and the contemporary, high-end technology such as satellites and low-end video. Aesthetically, they hybridize form, content, argument, and reception, linking technologies to marginalized politics to produce new potentially democratic spaces.

In *Spin* (1995), Brian Springer has explored how U.S. commercial television stifles public debate by reediting more than six hundred hours of on- and off-air satellite feeds into a seventy-six-minute compilation tape. Springer recorded these unscrambled satellite feeds during 1992, the year of the Los Angeles rebellion following the acquittals of the officers who beat Rodney King, the year of increased agitation over reproductive rights, and the year of a presidential election. The tape shows the off-air segments between national broadcasts, during which reporters talk to their producers, Larry King schmoozes his guests about how to obtain drugs, and Clinton and Gore discuss how to act on a live broadcast. Describing his work process, Springer explains:

> As far as the fair use issues, my public position on this is that images were transmitted unscrambled and visible to over 3.5 million dish owners across North America. So to me, the images are in the public. That's my position— I'm not a lawyer and others may have a different view based on the communications acts. Once the images are in a public realm, then they can be reused under fair use. I recorded them with my own dish.[59]

In these feeds, the performative mode of television, which packages news and sanitizes private discourses, recedes. *Spin* crawls between the interstices of television, the spaces of live, nonstop satellite hookups in between national and international broadcasts, in effect, working the seams rather than the programs. Indeed, because copyright issues regarding downlinking satellite feeds are both ambiguous and unresolved, the tape itself cannot be broadcast or commercially distributed; its own distribution and reception are thrown into other in-between spaces outside traditional distribution channels.

Presidential candidate Bill Clinton getting prepped on camera before a 1992 CNN broadcast in a live satellite feed from *Spin* (1995). Dir. Brian Springer. Photograph courtesy of Video Data Bank.

Spin serves as a montage of the national imaginary that is always repressed in the unconscious; like psychoanalysis, its editing and selection process zeros in on slippages, hysterias, and repetitions that in their alterity to the national public fantasies, divulge racism, corporatization, and the end of the public sphere. In one sequence, a host from a network morning show talks with her guest, a medical doctor who administers a major Los Angeles hospital. He admits that the cases admitted to his emergency unit are worse than anything he has seen in the Third World. The host asks him to discuss something else during the broadcast. Later, 1988 presidential candidate Pat Robertson comments to a staffer, "That guy was a homo, as sure as you're alive."

In other sequences, Larry King tells George Bush that the drug Halcyon can be secured without a doctor's prescription in Israel. Larry King is exposed toadying up to various politically powerful people for favors, from Ross Perot to Bush, to Clinton and Gore. To Clinton, Larry King exhorts: "Ted Turner changed the world. . . . He would serve you, you know what I mean. . . . I'd call him after you're elected." Throughout, reporters are shown primping, combing their hair, putting on lipstick, readying themselves for performance. Before reporting the verdict in the trial of the LAPD officers accused of beating Rodney King, a news anchor jokes, "Okay, I am standing by, ladies and gentlemen. We don't have shit to say. We don't have anything to do. But by god, the management of this company deems it necessary that I come on the air at seven in the morning and shock the shit out of all of you." By maneuvering through this national televisual unconsciousness in a slow editing rhythm permitting the unfolding of these intertexts, *Spin* disintegrates the technical velocity associated with commercial television by rerouting it via satellite, a space that holds more multifarious layers of communication. Consequently, *Spin* writes the end of the public sphere with these interstitial private utterances of racism, cronyism, power brokering, and regulated discourse.

As *Spin* refigures the reception of satellite feeds as a productive modality, *El Naftazteca: Cyber Aztec TV for 2000 A.D.* (1994) skyjacks satellite capabilities for cross-border production. A joint project between the iEAR Studios at Rensselaer Polytechnic Institute in Troy, New York, and Mexico City–born performance artist Guillermo Gómez-Peña and produced and directed by Branda Miller and Adriene Jenik, *El Naftazteca* was taped during a ninety-minute live satellite broadcast that addressed cross-cultural issues and American-Latino relations as they intertwined with issues of such advanced technologies as computers, virtual reality, long-distance telephones, cable access, satellite, television, and film. Directed by Adriene Jenik, with Branda Miller as executive producer, the broadcast was part of the live satellite telecasts program at Rensselaer Polytechnic Institute called "In a Word, with Technology." Flyers were mailed around the country urging communities to set up public viewings of the broadcast that would have telephones to allow the audience to call Gómez-Peña during the performance. The program was provided free to anyone with the technical capacities to downlink, and sites were encouraged to create public, communal viewings on Thanksgiving Day, November 22, 1994.[60]

Featuring Gómez-Peña as El Naftazteca, a name that combines the acronyn for the North American Free Trade Agreement (NAFTA) with Aztec, the name of Gómez-Peña's ancestral people, the tape assumes a visual look fusing the low-tech aesthetic of cable with the high-tech fast editing of MTV: a low-tech, self-reflexive mise-en-scène replete with computers decorated with Mexican toys, studio technicians dressed like gang members, and machinery jerry-built to look like homemade virtual reality machines mixed freely with state-of-the-art computers, editors, satellite transmitters, and glossy editing. Reverberating with this technological mixing and border crossing, a plethora of televisual styles are also referenced and revised, ranging from MTV clips of Hollywood spectacles about Mexico to computer animation, performance art, direct-address lecture, intertitles scrolling on the screens, and sermons. Thus *El Naftazteca* hybridizes all layers of the production, from genre to language to technology to form.

The tape "performs" piracy as in a simulacrum using interactive satellite television, posing as an illegal pirate transmission from an "underground *vato*-bunker, somewhere between New York, Miami, and Los Angeles." Throughout the tape, Gómez-Peña functions as host, shaman, intercultural translator, and pedagogue, constantly shape-shifting his own subject and performance position and freely intermixing Spanish, English, and Spanglish as he responds to live callers who ask about where to travel in Mexico, comment that the broadcast shows that "Third World countries are really capable of deconstructing the whole postmodern media paradigm," and joke about whether the performers will return to jail after the broadcast.

Prerecorded video sequences retrieve "cultural memories" of Mexican films, Gómez-Peña's own performances, and Hollywood representations of Mexicans through TECHNOPAL 2000, a "new technology" invented, Gómez-Peña explains, by "Mayans with the help of aliens from Harvard. Its CPU is powered by Habanero chili peppers, combined with this or DAT technology." Gómez-Peña is accompanied by a sidekick character called Cyber-Vato, who at one point dons "Chicano virtual reality machine" headgear to experience the subjectivity of an illegal alien attempting to cross the U.S. border.

Throughout, Gómez-Peña challenges everything—from language to computer and media technology, to film history, to the whole notion of interactivity—by assuming the role of pirate, the buccaneer who travels between cultures and nations, mixing bounty from different regions on a ship. The tape opens with a title in graffiti-style writing, "A TV Intervencion Pirata," and El Naftazteca announcing, "Good evening, post-NAFTA America. I'm sorry to inform you that this is a pirate TV broadcast. My name is El Naf-taz-teca: cross-cultural salesman, disc jockey *apocaliptico*, and information superhighway *bandido*, all in one, within, and vice versa, interrupting your coitus, as always."

Later in the broadcast, he exclaims:

> You lonesome *guerros* out there in TV land are witnessing a *historica* pirate broadcast. Two intelligent, live Mexicans on national televisions. So get off your *nalgas paldias* and be interactive, *carnales*. Call the bunker right now and let us know what you think you think. Remember: you are allowed to speak in any language you wish. Illegal aliens are welcome. You are allowed to be smart, performative, or poetic.[61]

El Naftazteca dematerializes technological power and copyright from exchange relations, not only severing them from commodification but also racializing them as new hybrid languages that defy borders. The tape suggests that piracy and hybridity are codependent, both tactics that displace monopoly controls over images, information, essentialized identities, technologies. In this tape, copyright and new technologies are virtually ignored and scorned as inconsequential to the emergent yet always circumscribed possibilities of interactive communications and the new communal spaces that can be provisionally and transitionally developed as technologies are repositioned and structurally amended.

▶

Fair Use and Fair Users

The monopoly character of copyright law is not totalized. Fair use provisions ensure that a small discursive terrain stays open for critical and educational usages. These provisions operate as a check and balance to the commodifying tendencies of copyright laws. The fair use provision imposes limitations on the exclusive ownership of images. Section 107 of the 1976 Copyright Act provides for use of copyrighted work for "criticism, comment, news reporting, teaching . . . and scholarship." Legally, four interconnected factors are exercised in the evaluation of the applicability of fair use: the purpose and character of the use, the nature of the copyrighted work, the amount and substantiality of the portion used in relation to the whole work, and the effect of the use on the potential market value of the original.[62]

In the post-1989 new world order, where information and entertainment are central components of the transnational economy, fair use provisions have emerged as a site of enormous system disturbance about the traffic in images. These debates on the boundaries of fair use underscore how new technologies that increase access to and democratize media production (camcorders, VCRs, home satellite dishes, tape recorders, fax machines, photocopiers, computers, e-mail systems) challenge older, more exclusionary elitist standards of authorship.[63] For example, corporations and national governments such as the United States under the Clinton administration have often argued for restrictions and delimiting of fair use in GATT and the Berne Conventions, a corporate protectionist stance that many artists and public access advocates view as dangerous.

Media pirates, who catapult images from a privatized realm to a public realm in different textual contexts, have invoked the fair use provision to question the legal and economic boundaries of what Guy Debord has called "the society of the spectacle." In their fair use manifesto, the found-sound band Negativland argues that the saturated mass-media environment is natural cultural material for artists to sample and collage as a way to intervene against the increasingly conservative interpretation of fair use:

> We think it's about time that the obvious aesthetic validity of appropriation begins to be raised in opposition to the assumed preeminence of copyright laws prohibiting the free reuse of cultural material. . . . the act of appropriating from this media assault represents a kind of liberation from our status as helpless sponges. . . . it is a much needed form of self defense against the one-way, corporate-consolidated media barrage. . . . appropriators claim the right to create with mirrors.[64]

For Negativland, the Fair Use Doctrine represents the only protection for artistic freedom, freedom of speech, and democracy within an increasingly corporate-controlled media landscape that inhibits critical public discussion. It is important to note here that Negativland and other media pirates do not reject copyright law in its entirety; they support the intention of copyright to protect authors and creators by requiring fair compensation for the use of work. The argument rests on the expansion of the liberalized interpretation of fair use, especially in the rapidly changing new media technological environment, where new artistic forms based on sampling and fragmenting existing cultural practices are surfacing.[65]

In effect, while copyright represents the privatization of images within a market economy, fair use sustains the public access environment surrounding the use of images and their circulation within different discursive networks. Fair use, then, theoretically functions as a mechanism to make images public and to allow individuals to insert them into public spheres defined by critique, parody, or education. Media piracy detaches and displaces images and words from the syntax of corporatized speech and creates new metonymic and metaphoric relations that attempt to emphasize the publicness of the image.

Two legal cases that transpired during the 1990s foreground the great philosophical divides between commerce and artists in relation to the Fair Use Doctrine and the pressures exerted on it by new artistic forms derived from new technologies: the 2 Live Crew case, which raised the issue of digital sampling and parody, and the Jeff Koons case, which queried the extent of protection for postmodern appropriated art.

In 1993, the rap group 2 Live Crew parodied the 1964 Roy Orbison song "Oh, Pretty Woman," recasting the woman as a grotesque hooker. Acuff-Rose Music, owner of the rights to the Orbison song, contended that the context of the usage constituted a copyright infringement, because the rap group was engaged in a commercial, for-profit undertaking. The U.S. Supreme Court upheld the Fair Use Doctrine, arguing that parody is protected, and ruled in favor of 2 Live Crew.[66]

However, in contrast, the federal appeals court ruled against postmodern sculptor Jeff Koons, who had copied a commercially produced photograph of two people sitting on a bench shot by Art Rogers in a sculpture called *String of Puppies*. In supporting Rogers's argument, the court stated that Koons had committed an act of piracy, arguing that his work was less a critical parody than a commercial enterprise.[67] In assessing the implications of the Koons/Rogers case for the art world, Martha Buskirk has asserted that the case points to a conflict between two different discursive practices: the court found no difference between a mass-produced product and an artistic product, suggesting a collision between two distinct types of authors who operate in different contexts of exchange relations.[68]

Although these cases represent two extremely differently inscribed sites—commercial music and the New York art gallery scene—the divergent court opinions suggest that both sampling and postmodern art elaborate the ambiguous parameters of fair use as it is challenged and stressed by technological and artistic restructurings. However, this legal articulation of fair use addresses only the judiciary layer of recycled imagery, minimizing and obscuring the evolution of new social spaces and the changes in property relations that new technologies intensify. The very ambiguities inherent in the Fair Use Doctrine, as it abuts the digital age, have emerged as a new subcultural territory occupied by culture jammers, computer hackers, media pranksters, ravers, billboard bandits, and critical theorists. This technosubculture exploits the contradictions between concentrated transnationalized media that crimp access and the diffusion of new consumer-based technologies that expand it. Rather than concentrating on the Fair Use Doctrine as a signifying system, this subculture emphasizes fair users as producers of new signification systems.

Extending Umberto Eco's call for "semiological guerrilla warfare," Mark Dery has explained that culture jammers of all types "introduce noise into the signal," always asking the central question, Who has access to information?[69] Dery contends that these pirate utopias constitute "temporary autonomous zones," provisional, transitory, nomadic places where the force of existing social and political restraints is suspended for limited periods of time.

Similarly, the Immediast Underground, in a series of public-domain, no-copyright manifestos, also notes the collusion between the state and media corporations to interpellate a collective identity devoid of public discussion, accountability, or resistance. Immediast tactics reverberate with a reclamation of public space suggested by the Fair Use Doctrine, but provoke a more access- and production-oriented position, far beyond the domain of copyright regulations. Immediast advances "empowerment through the liberation of public space, and the spread of insurgent projects that feed or fuel the democratic power necessary for glasnost and perestroika in America and Europe. . . . We envision a bibliocentric public sphere. We advance Freedom of Speech to mean the facilitated ability to both access and produce information and cultural material."[70]

Both culture jammers and Immediasts position democratic media as requiring access and production as central operative, active modes of subjectivity, displacing consumption and reception as positions infused with corporatist agendas of passivity, commodity identification, and delimitation of the public sphere. In other words, rather than working within the gray areas of the Fair Use Doctrine, these arguments elevate fair users over the text itself, because the text, as both object and discursive relation, is itself severed from its property relations and recoded as bibliophilia, a text to be endlessly revamped in new contexts that radically alter its semiotic relations. This move constitutes pirate documentary as always already manufacturing new documents out of old, a process of infinite citation and reconstruction.

Craig Baldwin's *Sonic Outlaws* (1995) is perhaps one of the most notorious of pirate media productions that deliberately play with these ideas of fair use versus fair users as a highly politicized zone where a new cultural politics is being hammered out. A feature-length film, *Sonic Outlaws* is ostensibly "about" the legal case in which the San Francisco-based sound collage group Negativland was sued by Island Records for illegally appropriating a song and image from the Irish rock band U2. The band mixed this material with outtake sound from famous disc jockey Casey Kasem in which he makes less than flattering comments about U2.

Negativland sampled the U2 song "I Still Haven't Found What I'm Looking For." The film maps the legal conflict between a broad, artistic, public-based interpretation of the Fair Use Doctrine by fair users and the limited, corporatized application of the doctrine by Island Records. In one scene, for example, one of the members of U2, during a phone call between the band and Negativland to discuss the case, asks what they want. They reply, "Money," and describe how the lawsuit has bankrupted them. *Sonic Outlaws* cast the legal case as a David and Goliath struggle between artists and megacorporations, serving as a kind of amicus curiae brief to the courts arguing that the disparity of resources between the defendants and the plaintiffs destabilizes the conservative interpretation of the Fair Use Doctrine.

However, *Sonic Outlaws* structurally displaces the linearity of the legal conflict between Negativland and Island Records by constantly expanding into a wider context of new technologies and media practices that

Mark Hosler of the San Francisco band Negativland explaining the image of the U2 plane used on Negativland's album cover in a scene from *Sonic Outlaws* (1995). Dir. Craig Baldwin. Photograph courtesy of the artist.

decenter the privileging of copyright through montage. By creating a swirling mix of a range of pirate media practices, *Sonic Outlaws* functions not only as feisty, militant manifesto for piracy that physically decomposes copyright in its layered structuration, but as an operations manual for how to engage in such piracy. The film, then, is a call to action, a *Man with a Movie Camera* upgraded with a new operating system for the new world order that calls for seeing the world with different eyes through technological appropriation.

Throughout, *Sonic Outlaws*'s editing strategy is to apply centrifugal force to the legal case, spinning it out into a larger context of culture jammers to yank it out of the gravitational pull of judicial discourse as a monologic position. In a Foucauldian way, Baldwin deauthorizes even the case, illustrating the end of authorship with the layers of discourse encircling the production of pirated works. The film itself is structured as an interrogation into the murky territories of fair use, parody, the mass-mediated landscape, and new media technologies, as much an analytic deconstruction of copyright as a materialization of anticopyright practice.

Sequences in the film feature a who's who of media piracy: writer Douglas Kahn explains how folk art uses appropriation, the Barbie Liberation Organization changes Barbie voice boxes, the Emergency Broadcast

Network pulls down satellite footage, the Tape-Beatles remake commercials, kids steal images from newspapers with Silly Putty, ACT UP infiltrates a Dan Rather broadcast, a member of Negativland eavesdrops on cell phone conversations.

A plethora of technologies and formats similarly deauthorize a technological essentialism that would argue for a formal unity: *Sonic Outlaws* edits together Pixelvision, camcorder footage, 16mm, computer imagery, and captured video and shows media piracy through almost every conceivable technology—computers, commercial television, camcorders, VCRs, audio tape, satellites, cellular phones, samplers. In the film, images-as-texts and technologies-as-apparatuses are annexed, destroying their boundaries and metamorphosing into a new cyborg of productive, interventionist communication. However, while *Sonic Outlaws* provides a tutorial in active spectatorship that seems an invocation of Dziga Vertov's kino-eye, it also reclaims the pleasure of production: it announces in an intertitle, "Copyright infringement is your best entertainment value."

▶

Technophobias and Technopublics

In February 1996, President Clinton signed into law the Public Telecommunications Act of 1996, the most major overhaul of telecommunications regulations since 1934. The *New York Times,* CNN, and all the networks analyzed the effectiveness of the V-chip—a salient provision in the bill almost obsessively highlighted by CBS, NBC, and CNN—to inhibit children from overdosing on unsupervised television violence. All the mainstream media focused attention on problematics of transgressive texts, passive audiences, and the susceptibility of underage youth to technological invasions into domesticated, private space. Clearly, new tactics for media democracies are called for in this chilling environment.

What was more frightening than television violence twisting the minds of minors, however, was the complete absence of debate about the telecommunications bill prior to its passage. An almost complete blackout by the corporate-owned mainstream news organizations that were bound to profit by the bill paralleled a congressional tactic of almost no debate on the bill, with deal making behind closed doors inaccessible to progressive lobbying groups.[71]

But more politically, the V-chip colloquy symbolized the social, political, and psychic instabilities that attend to the complete restructuring of the borders between public and private, nation and globe, that new technologies such as satellite, cable, and computer networks facilitate. The enormous amount of discussion surrounding the institution of the V-chip as the savior of the polluted airwaves in Clinton's 1996 State of the Union Address provided a convenient smoke screen for the provisions of the new telecommunications bills that paved the way for unprecedented, unregulated mergers between major media transnationals across different industries, closing down access to communication.

In her book *Communications Policy and the Public Interest,* Patricia Aufderheide refers to the bill as impoverishing public sites and noncommercial arenas. She points out that the bill ratifies transnational communications' vertical and horizontal integration in unprecedented ways, greasing the way for the formation of culture trusts that have the dangerous potential to annihilate public debate.[72] This battle cry for a newly invigorated critique of media concentration was echoed in a speech delivered at the Media and Democracy Conference by Tom Frank, which appeared as an article in *The Nation* titled "Hip Is Dead: The Howl of Unreflective Consumerism." Frank cautioned that the new culture trusts needed to be scrutinized and railed against with a newly rekindled muckraking fervor, exposing their demolition of democratic communications, their incorporation of a "hip" multiculturalism and culture of dissent gobbled up by consumerist advertising. He pointed out that most of the discussion about the new information age is optimistic and not critical, arguing that concentration of media power will "make each of us more autonomous." "Why haven't these gigantic developments aroused public anger?" Frank intoned. "What happened to that older model of dissent under which trusts were always suspect? And why is the model by which today we all understand liberation so powerless and backward, so susceptible to hijacking by the likes of Geffen and Eisner?"[73]

"Were the alternative media locked in their own insular world, in which only National Public Radio beams in news from the outside?" queried *New York Times* op-ed columnist Frank Rich. In a piece titled "Mixed Media Message," he tellingly quoted one participant at the progressive Media and Democracy Conference held in San Francisco in February 1996: "I feel like these are all the people I marched on the Pentagon with 20 years ago."[74]

The first ever Media and Democracy Conference—organized by the Institute for Alternative Journalism to rethink a progressive media strategy for the transnational–media-concentrated 1990s—featured a diverse array of media activists and writers, such as Lillian Jimenez, Barbara Ehrenreich, Salim Muwakkil, DeeDee Halleck, Jay Walljasper, Jonathan Tasini, and Urvashi Vaid, as well as media producers ranging from zines and Internet user groups to Globalvision and Paper Tiger.[75] "In my day's worth of panel-hopping," mused Rich, "I often felt I was trapped in the time warp of the old fratricidal left."[76]

Rich's piece emanates despair. Despite his good intentions, he failed to grasp the new mobilities offered by new media technologies and new pirate media practices. He bemoans outdated media practices that hermetically seal provocations to the new world order within the safe borders of the "left," paralyzed from puncturing the large transnational media webs encircling all public space and suffocating most public debate. Decrying how the ever-growing transnational behemoths block democratic communications, Rich describes Johns Hopkins University media studies professor Mark Crispin Miller's handout on the new culture trusts of the "four huge media conglomerates of Time-Warner, General Electric, Disney/Cap Cities, and Westinghouse."

However, although media concentration has without question progressed with almost unprecedented and unregulated frenzy since 1989, the border between transnationals and independent media is now much more porous, provisional, and mobile than in Frank's almost nostalgic conception of big bad media and good little media.

Media piracy has assumed a multitude of different performance styles. Two very different recent documentaries illustrate how this fluidity and malleability unsettle the very location of independent documentary media. These works necessitate analysis of the emerging spaces that can be created, occupied, warped, or imagined as different registers and acts of piracy: a censored segment of *TV Nation* from 1995 called "Savings and Loan Crooks" and a 1996 Paper Tiger Television video titled *Narrowcasting: Technology and the Rise of the Christian Right.*

Although different in style and in location, these two pieces disassemble the national imaginary and then trace how inside/outside segregations between the state and its opposition are much more transitory and mutable. These two pieces show how the inside of power is now outside and how the outside is inside: savings and loan executives bailed out by the government are sneered at as rich felons, while the religious right marshals new technologies such as cable, satellite, and the Internet to create a mass movement through narrowcasting.

Produced by Michael Moore, renowned for his anticorporate cinema verité film *Roger & Me, TV Nation* was first broadcast on NBC—owned by General Electric—in 1994. Canceled after six weeks during the summer, the maverick Fox network—owned by international media mogul Rupert Murdoch, owner of the News Corporation—picked it up for the 1995 season. *TV Nation* programs recycled the newsmagazine format reminiscent of *20/20* or *60 Minutes,* a low-cost, although neutralized, format for the networks that is extremely attractive to sponsors. Moore served as host, and often as aggressive interviewer. However, *TV Nation* openly called the bluff of the newsmagazines, which performed a masquerade of objectivity and fairness and avoided topics with any political and economic bite.[77]

TV Nation segments often were set up—an infraction against the tenets of nonmanipulation embedded in direct cinema—recalling Allen Funt more than Dan Rather. However, these fabricated scenarios did not trivialize individuals, but instead used the situations to open up institutional political analysis, exposing, for example, the racism of New York City taxi drivers or the exploitation of poor Mexican workers by American transnational *maquiladoras* as a result of NAFTA.

TV Nation also rejected the serious, reverential tone of network newsmagazines and reporters, substituting irreverence, irony, witticism, humor, and muckraking of politics and economics for stories about celebrities or victims. Episodes freely intermingled cinema verité with compilation techniques and a strategy of intervention invoking performance art or guerrilla theater. Editing was disjunctive, using the quick-cutting techniques of commercials to highlight analytic points. Borrowing from MTV, most of the segments used music for irony or for ideological effect, a strategy disdained by most network magazine producers as too editorializing.

"Savings and Loan Crooks," produced by veteran documentary filmmaker Pamela Yates (director of *Resurgence, When the Mountains Tremble,* and *Take Over*), was one of several *TV Nation* episodes that Fox refused to air. The nixed episodes were not permanently shelved, however, but were broadcast on the BBC and Channel Four in England, indicating the globalization of the market for independent media. "Savings and Loan Crooks" asks a simple question: Where are the crooks from the savings and loan scandal now? It blasts the posture of victimization assumed by the savings and loan executives. With visual evidence of their easy life of class privilege, the piece exposes the ramifications of the enormous government bailout of these bankers. Invoking populism, the piece rails against economic elites and refigures their lamentations of innocence as outrageous utterances.

"Savings and Loan Crooks" begins with a series of dissolves between medium close-ups of white male corporate executives in suits in front of a black background saying, "I am innocent," creating a surreal montage of corporate power effacing itself through pleas of victimization. This strategy is repeated two other times, evoking hall of fame or "most wanted" posters. In an archival news image, Ronald Reagan signs legislation to deregulate the banking industry and exclaims: "I think we hit the jackpot." The voice-over explains that bank officers broke the law by making improper loans, forcing the government to salvage the savings and loan industry at a cost of five hundred billion dollars.

The middle segment of the piece visually exposes how the U.S. government bailouts bolstered the lavish lifestyles of savings and loan officials, including Neil Bush, Thomas Spiegel, Craig Hall, "Bum" Bright, and Henry Hyde, by totaling their fines and government assistance over montage sequences of polo, tennis, limousines, elegant restaurants, and financial investments in other industries.

Hammering on the ludicrous claim of their personal pain, the final section of "Savings and Loan Crooks" is marked by dissolves of corporate executives proclaiming their distress and anger in front of black backgrounds. Using a scene from the Savings and Loan Support Group to undermine their individualistic remorse, the segment then cuts to a montage of upper-class leisure—polo, golf, limousines—with a voice-over that exclaims that it will cost Americans a total of one trillion dollars to remedy the savings and loan crisis. The capitalist hubris of these executives is divulged once more by a medium close-up interview with one executive who quietly reveals, "I'm a convicted felon, and I'm still doing business and my firm is doing well." The segment ends with a group portrait of about fifteen white, mostly male executives, with a voice-over asking, "Still, isn't it worth a trillion dollars to make a bunch of businessmen happy again? Because second chances are what America is all about."

"Savings and Loan Crooks" performs a series of inversions, hijackings, crossings, and warpings. It inverts the hidden network agenda of complicity with the ruling elites by exposing savings and loan executives as crooks who have used the government to finance their lifestyle. It hijacks the accessible, short, light, human interest story from corporate news agendas, refueling it with evidence, analysis, and argumentation of corruption. It crosses different strategies, combining experimental, highly stylized techniques of posed interviews with aggressive compilation editing recalling Vertov or Marker. And it warps the space for radical analysis by infiltrating national network and cable broadcasting with humor. Even when the segment was not aired, it was indomitable: it recirculated in the global television market.

Narrowcasting: Technology and the Rise of the Christian Right, produced by the cable-access, low-end media collective Paper Tiger Television, tracks another kind of inversion and warping from the other side of the political spectrum: it shows how the right has utilized new technologies and media alternatives to the networks to create space for a forceful conservative political agenda in the mass media and Congress. *Narrowcasting* argues that the Christian right has developed alternative media infrastructures for itself through an aggressive use of new technologies, such as satellite, cable, talk shows, the Internet, the World Wide Web, and home video. The Paper Tiger tape exposes the various media strategies of the Christian right: using new technologies, creating wedge issues, conducting stealth campaigns, disseminating free videos on antigay and antiabortion agendas, infiltrating school boards and curricula with untested scientific information.

"Savings and Loan Crooks" and *Narrowcasting* signify almost opposite maneuvers for institutional space, the location of independent producers, access to technology, and rhetorical address. Although both pieces were produced by independents, "Savings and Loan Crooks" is an example of independents who have effectively infiltrated corporatized media, whereas the Paper Tiger tape represents the creation of a new zone of production outside corporations entirely. The savings and loan piece employs extremely high-end production techniques of well-lit, stylized interviews; utilization of network television images of Reagan, Bush, and savings and loan scandal guys; and quick editing between segments. Conversely, the Paper Tiger piece uses camcorder interviews of various scholars and activists tracking the religious right, pirated satellite TV images from religious broadcasters, and a deductive structure heavily reliant on exposing the tactics of the religious right. Whereas "Savings and Loan Crooks" constantly uses an ironic voice-over that exposes the absurdity of these criminals' actually prospering from the government bailout, *Narrowcasting* deploys what Bill Nichols has termed a discourse of sobriety, mounting an explanatory argument on the tactics of the religious right.

However, the textual and rhetorical differences between "Savings and Loan Crooks" and *Narrowcasting* in the end do not sufficiently illuminate the new media politics they rouse. Rather, it is their strategic commonalities that represent significant and hopeful deviations from the forms of hermetically sealed, ghettoized independent media Frank Rich chastises. Both pieces morph the borders of and locations for independent media, moving around and within different economic and discursive terrains: networks, cable networks, political action groups, satellite, public access, home video, and global media outlets.

Each piece offers a critique of existing power relations through testimony and evidence and deploys disruptive visual techniques to produce fissures in the smooth presentation of the savings and loan crooks or the Christian right. Each piece pirates work from other sources to critique it as discursive construction and mythmaking, not as the more traditional form of compilation filmmaking that contains footage for its transparent evidentiary and explanatory qualities.

Both pieces operate within a different rubric of documentary than that of the classic television journalism documentary dedicated to exposing factual information, because in both, information itself is not only viewed with skepticism, but actually deconstructed as fantasy. Although both pieces borrow from postmodern documentary styles for their disjunctive editing and the combination of seemingly disparate visual elements, they implicitly refute a documentary practice that remains solely on the level of analysis of representation. Anchored to social and political agendas and struggles, to specific points of contestation, the pieces critique representation as social fantasies with evidence that redirects the viewer toward moral and social constituencies.

In both production and distribution, their strategy borrows more from computer hackers' infiltration and penetration of coded systems to expose system weaknesses than from either the classic documentary of sobriety or the more postmodern documentary of visual flourish and irony. Andrew Ross has persuasively argued for a wider conceptualization of the term *hacker* to dislodge social critics and radical practices from their folkloric invocations of dissent. He maintains:

> If there is a challenge here for cultural critics, then it might be presented as the obligation to make our knowledge about technoculture into something like a hacker's knowledge, capable of penetrating existing systems of rationality that might otherwise be seen as infallible; a hacker's knowledge, capable of reskilling, and therefore rewriting the cultural programs and reprogramming the social values that make room for new technologies; a hacker's knowledge, capable also of generating new popular romances around the alternative uses of human ingenuity.[78]

For documentary practice to survive as more than an antiquated relic of an idealized and pure radical practice that no longer exists in the new world order of transnational media, privatization, deregulation, and the closing down of political debate, it will be necessary, to extend Ross's argument to other forms of media, to reskill, rewrite, and reprogram it for penetration and popular desire. "Savings and Loan Crooks" and *Narrowcasting* demonstrate how to hack between the false divides between texts and structures, between production and distribution, between argument and deconstruction, between high- and low-end technologies, between radical interventions and popular desires.

▶
_____

Warping Space for the Translocal Imaginary

Pirates never return home, as the act of piracy itself disassociates from territories, nations, essentialized identities, master narratives, homogenized

Electronically layered image of shots from classical British and Hollywood films depicting mass-media representations of South Asians, from *It Is a Crime* (1996). Dir. Meena Nanji. Photograph courtesy of Video Data Bank.

places, a perpetual motion of moving booty across seas of images. To invoke the metaphor of the sea and boats, which are principal tropes in both postcolonial theory and piracy, the pirate moves between territories, between the land and the sea, between different images circulating in the transnational commodity flows, between the global and the local, always producing interstitial localities and provisional locations for democratic media.[79] This pirate world, then, is not a text but a series of relations that are in a constant shuttle between different modalities. As Arjun Appadurai argues, media and migration are central to the new global imaginaries, forming what he has termed "diasporic public spheres."[80]

Meena Nanji's *It Is a Crime* (1996) exemplifies how pirate work pilots between these multiple gaps. Nanji destabilizes images stolen from Hollywood films that exoticize and Orientalize India by digitizing them, fragmenting them into multiple boxes that are layered on top of other boxes of images that are rapidly edited to sitar music. *It Is a Crime* removes these images from their circulation as global imagery/imaginaries and locates them as a space of diasporas. Words from a Shani Mootoo poem are superimposed on these images restrung as pieces of the narrative othering process: "It is a crime that I should have to use your language to tell you how I feel that you have taken mine from me." *It Is a Crime* then creates a new diasporic space, between the global flows of Hollywood narratives populated with South Asians and new locations that are disjunctural and discursive, taking space as much as images, to quote Nanji's footage credits, "taken from a bunch of films made in Britain and Hollywood."

Piracy itself imprints a constant process of image production, of movement, of change, of creolization, rather than a fixed identity; it is not a text that is fixed, then, but is instead writing, always being written, and, in writing, making new spaces and locations. Discussing the radical potentialities of a postcolonial reading of *The Wizard of Oz*, for example, Salman Rushdie observes that "there is no longer any such place *as* home: except of course, for the home we make, or the homes that are made for us, in Oz: which is anywhere, and everywhere, except the place from which we began."[81]

Piracy, then, revises the whole concept of independent documentary: it is no longer a practice defined by constitutive positions vis-à-vis static structures and fixed locations, but dynamic, ever shifting, fluid, democratic strategies in perpetual motion that, like the nomad summoned by Gilles Deleuze and Félix Guattari, are not so simply stabilized texts, but a "space of contact."[82] For Deleuze and Guattari, space stages nomadism: "The nomad reterritorializes on deterritorialization itself."[83] They argue that nomadism dismantles the state, the nation, the law through heterogeneity: the media pirate, then, performs a similar dismantling, performing outside work inside. Like the nomad, the pirate takes the deterritorializations of the global circulation of images and the technologies of representations and reterritorializes them in new and different spaces, forming new locations that are simultaneously real and virtual, here and there, to be moved into and out of.

Ellen Spiro's *Roam Sweet Home* (1997) illustrates how nomadism is not only about taking images from the global flows but also, if not equally, about seizing spaces from transnationalized territories through mobile vectors. *Roam Sweet Home* follows an assortment of elderly nomads who travel the American West in recreational vehicles, fashioning their own utopian, mobile communities at various sites, among them a discarded bomb testing ground. One community runs an open food kitchen to feed people who can't cook for themselves. In another community, a group of elderly widows gather around a campfire to discuss self-protection on the road.

Spiro's cinema verité-inflected camcorder shooting style, however, displaces the camera as a site of authority and surveillance by repositioning it as a membrane through which interactions between the maker and the subjects achieve mobility and escape from the stasis associated with the

Ellen Spiro and her camcorder visit a trailer park to interview elderly nomads. Production still from *Roam Sweet Home* (1997). Dir. Ellen Spiro. Photograph courtesy of Video Data Bank.

elderly. The camera, then, does not simply interview these elderly nomads about their lifestyle, but manufactures a virtual space that is itself simultaneously specifying nomadic deterritorialization at the same time it practices an act of radical reterritorialization, a making of a new discursive and physical space for marginalized elderly people. Indeed, throughout the tape, the elderly travelers are shown doing various life-affirming folk art projects, such as songwriting, painting, decorating the insides of their trailers, painting rocks, walking across the country, affirming the creativity of life as they progress toward death. In fact, only dogs die in the tape, standing in for the inevitable decline of old age. These tasks of self-creation parallel Spiro's own videomaking, which is not a privileged activity at all, but a condensed metaphor for mobility and creating new spaces by pirating whatever is left—camcorders, Airstream trailers, old rocks, dogs, songs—and bestowing it with hope.

The local has emerged in discussions of transnationalization as a salient concept to anchor the deterritorialization of global image culture, a site from which to map new positions of resistance. It is described multifariously as an antidote, a residual formation, a nostalgia, a place of resistance, a place of material relations, a place of concrete struggles, a fantasy, a projection of stability.[84] However, several theorists suggest a different view of the local that counters the fixity of place with the movement of spaces and identification, and it is this view that offers promising ways for independent documentary to rethink its own practices for the new millennium.

Arif Dirlik has stated, "The local must be translocal." For him, the boundaries of the local are open, porous, constantly shifting and evolving within the deterritorialization of globalization. The local, for Dirlik, is "a site of invention," a space for imagining.[85] Along these same lines, Arjun Appadurai has advanced a notion of the local as always being in production and consequently relational, disjunctural, and contextual rather than simply spatial, creating a "multi-centric world."[86] Expanding on these ideas of the translocal as always defined by process, Caren Kaplan has emphasized that the local is always plural, populated by multiply placed and multiply linked subjectivities in a multiplicity of dialogues.[87]

However astute these various descriptions of the translocal are theoretically, and however useful they are for rethinking documentary as a relational process rather than as a fixed representation, these arguments frequently return to an invocation of concrete local organizing efforts around women's or environmental or race issues, which, in and of themselves, are to be saluted as political interventions. The matrix of "media" is still left within a corporatized, narrativized confine, the commercial current through which the global flow of images float, in effect codifying, by default, a binary opposition between bad media and good social practice. In the new world order, the metaphor of piracy can teach us that these kinds of distinctions ignore the democratic possibilities of all forms of new media—from camcorders to digitality to beyond—to join with resistant social practices to create translocal social spaces, which, in some ways, can exist only in these liminal zones between media spaces and practical politics.

For example, Austin Allen's *Claiming Open Spaces* (1996) investigates the end of public space for communities of color as a concerted effort by governments and corporations to privatize both activity and space. He begins with a battle between the African American community in Columbus, Ohio, and the local government, which was wooing an international flower show to a park heavily used by African Americans as public space. Allen links this fight to retain rights to public space for leisure and political activities to parks in Detroit, New Orleans, and Oakland that figured heavily in African American local history as gathering places for music, talking, and marching. *Claiming Open Spaces* writes the translocal as a montage of differently inflected African American histories, from slavery to civil rights, to the Black Panthers, to fights against transnational corporations that manufacture ersatz public space. The tape itself then emerges as translocal space, a space that reconnects local history to histories of resistance and reclamations of public space.[88]

The media campaigns of the National Labor Committee to expose the exploitation of workers by transnational clothing manufacturers in *maquiladora* sweatshops in Honduras and Haiti also exemplify this processual translocal by showing the connections between transnational textile manufacturing and international labor solidarities that are obscured by the products and publicity. These highly successful media campaigns, which achieved major concessions from the companies as well as propelled human rights campaigns internationally, attacked two high-profile transnational companies that target the youth market: the Gap and the Walt Disney Company.

Combining demonstrations at Gap and Disney stores with a sophisticated media outreach that organized diverse communities such as religious groups, schools, unions, and feminists across borders, the National Labor Committee produced two videos that were widely distributed within these community networks as extremely moving and effective organizing tools to mobilize support in the North for workers and children in the South. Shot with a camcorder, *Zoned for Slavery* (1995) reveals the oppressive working conditions of young teenage girls in Gap clothing plants in Central America. The tape refutes the idea that corporate space is private space by showing footage taken by a cameraperson who walked into the guarded plant with a camcorder to record the degrading working conditions despite being asked to turn off the camera and leave. *Mickey Mouse Goes to Haiti* (1996) chronicles the impoverishment of Haitian clothing workers who sew Walt Disney T-shirts, destroying the myth of the Disney Company as family-friendly. Both of these tapes function not as stand-alone artistic practices

"OUR ANIMALS WERE TREATED BETTER THAN MOST HUMANS...IN THE WORLD"

-Disney's 101 Dalmations press kit

UNBELIEVABLE!

"DURING FILMING, THE DOGS WHO STARRED IN DISNEY'S 101 DALMATIANS WERE VERY WELL TAKEN CARE OF. THEY STAYED IN SMALL DOG MOTELS, HAD ROUND-THE-CLOCK CARE, *AND* HAD PERSONAL TRAINERS."

-McDonald's 101 Dalmatian toy package

"GREAT EXPLOITATIONS!

IN HAITI, WOMEN SEWING DISNEY'S 101 DALMATIANS CHILDREN'S CLOTHING ARE PAID STARVATION WAGES OF SIX CENTS FOR EVERY $19.99 GARMENT THEY SEW."

-National Labor Committee

"PHENOMENAL MISERY!

FOR THE LAST YEAR, DISNEY'S CHILDREN'S CLOTHING HAS BEEN PRODUCED IN BURMA, IN A FACTORY LARGELY OWNED BY THE RUTHLESS MILITARY DICTATORS. AVERAGE WAGES IN BURMA ARE SIX CENTS AN HOUR, THE AVERAGE WORK WEEK IS 60 HOURS!"

-National Labor Committee

FOR MORE INFORMATION CONTACT: NATIONAL LABOR COMMITTEE, 275 SEVENTH AVE. NY, NY 10001 212/242-3002

Political organizing flyer from the National Labor Committee's Disney campaign, "101 Sweatshops." Reproduced courtesy of the National Labor Committee.

but as simply one strand of much larger media campaigns that included commercial television, *New York Times* op-ed pieces, flyers, demonstrations, public speeches, and radio call-in shows. The aim of this work was to reconnect the communities of the North with communities of the South, demonstrating that the translocal means rejecting false borders.[89] In these tapes, the low-end camera operates like a ship, moving in and out of ports to bring images home to be used, a piracy of that which transnationals attempt to conceal. Although shot in a conventional realist mode, the social uses of these documentaries typify Trinh T. Minh-ha's distinction between a narrative, which sustains domination through closure, and a story, which overflows patriarchal time and truth: "A story told is a story bound to circulate."[90]

Independent documentaries endure as an endangered species as arts defunding, public television retrenchments, attacks against cultural difference, and conservative assaults against interventionist public discourses chisel away public space. Yet, simultaneously and congruently, new media technologies continually recombined with a radical rethinking of political organizing across communities may provide the possibility of splicing documentaries to democracies once again. New media ecologies for a survival of the species in the new world orders that are yet to be known may open up closed-down public space.

As radical intervention straddling the end of the current millennium and the dawn of the new one, media piracy suggests that independent documentary itself needs to be pluralized into multiple strategies, decentered sites, hybridized technologies, and interconnected communities, where media practice itself is reconditioned for the future. And finally, documentary media piracy, as a performative and pedagogical act, teaches us that readers are authors and spectators are artists. It reminds us that in a more democratically imagined new world order, everyone is a potential producer: of critique, of documentaries, of democracies, of healing, of hope.

Notes

Introduction

Some of the ideas developed in this introduction were first expressed in somewhat different form in two short journalistic essays published for media arts organizations. I thank Helen De Michel, director of the National Media Arts Coalition, for pushing me to develop some of these overview arguments for her newsletter, and John Columbus, director of the Black Maria Film and Video Festival, for asking me to write a catalog essay for the 1998 program assessing the state of the arts. See Patricia R. Zimmermann, "The New World Image Orders," 17th Annual Black Maria Film and Video Festival *1998 Exhibition Catalog*, 2–11; and Patricia R. Zimmermann, "States of Emergency," *Main* (Media Arts Information Network), fall 1997, 1, 3.

1. For lucid discussions of the unprecedented growth of media transnationals since 1989, see Erik Barnouw et al., *Conglomerates and the Media* (New York: New Press, 1997); Robert W. McChesney, *Corporate Media and the Threat to Democracy* (New York: Seven Stories, 1997); Robert W. McChesney, Ellen Meiksins Wood, and John Bellamy Foster, *Capitalism and the Information Age: The Political Economy of the Global Communication Revolution* (New York: Monthly Review Press, 1998); John Hess and Patricia R. Zimmermann, "Transnational Documentaries: A Manifesto," *Afterimage* (January/February 1997): 10–14.
2. For an analysis of transnationalization of national economies and its relationship to digitality, see Saskia Sassen, *Globalization and Its Discontents* (New York: New Press, 1998).
3. Arjun Appadurai, *Modernity at Large: Cultural Dimensions of Globalization* (Minneapolis: University of Minnesota Press, 1996), 27–47
4. Leslie Sklair, "Social Movements and Global Capitalism," in *The Cultures of Globalization*, ed. Fredric Jameson and Masao Miyoshi (Durham, N.C.: Duke University Press, 1998), 291–331.
5. For a penetrating look at what film historians term "the post-classical Hollywood era," see Richard Maltby, " 'Nobody Knows Everything': Post-classical Historiographies and Consolidated Entertainment," and Tino Balio, " 'A Major Presence in All of the World's Important Markets': The Globalization of Hollywood in the 1990s," both in *Contemporary Hollywood Cinema*, ed. Stephen Neale and Murray Smith (New York: Routledge, 1998).
6. For a detailed review of the various controversies over international politics, sexuality, race, and gender engulfing independent documentary during this period, see B. J. Bullert, *Public Television: Politics and the Battle over Documentary Film* (New Brunswick, N.J.: Rutgers University Press, 1997).
7. Toni Morrison, "The Site of Memory," in *Out There: Marginalization and Contemporary Cultures*, ed. Russell Ferguson, Martha Gever, Trinh T. Minh-ha, and Cornel West (Cambridge: MIT Press, 1990), 299–305.
8. For an insider's view of *Titanic* and the economics of its excessive use of digital effects within the nexus of new media development and the Hollywood studio system, see the special dossier titled "Digital Hollywood," *Red Herring*, January 1998, 59–96.
9. For an insider's view of the development of commercial independent cinema in the 1980s and 1990s, see John Pierson, *Mike, Spike, Slackers and Dykes: A Guided Tour across a Decade of Independent American Cinema* (London: Faber, 1996).
10. For a look into the relationship between black independent cinema and the Hollywood studio

system, see Jesse Algeron Rhines, *Black Film/White Money* (New Brunswick, N.J.: Rutgers University Press, 1996).

11. For a historical analysis of the function of B pictures within the classical Hollywood studio system, see Thomas G. Schatz, *The Genius of the System: Hollywood Filmmaking in the Studio Era* (New York: Henry Holt, 1988).

12. See Justin Wyatt, "The Formation of the 'Major Independent': Miramax, New Line and the New Hollywood," in *Contemporary Hollywood Cinema*, ed. Stephen Neale and Murray Smith (New York: Routledge, 1998), 74–90.

13. See Monica Roman, "Filmmakers Get into Designers' Pants," *Variety*, September 7–13, 1998, 1, 86. This article exposes how fashion designers and clothing manufacturers such as Ralph Lauren, Tommy Hilfiger, Calvin Klein, and Levi Strauss are courting independent filmmakers for product tie-ins and exhibition underwriting in order to target the under-thirty market for T-shirts and jeans.

14. Thomas Waugh has used the term *committed documentary* to describe the history of politically engaged work as a major legacy of the documentary tradition. See Thomas Waugh, ed., *"Show Us Life": Toward a History and Aesthetics of the Committed Documentary* (Metuchen, N.J.: Scarecrow, 1984).

15. See DeeDee Halleck, "Guerrillas in Our Midst," *Afterimage* (September/October 1998), 16–17. Halleck points out how the surge of academic work in cultural studies has de facto supported and prioritized commercial media practices rather than analyzed independent media, thereby separating theoretical work from practice.

16. For a discussion of commercial feature-length documentary that markets marginality, see Jillian Sandell, "Out of the Ghetto and into the Marketplace: *Hoop Dreams* and the Commodification of Marginality," *Socialist Review* 25, no. 2 (1995), 57–82.

17. For example, Janice R. Welsch has argued that feminist documentary filmmaking has dispensed with the idea of a monologic style of documentary and opted instead for a more radical heteroglossic style that is multivocal. See her "Bakhtin, Language, and Women's Documentary Filmmaking," in *Multiple Voices in Feminist Film Criticism*, ed. Diane Carson, Linda Ditmar, and Janice R. Welsch (Minneapolis: University of Minnesota Press, 1994), 162–75.

18. See Patricia R. Zimmermann, "Turn Back the Fight," *Socialist Review* 25, no. 2 (1995): 5–7.

19. Bill Nichols, *Representing Reality: Issues and Concepts in Documentary* (Bloomington: Indiana University Press, 1991), 28–30.

20. See Wahneema Lubiano, "Shuckin' Off the African-American Native Other: What's 'Po-Mo' Got to Do with It?" in *Dangerous Liaisons: Gender, Nation, and Postcolonial Perspectives*, ed. Anne McClintock, Aamir Mufti, and Ella Shohat (Minneapolis: University of Minnesota Press, 1997), 204–29. In discussing the need for African American writing to rethink the consequence of linear narrative as a hegemonizing force, Lubiano contends, "Neither this narrative nor this narrator is part of a pattern for unproblematic and centered control, for a unified subject. The story is, however, a sure ground for exploration, for problematizing, and for decentering" (222).

21. For an explanation of how hypertextual modes reorient linearity and deductive logical reasoning into a path of navigation and exploration of linkages, see George P. Landow, *Hypertext 2.0: The Convergence of Contemporary Critical Theory and Technology* (Baltimore: Johns Hopkins University Press, 1997).

1. The War on Documentary

1. See People for the American Way, *Attacks on Public Broadcasting: Who's Who on the Right* (Washington, D.C.: People for the American Way, 1992), 11–19.

2. For discussions of the demise of critical investigative news and documentary even within transnational media corporations, see James Fallows, *Breaking the News: How the Media Undermine American Democracy* (New York: Random House, 1996); Dennis W. Mazzocco, *Networks of Power: Corporate TV's Threat to Democracy* (Boston: South End, 1994); Mark Crispin Miller, "Free the Media," *The Nation*, June 3, 1996, 9–15.

3. Masao Miyoshi, "A Borderless World? From Colonialism to Transnationalism and the Decline of the Nation-State," *Critical Inquiry* 19, no. 4 (1993): 736.

4. Miller, "Free the Media," 9.

5. Quoted in People for the American Way, *Attacks on Public Broadcasting*, 18.

6. Cornel West, "A New Cultural Politics of Difference," in *Out There: Marginalization and Contemporary Cultures*, ed. Russell Ferguson, Martha Gever, Trinh T. Minh-ha, and Cornel West (Cambridge: MIT Press, 1990), 19–36.

7. See David Horowitz and Laurence Jarvik, eds., *Public Broadcasting and the Public Trust* (Los Angeles: Second Thoughts, 1995).

8. See ibid.

9. See Tom White, "Heston and the NEA: Long Allies," *Los Angeles Times*, January 28, 1995, F1;

Jacqueline Trescott, "Private Sector's Shortfall Specter: If Endowments Vanish, Donors Say They Can't Fill the Gap," *Washington Post*, February 26, 1995, G2; Sam Walker, "Proposals to Revamp Agency Include 'Privatizing' It: NEA Advocates and Opponents Say Some Change is Inevitable," *Christian Science Monitor,* February 23, 1995, 10; Dan Hulbert, "Is It Lights Out for the NEA?" *Atlanta Journal*, January 1, 1995, K1; Thomas Goetz, "Public Broadcasting Death Watch: Big Bird vs. Tony the Tiger," *Village Voice*, July 4, 1995, 45; Jerry Gray, "House Accord Would Kill Arts Endowment by 1997, " *New York Times,* July 14, 1995, 1, 17.

10. Laurence Jarvik, "The Myth of Independent Film," in Horowitz and Jarvik, *Public Broadcasting*, 119.

11. David Horowitz, "The Problem with Public TV," in Horowitz and Jarvik, *Public Broadcasting*, 12.

12. Ibid., 20.

13. David Horowitz, "Panther Outrage," in Horowitz and Jarvik, *Public Broadcasting*, 60.

14. Jarvik, "The Myth of Independent Film," 106.

15. Quoted in Peter M. Nichols, "Smile When You Say Documentary," *New York Times,* June 2, 1996, H11.

16. C. Carr, "Documentary," *Village Voice*, May 23, 1995, 13.

17. Homi K. Bhabha, "DissemiNation: Time, Narrative, and the Margins of the Modern Nation," in *Nation and Narration*, ed. Homi K. Bhabha (New York: Routledge, 1990), 184–322.

18. See Bruno Bosteels, Loris Mirella, and Peter A. Schilling, "The Politics of Totality in Magic Realism," in *Challenging Boundaries*, ed. Michael J. Shapiro and Hayward R. Alker (Minneapolis: University of Minnesota Press, 1996), 111–33; Fredric Jameson, *The Geopolitical Aesthetic: Cinema and Space in the World System* (Bloomington: Indiana University Press, 1992); Jim Pines and Paul Willemen, *Questions of Third Cinema* (London: British Film Institute, 1989).

19. Homi K. Bhabha, "Introduction," in *The Location of Culture* (London: Routledge, 1994), 7.

20. Zillah R. Eisenstein, *Hatreds: Racialized and Sexualized Conflicts in the 21st Century* (New York: Routledge, 1996).

21. Trinh T. Minh-ha, *Woman, Native, Other: Writing Postcoloniality and Feminism* (Bloomington: Indiana University Press, 1989), 98.

22. For discussions of the relationship between national formation and fiction, see Homi K. Bhabha, ed., *Nation and Narration* (New York: Routledge, 1990); Frederick Buell, *National Culture and the New Global System* (Baltimore: Johns Hopkins University Press, 1994); Andrew Parker, Mary Russo, Doris Sommer, and Patricia Yaeger, eds., *Nationalisms and Sexualities* (New York: Routledge, 1992).

23. Bhabha, "DissemiNation," 300.

24. See Zillah R. Eisenstein, *The Color of Gender: Reimaging Democracy* (Berkeley: University of California Press, 1994), 1–69. For discussions of the political changes in Eastern Europe and the Soviet Union, see William E. Griffith, *Central and Eastern Europe: The Opening Curtain?* (Boulder, Colo.: Westview, 1989); Tariq Ali, *Revolution from Above: Where Is the Soviet Union Going?* (London: Hutchinson, 1988).

25. Cited in Maureen Dowd, 'Jesse Helms Takes No-Lose Position on Art," *New York Times*, July 28, 1991, 1. For examples of how the press covered the arts funding debates, see, for example, Barbara Gamarekian, "Corcoran Board to Meet on Dismissing Director," *New York Times*, September 25, 1989, C17; Gary Indiana, "Democracy, Inc.," *Artforum*, September 1989, 11–12; Brian Wallis, "Can Crippled Corcoran Survive?" *Art in America*, November 1989, 41; Brian Wallis, "Fallout from Helms Amendment," *Art in America*, October 1989, 29; William H. Honan, "Arts Endowment Withdraws Grant for AIDS show," *New York Times,* November 9, 1989, 1, C28; Barbara Gamarekian, "Curator for Mapplethorpe Show Resigns Corcoran Posts," *New York Times*, September 14, 1989, B3.

26. Quoted in Richard Goldstein, "Crackdown on Culture: Art and Entertainment in the Age of Helms," *Village Voice*, October 10, 1989, 29.

27. Dowd, 'Jesse Helms," 1. See also Grace Glueck, "Border Skirmish: Art and Politics," *New York Times*, November 19, 1989, sec. 2, pp. 1, 25.

28. For a fuller discussion of the intricate relationship between documentary and glasnost in the Soviet Union in the late 1980s and early 1990s, see Patricia R. Zimmermann and Michael Selig, eds., "International Issues" (special issue), *Journal of Film and Video* 44, nos. 1–2 (1992). For a discussion of Gorbachev's opening up of historical debate and national memory under glasnost, see R. W. Davies, *Soviet History in the Gorbachev Revolution* (Bloomington: Indiana University Press, 1989).

29. Johnnie L. Roberts, 'The Men behind the Megadeals," *Newsweek*, August 14, 1995, 22–27. For a fuller discussion of the reorganization of the Hollywood film industry in the past decade, see Janet Wasko, *Hollywood in the Information Age* (Austin: University of Texas Press, 1994), 41–70.

30. See Erik Barnouw et al., *Conglomerates and the Media* (New York: New Press, 1997), for a discussion of this cross-merger activity across a range of media industries such as film, radio, television, cable, and print news.

31. See Salman Rushdie, *The Satanic Verses* (Dover, Del.: Consortium, 1992); Aamir Mufti, "Reading the Rushdie Affair: 'Islam,' Cultural Politics, Form," in *The Administration of Aesthetics: Censorship, Political Criticism, and the Public Sphere*, ed. Richard Burt (Minneapolis: University of Minnesota Press, 1994), 307–39. For a collection of responses to the Rushdie affair, including Rushdie's own written reaction, see Lisa Appignanesi and Sara Maitland, *The Rushdie File* (Syracuse, N.Y.: Syracuse University Press, 1990).

32. John Updike, "Modern Art: Always Offensive to Orthodoxy," *Wall Street Journal*, August 10, 1989, 16.

33. Slavoj Zizek, *The Sublime Object of Ideology* (London: Verso, 1989), 73.

34. Salman Rushdie, "In Good Faith," in *Imaginary Homelands 1981–1991* (London: Penguin, 1992), 394.

35. Anouar Abdallah, "Why Is It Necessary to Defend Salman Rushdie? " in *For Rushdie: Essays by Arab and Muslim Writers in Defense of Free Speech*, ed. Anouar Abdallah (New York: George Braziller, 1994), 13.

36. Etel Adnan, "On the Subject of Rushdie," in *For Rushdie: Essays by Arab and Muslim Writers in Defense of Free Speech*, ed. Anouar Abdallah (New York: George Braziller, 1994), 16.

37. For one of the most influential discussions of the multiple layers of global flows, see Arjun Appadurai, "Disjuncture and Difference in the Global Cultural Economy," in *The Phantom Public Sphere*, ed. Bruce Robbins (Minneapolis: University of Minnesota Press, 1993), 269–96.

38. U.S. Congress, Public Telecommunications Act, Public Law 100–626, November 7, 1988, 629–30.

39. U.S. Congress, International Trade Act, Public Law 100–418, August 23, 1988, 331–32.

40. The idea of the palimpsest as a figuration of the relationship between national identity and layers of representation is narrativized in Salman Rushdie, *The Moor's Last Sigh* (New York: Pantheon, 1996).

41. See Patricia R. Zimmermann, "Midwives, Hostesses and Feminist Film," in "The Flaherty: Four Decades in the Cause of Independent Cinema" (special issue), ed. Erik Barnouw and Patricia R. Zimmerman, *Wide Angle* 17, nos. 1–4 (1995): 197–216. See also Peter Steven, ed., *Jump Cut: Hollywood, Politics, and Counter Cinema* (New York: Praeger, 1985).

42. For excellent histories of the formation of the Association of Independent Video and Filmmakers and the struggle for independent film in the 1970s and 1980s, see Lawrence Sapadin, "Adventures in Advocacy," *Independent*, June 1994, 30–34; B. Ruby Rich, "Field of Dreams," *Independent*, June 1994, 35–38; Larry Loewinger, "The Fab Formation (of a Media-Arts Organization)," *Independent*, June 1994, 12–18.

43. Rich, "Field of Dreams," 36.

44. Testimony of David Brugger of the National Association of Public Television Stations, U.S. Congress, hearings on public television, March 15, 1988, 437.

45. James Day, *The Vanishing Nation: The Inside Story of Public Television* (Berkeley: University of California Press, 1995), 273–330.

46. Testimony of Bruce Christensen, president of the Public Broadcasting System, U.S. Congress, hearings on public television, March 10, 1988, 468.

47. Testimony of Lawrence Sapadin, U.S. Congress, hearings on public broadcasting, March 15, 1988, 189.

48. For a discussion of the effects of these transnationalized media giants on world politics before the 1995 mergers (although unfortunately mired in an old-fashioned opposition between corporate domination and nationalist civil wars), see Benjamin R. Barber, *Jihad vs. McWorld: How the Planet Is Both Falling Apart and Coming Together and What This Means for Democracy* (New York: Random House, 1995). For a discussion of the consequences of the 1995 transnational media merger activities on democratic agendas, see Mark Crispin Miller, "Demonopolize Them," in *Media and Democracy*, ed. Don Hazen and Larry Smith (San Francisco: Institute for Alternative Journalism, 1996), 15–20. For a chart tracking the extent of "synergy" across media industries in the transnational mergers, see "Lest You Forget: These Three Companies Own the World," in *Media and Democracy*, 94–95.

49. For discussions of this opening up of dominant media discourse as a staging area for difference and identity politics, see John Fiske, *Media Matters: Everyday Culture and Political Change* (Minneapolis: University of Minnesota Press, 1994); Jane Shattuc, *The Talking Cure: Television Talk Shows and Women* (New York: Routledge, 1996); "On Thinking the Public Sphere" (special issue), *Public Culture* 7, no. 1 (1994); Lawrence Grossberg, *We Gotta Get Out of This Place: Popular Conservatism and Postmodern Culture* (New York: Routledge, 1992); Toni Morrison, ed., *Race-ing Justice, En-gendering Power: Essays on Anita Hill, Clarence Thomas, and the Construction of Social Reality* (New York: Pantheon, 1992).

50. See Penn Kimball, *Downsizing the News: Network Cutbacks in the Nation's Capital* (Baltimore: Johns Hopkins University Press, 1994), 23–34, 93–152.

51. For a similar line of argument, see Andrew Ross, "The Fine Art of Regulation," in *The Phantom Public Sphere*, ed. Bruce Robbins (Minneapolis: University of Minnesota Press, 1993), 257–68.

52. For discussions of the move toward economic and cultural privatization in the post–Cold War era, see Herbert I. Schiller, *Culture Inc.: The Corporate Takeover of Public Expression* (Oxford: Oxford University Press, 1989); Edward S. Herman, *Triumph of the Market: Essays on Economics, Politics, and the Media* (Boston: South End, 1995); Herbert I. Schiller, *Information Inequality: The Deepening Social Crisis in America* (New York: Routledge, 1996).

53. For a cogent discussion of the emergence of privacy as an issue in the politics of post-1989, see Eisenstein, *The Color of Gender*.

54. One of the most thoroughly documented analyses of the transnationalization of telecommunications across borders, with excellent case studies of the global media giants Sony and Bertelsmann, can be found in Richard J. Barnet and John Cavanaugh, *Global Dreams: Imperial Corporations and the New World Order* (New York: Simon & Schuster, 1994).

55. For examples of analyses of the right's attack against sexually explicit art with homoerotic content that evidences this depoliticization of larger structural and ideological interventions, see Richard Bolton, ed., *Culture Wars: Documents from the Recent Controversies in the Arts* (New York: New Press, 1992); Alice Goldfarb Marquis, *Art Lessons: Learning from the Rise and Fall of Public Arts Funding* (New York: Basic Books, 1995). For an excellent analysis of the narrowing of public space, see Schiller, *Culture Inc.*

56. See Jean Beaudrillard, *Simulations*, trans. Paul Foss, Paul Patton, and Philip Beitchman (New York: Semiotext[e], 1983).

57. John Guillory, *Cultural Capital: The Problem of Literary Canon Formation* (Chicago: University of Chicago Press, 1993), 18.

58. Quoted in Richard Bolton, "Introduction," in Bolton, *Culture Wars*, 9.

59. For discussion of the controversy, see Hal Hinson, "Censuring the Censors," *Washington Post*, January 29, 1993, C7; Joe Brown, "Censorship Uncensored," *Washington Post*, January 29, 1993, *Weekend Magazine*, 39; Vincent Canby, "About Arts, Reporters and Censors," *New York Times*, November 13, 1992, C11; William Stevenson, "Damned in the USA," *Variety*, September 23, 1991, 78–79; Gara LaMarche, "Festival Furore," *Index on Censorship* 21, no. 7 (1992): 16; James R. Petersen, "Damned in the U.S.A.," *Playboy*, May 1992, 44–45; William Stevenson, "Wildmon Hearing Set for May 1 in Gotham," *Variety*, April 20, 1992, 3, 8; Amy Taubin, "Damned in the USA," *Village Voice*, November 17, 1992, 102.

60. People for the American Way, "People for Joins Anti-censorship Lawsuit against Don Wildmon" (press release), April 9, 1992, 1–2.

61. See Edward Arian, *The Unfulfilled Promise: Public Subsidy of the Arts in America* (Philadelphia: Temple University Press, 1989), 69–102.

62. Paul J. DiMaggio, "Decentralization of Arts Funding from the Federal Government to the States," in *Public Money and the Muse: Essays on Government Funding for the Arts*, ed. Stephen Benedict (New York: W. W. Norton, 1991), 247.

63. See New York State Council on the Arts, *Set in Motion* (catalog) (Albany: New York State Council on the Arts, 1994).

64. See Karen Rosenberg, "To Halve and Halve Not: Massachusetts Cuts Arts Funding," *Independent*, May 1989, 2–3; Lucinda Furlong, "In Dire Straits: Downsized by Half, the New York State Council on the Arts Restructures," *Independent*, April 1993, 20–23; Jon Burris, "No Silver Lining: States Announce Declining Arts Budgets," *Independent*, November 1991, 12–13; Wendy Greene, "ETC Extinguishes AIR," *Independent*, January/February 1993, 6–7; Barbara Osborn, "Sacramento Sacrilege: California Arts Council Struggles to Survive," *Independent*, May 1993, 5; Michelle Yasmine Valladares, "Native American Producers Form Alliance," *Independent*, May 1993, 5–7; Barbara Bliss Osborn, "Out of Focus: WNET Gives *Independent Focus* the Heave Ho," *Independent*, October 1993, 7–8; Scott Briggs, "The Big Chill: Film in the Cities' Shutdown Bleakens Outlook for Media Arts Centers," *Independent*, November 1993, 5–7.

65. National Endowment for the Arts, *America in the Making: A Prospectus for the Arts* (Washington, D.C.: National Endowment for the Arts, 1995), 12.

66. George Yúdice, "For a Practical Aesthetics," *Social Text* 25/26 (1990): 142.

67. People for the American Way, *Artistic Freedom under Attack*, vol. 2 (Washington, D.C.: People for the American Way, 1994), 10.

68. People for the American Way, *Artistic Freedom under Attack*, vols. 1–4 (Washington, D.C.: People for the American Way, 1992–95).

69. People for the American Way, *Artistic Freedom under Attack*, vol. 1, pp. 24, 60, 61, 84–85.

70. People for the American Way, *Artistic Freedom under Attack*, vol. 2, pp. 30–31, 73, 132, 155.

71. DiMaggio, "Decentralization of Arts Funding," 216–52.

72. Glenn Pierce, "NEA under Seige," *Museum and Arts*, November/December 1989, 56, 139.

73. DiMaggio, "Decentralization of Arts Funding," 222.

74. Nina J. Easton, "PBS: Behind the Sound and the Fury," *Los Angeles Times*, January 31, 1995, 1.

75. Marquis, *Art Lessons*, 52–88.

76. Ibid., 60–63.

77. William Stott, *Documentary Expression in 1930s America* (New York: Oxford University Press, 1973).

78. For feminist discussions of these assaults against the welfare state, see Eisenstein, *The Color of Gender*; Cynthia Enloe, *The Morning After: Sexual Politics and the End of the Cold War* (Berkeley: University of California Press, 1993); Linda Gordon, ed., *Women, the State and Welfare* (Madison: University of Wisconsin Press, 1990).

79. Slavoj Zizek, "Caught in Another's Dream in Bosnia," in *Why Bosnia? Writings on the Balkan War*, ed. Rabia Ali and Lawrence Lifschultz (Stony Creek, Conn.: Pamphleteer's Press, 1993), 235.

80. Sam Walker, "After Spirited Debate, Senate Vote Jolts NEA," *Christian Science Monitor*, August 2, 1994, 14.

81. See Arian, *The Unfulfilled Promise*, 31–67.

82. See Stephen Benedict, ed., *Public Money and the Muse: Essays on Government Funding for the Arts* (New York: W. W. Norton, 1991); Arian, *The Unfulfilled Promise*.

83. Martha Wallner, advocacy coordinator, Association of Independent Film and Video Makers, telephone interview with the author, August 2, 1995.

84. Pamela Yates, Skylight Pictures, telephone interview with the author, June 14, 1996.

85. National Endowment for the Arts, *National Endowment for the Arts Annual Report 1993* (Washington, D.C.: National Endowment for the Arts, 1993), 98–99

86. Ibid., 100–103.

87. For discussions of the profusion of camcorders in the 1990s, see Brent Butterworth, "Art of the Win," *Video*, April 1992, 29, 78, 80; Brent Butterworth, "Home Video Contest Winners," *Video*, November 1992, 56–58; Gordon McComb, "50 Ways to Use Your Camcorder," *Video*, November 1988, 73–75; Ellen Spiro, "What to Wear on Your Video Activist Outing (Because the Whole World Is Watching): A Camcordist's Manifesto," *Independent*, May 1991, 22–24. For a discussion of how the various endowments increased funding to underserved communities in the 1980s, see Robert Garfias, "Cultural Diversity and the Arts in America," and Gerald D. Yoshitomi, "Cultural Democracy," both in Benedict, *Public Funding and the Muse*.

88. See Catherine Saalfield, "Tongue Tied: Homophobia Hamstrings PBS," *Independent*, October 1991, 4–5; Stuart Klawans, "Damned Ban," *The Nation* December 7, 1992, 455; Erwin Knoll, "Conflict of Interest," *Progressive*, March 1993, 4; Patricia Thomson, "Promises, Promises: Programs on the Palestinian Intifada Accused of Bias," *Independent*, June 1989, 4–6; Rob Edelman, "An Epic of an Epoch," *Independent*, January/February 1991, 23–25.

89. Hilton Kramer, "Studying the Arts and Humanities," in *Against the Grain: The New Criterion on Art and Intellect at the End of the Twentieth Century*, ed. Hilton Kramer and Roger Kimball (Chicago: Ivan R. Dee, 1995), 78.

90. Michael Berube, *Public Access: Literary Theory and American Cultural Politics* (London: Verso, 1994). For more specific discussion of the debate surrounding political correctness, see Patricia Aufderheide, ed., *Beyond P.C.: Toward a Politics of Understanding* (St. Paul, Minn.: Graywolf, 1992).

91. Gene Edward Veith, "Art and the Free Market," in *The National Endowments: A Critical Symposium*, ed. Laurence Jarvik, Herbert I. London, and James F. Cooper (Los Angeles: Second Thoughts, 1995), 92.

92. Quoted in Christine Dolen, "The Clash over Federal Arts Funding: Putting a Price on Culture," *Miami Herald*, March 16, 1995, 10.

93. Quoted in Rod Dreher, "Many Faces of Liberalism Survive Elections," *Washington Post*, November 13, 1994, 1.

94. Quoted in Thomas B. Edsall, "Defunding Public Broadcasting: Conservative Goal Gains Audience," *Washington Post*, April 15, 1995, 4.

95. Hilton Kramer, editorial, *All Things Considered*, National Public Radio, March 13, 1995.

96. Robert H. Knight, senior fellow, "The National Endowment for the Arts: Misusing Taxpayers Money" (Heritage Foundation "Backgrounder" pamphlet), January 18, 1991, 7.

97. For example, see Anne-Imelda Radice, "What Can Be Done"; Gordon Wysong, "The NEA and Public Purpose"; and Stanley Crouch, "The Inevitability of Corruption," all in *The National Endowments: A Critical Symposium*, ed. Laurence Jarvik, Herbert I. London, and James F. Cooper (Los Angeles: Second Thoughts, 1995).

98. Peter Shaw, "The Way the NEH Works," in *The National Endowments: A Critical Symposium*, ed. Laurence Jarvik, Herbert I. London, and James F. Cooper (Los Angeles: Second Thoughts, 1995), 9.

99. See, for example, Heather MacDonald, "Certain Paradoxes," and David Horowitz, "Funding the Left," both in *The National Endowments: A Critical Symposium*, ed. Laurence Jarvik, Herbert I. London, and James F. Cooper (Los Angeles: Second Thoughts, 1995). See also Hilton Kramer, "Studying the Arts and Humanities"; Roger Kimball, "The Perversions of Michel Foucault";

Maurice Cowling, "Raymond Williams in Retrospect"; and Richard Vine, "The 'Ecstasy' of Jean Baudrillard," all in *Against the Grain: The New Criterion on Art and Intellect at the End of the Twentieth Century,* ed. Hilton Kramer and Roger Kimball (Chicago: Ivan R. Dee, 1995).

100. Knight, "The National Endowment for the Arts," 1, 2.

101. Ibid., 5–8, 18.

102. Frederick Turner, "An Embattled Establishment," in *The National Endowments: A Critical Symposium,* ed. Laurence Jarvik, Herbert I. London, and James F. Cooper (Los Angeles: Second Thoughts, 1995), 76.

103. Ibid., 79–80.

104. Arlene Raven, "Dare to Deviate," *Village Voice,* November 21, 1989, 109.

105. For discussions of the operations of transnational media systems across borders, see, for example, David Morley and Kevin Robbins, *Spaces of Identity: Global Media, Electronic Landscapes, and Cultural Boundaries* (New York: Routledge, 1995); *The Case against "Free Trade": GATT, NAFTA, and the Globalization of Corporate Power* (San Francisco: Earth Island, 1993); Malcolm Waters, *Globalization* (New York: Routledge, 1995), 124–57; Barber, *Jihad vs. McWorld,* 1–151; and Robert B. Reich, *The Work of Nations* (New York: Vintage, 1992).

106. Quoted in Nina J. Easton and Judith Michaelson, "PBS: Behind the Sound and Fury," *Los Angeles Times,* January 31, 1995, 1.

107. Both quoted in David Dillon, "Voices from the Arts World," *Dallas Morning News,* January 29, 1995, 1C.

108. C. Carr, "Hanging by a Thread," *Village Voice,* January 25, 1995, 25.

109. Ibid., 26.

110. People for the American Way, "Purchase of PBS by Private Companies Would Risk the Cannibalization of Public TV" (press release), January 23, 1995, 1.

111. Corporation for Public Broadcasting, "Statement of Richard W. Carlson, President and CEO" (press release), December 7, 1994.

112. Jacqueline Trescott, "NEA Chief Told to Face 'All Options,'" *Washington Post,* January 27, 1995, C4.

113. Letter to all AIVF members from Martha Wallner, advocacy coordinator, AIVF, February 25, 1995; letter to colleagues and supporters of public service media and the cultural arts from James Yee, executive director, ITVS, January 13, 1995; letter to media colleagues from Deann Borshay, executive director, NAATA, January 2, 1995.

114. Quoted in Jacqueline Trescott, "Private Sector's Shortfall Specter," *Washington Post,* February 26, 1995, 12; Stephen Goode, "Is the Curtain Dropping on the Arts?" *Insight,* March 6, 1995, 6–9; Christopher Knight, "A Day in the Death of the NEA: Did Agency's Success Cause Its Demise?" *Los Angeles Times,* M3, M6. Quote from National Campaign for Freedom of Expression Flyer, "Letter from the Executive Director, David Mendoza," April 1995.

115. For a history of the media mergers of 1989, see Wasko, *Hollywood in the Information Age,* 41–70.

116. See the series of Heritage Talking Points papers written by Adam D. Thierer and published by the Heritage Foundation in 1995: "A Policy Maker's Guide to Deregulating Telecommunications: Part 1: The Open Access Solution"; "Part 2: Why the Cable Act of 1992 Was a Failure"; "Part 3: Solving the Local vs. Long Distance Dilemma"; "Part 4: Why Telecommunications Protectionism Should Be Ended"; "Part 5: Is the FCC Worth Its Cost?"; and "Part 6: A Free Market Future for Spectrum."

117. Hamid Mowlana, *Global Communications in Transition: The End of Diversity?* (Thousand Oaks, Calif.: Sage, 1996), 39–70. For a discussion of the economic interrelationships between deregulation and globalization, see Richard A. Gershon, "International Deregulation and the Rise of the Transnational Media Corporations," *Journal of Media Economics* (summer 1993), 3–22.

118. Cees J. Hamelink, "The Democratic Ideal and Its Enemies," in *The Democratization of Communications,* ed. Philip Lee (Cardiff: University of Wales Press, 1996), 33.

119. Fredric Jameson, "Five Theses on Actually Existing Marxism," *Monthly Review,* April 1996, 1–10.

120. Ralph Engelman, *Public Radio and Television in America: A Political History* (Thousand Oaks, Calif.: Sage, 1996), 165–78, 188–98.

121. Ibid., 193.

122. Richard Somerset-Ward, "Public Television: The Ballpark's Changing," in Twentieth Century Fund, *Quality Time? The Report of the Twentieth Century Fund Task Force on Public Television* (New York: Twentieth Century Fund Press, 1993), 96.

123. For discussions of privatization, its relationship to the new world order, and its narrowing of the public sphere, see Herman, *Triumph of the Market,* 3–53; Schiller, *Culture Inc.;* Schiller, *Information Inequality.*

124. For specific discussions of how news and public affairs programming has been reduced in Brazil, Italy, England, Canada, and Western Europe as a result of deregulation, see Tony Dowmunt, ed., *Channels of Resistance: Global Television and Local Empowerment* (London: British Film Institute, 1993).

125. Shelly Gabert, "Inside HBO: The Dish on the Documentary Division," *Independent*, December 1997, 26–29.

126. For documentation on the *Out at Work* controversy at PBS, see "Draft Resolution to the 1997 AFL-CIO Convention" (memo), AFL-CIO; letter to Lisa Heller, *P.O.V,* from Sandra Heberer, PBS, March 3, 1997; letter from Kathy Quattrone, PBS Programming Services, to *The Nation*, October 13, 1997; "Who's the Public in Public TV?" *Labor Party Press*, September 1997, 8; "Shut Out," *Providence Phoenix News*, October 24, 1997, 6; "PBS Strikes Labor" (editorial), *The Nation,* June 30, 1997, 5–6.

2. Mobile Battlegrounds in the Air

1. Bruce Cumings, *War and Television* (London: Verso, 1991), 86.

2. For discussions of nationalism and its psychic repressions, see David Trend, ed., *Radical Democracy: Identity, Citizenship and the State* (New York: Routledge, 1996); Homi K. Bhabha, ed., *Nation and Narration* (New York: Routledge, 1990); Andrew Parker, Mary Russo, Doris Sommer, and Patricia Yaeger, *Nationalisms and Sexualities* (New York: Routledge, 1992).

3. Cynthia Enloe, *The Morning After: Sexual Politics and the End of the Cold War* (Berkeley: University of California Press, 1993).

4. For examples from the war in Bosnia, see Milan Milosevic, "The Media Wars," in *Yugoslavia's Ethnic Nightmare: The Inside Story of Europe's Unfolding Ordeal*, ed. Jasminka Udovicki and James Ridgeway (New York: Lawrence Hill, 1995), 105–22; David Rieff, *Slaughterhouse: Bosnia and the Failure of the West* (New York: Touchstone, 1995). For penetrating examples from Latin America, see Alma Guillermoprieto, *The Heart That Bleeds: Latin America Now* (New York: Vintage, 1995).

5. See Michel Foucault, "Space, Knowledge and Power," in *The Foucault Reader*, ed. Paul Rabinow (New York: Pantheon, 1984), 239–56.

6. Marita Sturken, *Tangled Memories: The Vietnam War, the AIDS Epidemic, and the Politics of Remembering* (Berkeley: University of California Press, 1997), 37.

7. Bill Nichols, *Blurred Boundaries: Questions of Meaning in Contemporary Culture* (Bloomington: Indiana University Press, 1994).

8. Paul Virilio, *War and Cinema: The Logistics of Perception*, trans. Patrick Camiller (London:Verso, 1989), 5.

9. Avital Ronell, "Video/Television/Rodney King: Twelve Steps beyond *The Pleasure Principle*," in *Transmission: Toward a Post-Television Culture*, 2d ed., ed. Peter d'Agostino and David Tafler (Thousand Oaks, Calif.: Sage, 1995), 108.

10. Paul Gilroy, *There Ain't No Black in the Union Jack: The Cultural Politics of Race and Nation* (Chicago: University of Chicago Press, 1987), 43–69.

11. Slavoj Zizek, *The Sublime Object of Ideology* (London: Verso, 1989), 69.

12. For discussions of racialized demonization as an aspect of nationalism, see Ronald Takaki, *A Different Mirror: A History of Multicultural America* (Boston: Little, Brown, 1993); Ella Shohat and Robert Stam, *Unthinking Eurocentrism: Multiculturalism and the Media* (New York: Routledge, 1994), 137–247.

13. See Douglas Kellner, *Media Culture: Cultural Studies, Identity and Politics between the Modern and the Postmodern* (New York: Routledge, 1995), 198-226; Douglas Kellner, *The Persian Gulf TV War* (Boulder, Colo.: Westview, 1992).

14. Trinh T. Minh-ha, *Woman, Native, Other: Writing Postcoloniality and Feminism* (Bloomington: Indiana University Press, 1989), 119.

15. Ibid., 135.

16. See John R. MacArthur, *Second Front: Censorship and Propaganda in the Gulf War* (Berkeley: University of California Press, 1993); Cynthia Peters, ed., *Collateral Damage: The New World Order at Home and Abroad* (Boston: South End, 1992); Nancy Peters, ed., *War after War: The New Corporate/Military Order, the Middle East, Insurgencies on the Home Front* (San Francisco: City Lights Books, 1992).

17. Gilles Deleuze and Félix Guattari, "What Is a Minor Literature?" in *Out There: Marginalization and Contemporary Cultures*, ed. Russell Ferguson, Martha Gever, Trinh T. Minh-ha, and Cornel West (Cambridge: MIT Press, 1990), 67.

18. Ibid., 61.

19. See, for example, Edward S. Herman and Noam Chomsky, *Manufacturing Consent: The Political Economy of the Mass Media* (New York: Pantheon, 1988); Edward S. Herman, *Triumph of the Market: Essays on Economics, Politics, and the Media* (Boston: South End, 1995).

20. Armand Mattelart, *Mapping World Communication: War, Progress, Culture* (Minneapolis: University of Minnesota Press, 1994), 53.

21. Ibid., 85–99.

22. Daniel C. Hallin, *We Keep America on Top of the World: Television Journalism and the Public Sphere* (New York: Routledge, 1994), 4–7.
23. Ibid., 21, 46–86.
24. Todd Gitlin, *The Whole World Is Watching: Mass Media in the Making and Unmaking of the New Left* (Berkeley: University of California Press, 1980).
25. Virilio, *War and Cinema*, 7.
26. Ibid., 85.
27. Ibid., 31–69.
28. Christopher Norris, *Uncritical Theory: Postmodernism, Intellectuals, and the Gulf War* (Amherst: University of Massachusetts Press, 1992).
29. Kellner, *The Persian Gulf TV War*, 145–85.
30. Brian Winston, *Claiming the Real* (London: British Film Institute, 1995), 78.
31. Patricia R. Zimmermann, *Reel Families: A Social History of Amateur Film* (Bloomington: Indiana University Press, 1995), 45–98.
32. For discussions of recyclings of Vietnam imagery, see Sturken, *Tangled Memories*, 44–121.
33. For analysis of how the media recirculated military images as news, see Daniel C. Hallin, *The Uncensored War: The Media and Vietnam* (Berkeley: University of California Press, 1989).
34. Zizek, *The Sublime Object of Ideology*, 49.
35. Rey Chow, *Writing Diaspora: Tactics of Intervention in Contemporary Cultural Studies* (Bloomington: Indiana University Press, 1993), 67.
36. Dana Polan, "Above All Else to Make You See," in *Postmodernism and Politics*, ed. Jonathon Arac (Minneapolis: University of Minnesota Press, 1986), 61.
37. Ibid., 67.
38. bell hooks, "Marginality as a Site of Resistance," in *Out There: Marginalization and Contemporary Cultures*, ed. Russell Ferguson, Martha Gever, Trinh T. Minh-ha, and Cornel West (Cambridge: MIT Press, 1990), 340.
39. For primary material on the Chiapas uprising, see Ben Clark and Clifton Ross, eds., *Voice of Fire: Communiques and Interviews from the Zapatista National Liberation Army* (Berkeley, Calif.: New Earth, 1994).
40. See Zillah R. Eisenstein and Patricia R. Zimmermann, "The Olympics and Post–Cold War Femininities: Tonya and Nancy," in *Women on Ice: Feminism, Spectacle and Sport*, ed. Cynthia Baughman (New York: Routledge, 1995), 250–63.
41. Bill Nichols, *Representing Reality: Issues and Concepts in Documentary* (Bloomington: Indiana University Press, 1991), 32–75.
42. See Michael Schudson, *Discovering the News: A Social History of American Newspapers* (New York: Basic Books, 1978).
43. Winston, *Claiming the Real*, 40.
44. Ibid., 71.
45. Julia Lesage, "Feminist Documentary: Aesthetics and Politics," in *"Show Us Life": History and Theory of the Committed Documentary*, ed. Thomas Waugh (Metuchen, N.J.: Scarecrow, 1980), 246.
46. Bill Nichols, "The Ethnographer's Tale," in *Visualizing Theory: Selected Essays from V.A.R. 1990–1994*, ed. Lucien Taylor (New York: Routledge, 1994), 76.
47. Shoshana Felman and Dori Laub, *Testimony: Crises of Witnessing in Literature, Psychoanalysis, and History* (New York: Routledge, 1992), 69.
48. Ibid., xix.
49. Ibid., xix, 50.
50. Ibid., 85.
51. Ibid., 108.
52. Ibid., 204.
53. Ibid., 69.
54. Ibid., xix.
55. Nichols, *Blurred Boundaries*, 6. For an insightful analysis of how trauma and memory are transfigured in *History and Memory* and refute the realist mode of documentary, see Janet Walker, "The Traumatic Paradox: Documentary Films, Historical Fictions, and Cataclysmic Past Events," *Signs* 22 (summer 1997): 803–25.
56. Felman and Laub, *Testimony*, 85.
57. See Rabia Ali and Lawrence Lifschultz, eds. *Why Bosnia? Writings on the Balkan War* (Stony Creek, Conn.: Pamphleteer's Press, 1993); Susan L. Woodward, *Balkan Tragedy: Chaos and Dissolution after the Cold War* (Washington, D.C.: Brookings Institution, 1995).
58. Milosevic, "The Media Wars."
59. Slavenka Drakulic, *The Balkan Express: Fragments from the Other Side of War* (New York: W. W. Norton, 1993), 84.

60. Zillah R. Eisenstein, *Hatreds: Racialized and Sexualized Conflicts in the 21st Century* (New York: Routledge, 1996), 59.

61. See Alexandra Stiglmayer, ed., *Mass Rape: The War Against Women in Bosnia-Herzegovina* (Lincoln: University of Nebraska Press, 1994).

62. Fact sheet, *Calling the Ghosts* press kit, 1996.

63. hooks, "Marginality as a Site of Resistance," 343.

64. Filmmaker's statement, *Calling the Ghosts* press kit, 1996.

65. Felman and Laub, *Testimony,* 114.

66. Ibid., 25.

67. Michael Renov, "Introduction: The Truth about Non-Fiction," in *Theorizing Documentary,* ed. Michael Renov (New York: Routledge, 1993), 33.

68. Erik Barnouw, "How a University's Film Branch Released Long-Secret A-Bomb Pic," *Variety,* January 5, 1972.

69. Susan Buck-Morss, "Aesthetics and Anesthetics: Walter Benjamin's Artwork Essay Reconsidered," *October* 62 (fall 1992): 18.

70. Ibid., 17.

71. Ibid., 5.

72. Trinh T. Minh-ha, *When the Moon Waxes Red: Representation, Gender and Cultural Politics* (New York: Routledge, 1991), 11–26, 95–105.

73. Buck-Morss, "Aesthetics and Anesthetics," 6.

74. Marita Sturken, "What Is Grace in All This Madness: The Videotapes of Dan Reeves," *Afterimage* (summer 1985): 24–27.

75. Trinh, *When the Moon Waxes Red,* 23.

76. Ibid., 18–19.

77. Homi K. Bhabha, *The Location of Culture* (New York: Routledge, 1994), 36.

3. Ground Wars and the Real of Bodies

1. Caren Kaplan, *Questions of Travel: Postmodern Discourses of Displacement* (Durham, N.C.: Duke University Press, 1996), 160.

2. Chantal Mouffe, "Radical Democracy or Liberal Democracy?" in *Radical Democracy: Identity, Citizenship, and the State,* ed. David Trend (New York: Routledge, 1996), 19–26.

3. See Joris Ivens, *The Camera and I* (New York: International, 1969), 103–38.

4. Ibid., 137.

5. Thomas Waugh, "Joris Ivens' *The Spanish Earth:* Committed Documentary and the Popular Front," in *"Show Us Life": Toward a History and Aesthetics of the Committed Documentary,* ed. Thomas Waugh (Metuchen, N.J.: Scarecrow, 1984), 121.

6. Ibid., 133.

7. Jon Alpert, "Recollection," in "The Flaherty: Four Decades in the Cause of Independent Cinema" (special issue), ed. Erik Barnouw and Patricia R. Zimmermann, *Wide Angle* 17, nos. 1–4 (1995): 4.

8. For a discussion of the origins and history of guerrilla television in the 1970s, see Deirdre Boyle, *Subject to Change: Guerrilla Television Revisited* (Oxford: Oxford University Press, 1997).

9. Bill Nichols, *Representing Reality: Issues and Concepts in Documentary* (Bloomington: Indiana University Press, 1991), 47.

10. Ibid.

11. Ibid., 73.

12. Paula Rabinowitz, *They Must Be Represented: The Politics of Documentary* (London: Verso, 1995), 84.

13. Michel Foucault, "Nietzsche, Genealogy, History," in *The Foucault Reader,* ed. Paul Rabinow (New York: Pantheon, 1984), 76–100.

14. Stephen Tyler, "Postmodern Ethnography," in *Writing Culture: The Poetics and Politics of Ethnography,* ed. James Clifford and George Marcus (Berkeley: University of California Press, 1986).

15. Ibid., 87.

16. Marlon Fuentes offered this observation of new cinematic practices creating membranes for exchange between makers and subjects instead of representing subjects at the 42nd Annual Robert Flaherty Film Seminar, August 3-8, 1996, Wells College, Aurora, N.Y.

17. Merata Mita, comments made at the 42nd Annual Robert Flaherty Film Seminar, August 4, 1996, Wells College, Aurora, N.Y.

18. Gregg Bordowitz, "Operative Assumptions," in *Resolutions: Contemporary Video Practices,* ed. Michael Renov and Erika Suderberg (Minneapolis: University of Minnesota Press, 1996), 173–84.

19. Erik Barnouw, *Documentary: A History of the Non-fiction Film,* rev. ed. (Oxford: Oxford University Press, 1983), 253–93.

20. Alexandra Juhasz, *AIDS TV* (Durham, N.C.: Duke University Press, 1995).
21. Gregg Bordowitz, "The AIDS Crisis Is Ridiculous," in *Queer Looks: Perspectives on Lesbian and Gay Film and Video*, ed. Martha Gever, John Greyson, and Pratibha Parmar (New York: Routledge, 1993), 212–13.
22. Margot Lovejoy, *Postmodern Currents: Art in the Electronic Age* (New York: Prentice Hall, 1997), 128–53.
23. Mouffe, "Radical Democracy."
24. "Talking Heads: Black Planet's Cyrille Philpps and Art Jones," *International Documentary* 13, no. 1 (1994): 1, 12–15.
25. For an exposé of how the press misrepresented the Los Angeles rebellion as a chaotic black-and-white riot and repressed the historical and social contexts, see Don Hazen, ed., *Inside the L.A. Riots: What Really Happened and Why It Will Happen Again* (San Francisco: Institute for Alternative Journalism, 1992).
26. See Laurie Ouellette, "Sick and Tired of Being Sick and Tired: Deep Dish TV Examines the Health Care Crises," *Independent*, July 1995, 35–36.
27. Justin Wyatt, "Autobiography, Home Movies, and Derek Jarman's History Lesson," in *Between the Sheets, In the Streets: Queer, Lesbian, Gay Documentary*, ed. Chris Holmlund and Cynthia Fuchs (Minneapolis: University of Minnesota Press, 1997), 158–71.
28. See Robert Karl Manoff and Michael Schudson, eds., *Reading the News* (New York: Pantheon, 1986); Peter Dahlgren, *Television and the Public Sphere: Citizenship, Democracy and the Media* (London: Sage, 1995); Ben H. Bagdikian, *The Media Monopoly* (Boston: Beacon, 1990).
29. Jean Baudrillard, *Simulations* (New York: Semiotext[e], 1983), 119.
30. See Brian Winston, *Claiming the Real* (London: British Film Institute, 1996); Nichols, *Representing Reality*.
31. Nichols, *Representing Reality*, 125.
32. For a detailed discussion of how the Empowerment Project implemented this strategy, see Barbara Trent, W. B. Peale, and Joanne Doroshow, *Taking It to the Theaters: The Empowerment Project's Guide to Theatrical and Video Self-Distribution of Issue-Oriented Films and Videos* (New York: National Video Resources and the Empowerment Project, 1993).
33. See DeeDee Halleck, "The Experience of Citizens' Television in the United States: Public Access/Public Sphere," unpublished manuscript, spring 1997.
34. William Boddy, "Alternative Television in the United States," *Screen* 31, no. 1 (1990): 91–101; DeeDee Halleck, "Paper Tiger Television: Smashing the Myths of the Information Industry Every Week on Public Access Cable," *Media, Culture & Society* 6 (1984): 313–18; Charles Hagen, "Paper Tiger Television," *Artforum*, April 1985, 97; Kathleen Hulser, "Paper Tiger Television," *American Film*, March 1985, 61–63; Amy Taubin, "Paper Tiger: Local Access Makes Good," *Village Voice*, September 13, 1988, 73.
35. Taubin, "Paper Tiger," 73.
36. Sherry Milner, "Bargain Media," in *Roar! The Paper Tiger Television Guide to Media Activism*, ed. Paper Tiger Collective (New York: Paper Tiger Collective, 1991), 10.
37. Quoted in "Letting You See the Seams," *Index on Censorship* 1 (1993): 10.
38. Joan Braderman, "TV/Video: Reclaiming the Utopian Moment," in *Roar! The Paper Tiger Television Guide to Media Activism*, ed. Paper Tiger Collective (New York: Paper Tiger Collective, 1991), 21.
39. Helen De Michel, "Re-visioning the Electronic Democracy," in *Roar! The Paper Tiger Television Guide to Media Activism*, ed. Paper Tiger Collective (New York: Paper Tiger Collective, 1991), 15.
40. Deep Dish T.V. Network, "Your Organization Can Use Deep Dish T.V." (flyer), spring 1996.
41. Linda Yablonskaya, "The Visionary for the '90s: Deep Dish TV," *High Performance*, spring 1993, 28.
42. DeeDee Halleck, "Deep Dish TV: Community Video from a Geostationary Orbit," *Leonardo* 26, no. 5 (1993): 416.
43. Ibid.
44. Deep Dish T.V. catalog, spring 1996, 8.
45. Douglas Kahn, "Satellite Skirmishes: An Interview with Paper Tiger West's Jesse Drew," *Afterimage* (May 1993): 11.
46. Christopher Norris, *Uncritical Theory: Postmodernism, Intellectuals, and the Gulf War* (Amherst: University of Massachusetts Press, 1991), 26–27.
47. Bill Stamets, "DeeDee Halleck: Beaming Up," *In These Times*, May 1–8, 1991, 6.
48. Steve Seid, "Obsessive Becoming: The Video Poetics of Daniel M. Reeves," in *1996 Mill Valley Film Festival Souvenir Program* (Mill Valley, Calif.: Mill Valley Film Festival, 1996), 3, 137; Susan Christie, flyer on Daniel Reeves's *Obsessive Becoming*, Scottish Arts Council Travelling Gallery, Glasgow, 1996, 1–2.
49. Michael Taussig, *The Nervous System* (New York: Routledge, 1992), 9.
50. Ibid., 8, 9, 28.

51. Thich Nhat Hanh, *Being Peace* (Berkeley, Calif.: Parallax, 1987), 43.

52. I thank John Hess for this observation on the melodramatic structure of *Obsessive Becoming*.

4. Female Body Ambushes

1. For a fuller explanation of the consequences of *Bray v. Alexandria Women's Health Clinic*, see National Abortion Rights Action League, "Clinic Access" (pamphlet), n.d. For a compelling explication of why and how feminist politics needs to be combined with documentary practice, see Janet Walker and Diane Waldman, "Introduction," in *Feminism and Documentary*, ed. Diane Waldman and Janet Walker (Minneapolis: University of Minnesota Press, 1999), 1–35.

2. For discussions of how new media technologies such as satellite, cable, and laptop computers altered the public sphere of reporting the Gulf War, see Craig LaMay, Martha FitzSimon, and Jeanne Sahadi, eds., *The Media at War: The Press and the Persian Gulf Conflict* (New York: Gannett Foundation Media Center, 1991); Douglas Kellner, *The Persian Gulf TV War* (Boulder, Colo.: Westview, 1992); Hamid Mowlana, George Gerbner, and Herbert I. Schiller, eds., *Triumph of the Image: The Media's War in the Persian Gulf—a Global Perspective* (Boulder, Colo.: Westview, 1992); Bruce Cumings, *War and Television* (London: Verso, 1992).

3. See Donna J. Haraway, "A Cyborg Manifesto: Science, Technology, and Socialist-Feminism in the Late Twentieth Century," in *Simians, Cyborgs, and Women: The Reinvention of Nature* (New York: Routledge, 1991), 153.

4. Ibid., 174.

5. Larry Rohter, "Doctor Is Slain during Protest over Abortions" *New York Times*, March 11, 1993, 1, B10; Anthony Lewis, "Right to Life," *New York Times*, March 12, 1993, 29; David A. Grimes, Jacqueline D. Forrest, Alice L. Kirkman, and Barbara Radford, "An Epidemic of Antiabortion Violence in the United States," *American Journal of Obstetrics and Gynecology* 165, no. 5 (1991): 1263–68; Planned Parenthood, "Highlights of Recent Violence against Planned Parenthood Clinics" (flyer), March 11, 1993. See also a series of Planned Parenthood news releases issued on the heels of the Dr. Gunn shooting: "Statement by Pamela J. Maraldo, Ph.D., President of Planned Parenthood Federation of America Planned Parenthood Action Fund," March 11, 1993; "Statement by Pamela J. Maraldo, Ph.D., President Planned Parenthood Federation of America Planned Parenthood Action Fund," March 12, 1993; "Planned Parenthood Establishes Clinic Defense Fund in Aftermath of Florida Physician's Murder," March 12, 1993; "Statement by Alexander C. Sanger, President and CEO, Planned Parenthood of New York City," March 12, 1993; "Statement by Dr. Pamela J. Maraldo, President, Planned Parenthood Federation of America Planned Parenthood Action Fund," March 10, 1993. See also Planned Parenthood, "Unwanted in Any Florida City, David LaMond Gunn" (flyer of a clip from *Washington Times*, March 12, 1993).

6. Constance Penley and Andrew Ross, "Introduction," in *Technoculture*, ed. Constance Penley and Andrew Ross (Minneapolis: University of Minnesota Press, 1991), xv.

7. See, for example, E. Ann Kaplan, "Theories and Strategies of the Feminist Documentary"; Vivian C. Sobchack, "No Lies: Direct Cinema as Rape"; Patricia Erens, "Women's Documentary Filmmaking: The Personal Is Political"; and Linda Williams, "What You Take for Granted," Julia Lesage, "Feminist Documentary: Aesthetics and Politics," in *"Show Us Life": Toward a History and Aesthetics of the Committed Documentary*, ed. Thomas Waugh (Metuchen, N.J.: Scarecrow, 1984); Julianne Burton, "Transitional States: Creative Complicities with the Real in *Man Marked to Die*, *Twenty Years Later* and *Patriamada*," in *The Social Documentary in Latin America*, ed. Julianne Burton (Pittsburgh: University of Pittsburgh Press, 1990), 373–401.

8. Although recent writing on documentary invokes feminist film theorization on the body and the gaze, this work does not offer a theoretical interrogation of what would constitute a feminist documentary practice. See Bill Nichols, *Representing Reality: Issues and Concepts in Documentary* (Bloomington: Indiana University Press, 1991). Nichols insists, for example, that documentary is linked with history, ethics, and rhetoric. He masterfully outlines the various formal and rhetorical modes of address and organization that documentary occupies, yet he offers no distinctions in terms of gender. In his line of argument, gender is subsumed under the category of the social, but it is not viewed as a system of difference requiring different modes of theorization.

9. Margaret Cooper, "The Abortion Film Wars: Media in the Combat Zone," *Cineaste* 15, no. 2 (1986): 8–12.

10. Rosalind Pollack Petchesky, "Foetal Images: The Power of Visual Culture in the Politics of Reproduction," in *Reproductive Technologies: Gender, Motherhood, and Medicine*, ed. Michelle Stanworth (Minneapolis: University of Minnesota Press, 1987), 58.

11. Valerie Hartouni, "Containing Women: Reproductive Discourse in the 1980s," in *Technoculture*, ed. Constance Penley and Andrew Ross (Minneapolis: University of Minnesota Press, 1991), 51.

12. See, for example, Laurence H. Tribe, *Abortion: The Clash of Absolutes* (New York: W. W. Norton,

1990); Shirley L. Radl, *Over Our Live Bodies: Preserving Choice in America* (Dallas: Steve Davis, 1989); Susan E. Davis, ed., *Women under Attack: Victories, Backlash and the Fight for Reproductive Freedom* (Boston: South End, 1988). The most thorough study of abortion history and politics is Rosalind Pollack Petchesky's *Abortion and Woman's Choice: The State, Sexuality, and Reproductive Freedom* (Boston: Northeastern University Press, 1985).

13. See Michel Foucault, *The Archaeology of Knowledge and the Discourse on Language* (New York: Harper Colophon, 1972), 125–28, 186–88, 190–95.

14. Arthur S. DeMoss Foundation, "Life. What a Beautiful Choice" (brochure), n.d.

15. Ibid., 1.

16. Rebecca S. McKay, Arthur S. DeMoss Foundation, letter to the author, March 3, 1993.

17. These tropes of melodrama are elaborated in Laura Mulvey, "Notes on Sirk and Melodrama" and "Melodrama inside and outside the Home," both in *Visual and Other Pleasures* (Bloomington: Indiana University Press, 1989).

18. Carole A. Stabile, "Shooting the Mother: Fetal Photography and the Politics of Disappearance," *Camera Obscura* 28 (1992): 180.

19. E. Ann Kaplan, *Motherhood and Representation: The Mother in Popular Culture and Melodrama* (London: Routledge, 1992), 76–106.

20. Gwen Ifill, "Clinton Ready to Act on 2 Abortion Regulations," *New York Times*, January 17, 1993, 21; Robin Toner, "Anti-abortion Movement Prepares to Battle Clinton," *New York Times*, January 22, 1993, 1, 16; "Since Roe v. Wade: The Evolution of Abortion Law," *New York Times*, January 22, 1993, 11; Robin Toner, "Clinton Orders Reversal of Abortion Restrictions Left by Reagan and Bush," *New York Times*, January 23, 1993, 1, 10.

21. My argument here is based on analysis of Toner, "Clinton Orders Reversal," and the two photographs accompanying that article.

22. See, for example, Robert Pear, "Hillary Clinton Gets Policy Job and New Office," *New York Times*, January 22, 1993, 1, 23.

23. Deborah Sontag, "Increasingly, 2-Career Family Means Illegal Immigrant Help," *New York Times*, January 24, 1993, 1, 32; Gwen Ifill, "Clinton's Blunt Reminder of the Mood That Elected Him," *New York Times*, January 24, 1993, E3.

24. Linda Hutcheon, *The Politics of Postmodernism* (London: Routledge, 1989), 58.

25. Barry Smart, *Modern Conditions, Postmodern Controversies* (London: Routledge, 1992), 171.

26. Nina C. Leibman, "The Way We Weren't: Abortion 1950s Style in Blue Denim and Our Time," *Velvet Light Trap* 29 (spring 1992): 31–43.

27. Steven C. Dubin, *Arresting Images: Impolitic Art and Uncivil Actions* (New York: Routledge, 1992), 131–37.

28. "The Advertiser That Didn't Balk," *Ms.*, July 1989, 75; Judith Graham, "NBC's 'Roe' may turn off advertisers," *Advertising Age*, May 1, 1989, 1, 85; John Leonard, "Their Bodies, Their Selves," *New York Magazine*, May 15, 1989, 117; Mark Lasswell, "Movie of the Week," *Rolling Stone*, June 1, 1989, 40; Judith Graham, "'Roe' Advertisers Risk Boycotts," *Advertising Age*, May 15, 1989, 2; "Roe v. Wade," *People Weekly*, May 15, 1989, 9–10; Verne Gay, "'Roe v. Wade' Sells Out, but Did the Advertisers Sell Out to Boycott Threat?" *Variety*, May 17, 1989, 1.

29. Neil DeMause, "The Great Abortion 'Compromise,'" *Extra*, September 1992, 25, 26; "Can Men Spot Sexist Premises in Abortion Debate?" *Extra*, September 1992, 26.

30. B. Ruby Rich, "The Current State of Independent Film and Video," keynote address, University Film and Video Conference, Ithaca College, Ithaca, N.Y., June 16, 1990.

31. For a thorough discussion of the attack against public broadcasting and a clear description of the major players in the debate, see Josh Daniel, "Uncivil Wars: The Conservative Assault on Public Broadcasting," *Independent*, August/September 1992, 20–25. See also Walter Goodman, "Pull the Plug on PBS?" *New York Times*, March 22, 1992, H33; Martin Tolchin, "Public Broadcasting Bill Is Sidelined," *New York Times*, March 5, 1992, A14; Mark Schapiro, "Public TV Takes Its Nose Out of the Air," *New York Times*, November 3, 1992, H31; "Attacks on CPB and ITVS Threaten Funding for TV Documentaries," *Documentary*, May 1992, 1, 8–9.

32. Kim Masters, "Big Bird Meets the Right Wing," *Washington Post*, March 4, 1992, 21; William J. Eaton and Sharon Bernstein, "GOP Senators Blast Public Broadcasting," *Los Angeles Times*, March 4, 1992, 11; Kim Masters, "Hill Clash Set over Public TV," *Washington Post*, March 3, 1992, 14; Robert Knight, "Free Big Bird," *Miami Herald*, March 6, 1992, 8C; Laurence Jarvik, "Monopoly, Corruption, and Greed: The Problem of Public Television," speech delivered as part of the Heritage Foundation Lecture Series, February 25, 1992; Richard Zoglin, "Public TV under Assault," *Time*, March 30, 1992, 58; S. Robert Lichter, Daniel Amundson, and Linda S. Lichter, "Balance and Diversity in PBS Documentaries," unpublished manuscript, Center for Media and Public Affairs, March 1992.

33. Martin Tolchin, "Public Broadcasting Bill Is Sidelined," *New York Times*, March 5, 1992, 7; Patti Hartigan, "Targeting PBS," *Boston Globe*, March 4, 1992, 18; Howard Rosenberg, "On the Urge to

Purge Public TV," *Los Angeles Times*, March 6, 1992, 34; Mike Mills, "Charges of Liberal Bias Stall PBS Funding Bill," *Washington Times*, March 7, 1992, 16; John Wilner, "Stealth Senators Sought; One Admits He Placed Hold," *Current*, March 2, 1992, 3; Corporation for Public Broadcasting, "Statement by Donald Ledwig, President, Corporation for Public Broadcasting (CPBP) on the Reauthorization of CPB, Which Is Being Debated on the Senate Floor" (press release), March 3, 1992; Heritage Foundation, "Making Public Television Public" (Heritage Foundation "Backgrounder" pamphlet), January 18, 1992.

34. Mills, "Charges of Liberal Bias," 17.

35. Ben Bagdikian, *The Media Monopoly* (Boston: Beacon, 1992); Ken Auletta, *Three Blind Mice: How the TV Networks Lost Their Way* (New York: Random House, 1991); Douglas Kellner, "Public Access Television and the Struggle for Democracy," in *Democratic Communications in the Information Age*, ed. Janet Wasko and Vincent Mosco (Norwood, N.J.: Ablex, 1992), 100–113; Gladys D. Ganley, *The Exploding Political Power of Personal Media* (Norwood, N.J.: Ablex, 1992).

36. Richard O. Curry, *An Uncertain Future: Thought Control and Repression during the Reagan-Bush Era* (Los Angeles: First Amendment Foundation, 1992), 59–61.

37. Marjorie Heins, director, American Civil Liberties Union Arts Censorship Project, "The First Amendment, Censorship, and Government Funding of the Arts" (American Civil Liberties Union position paper), n.d., 3.

38. Ibid., 4.

39. Sean Cubitt, *Timeshift: On Video Culture* (London: Routledge, 1991), 13–14.

40. DeeDee Halleck, "Watch Out, Dick Tracy! Popular Video in the Wake of the *Exxon Valdez*," in *Technoculture*, ed. Constance Penley and Andrew Ross (Minneapolis: University of Minnesota Press, 1991), 217. For a discussion of the use of camcorders for AIDS education and empowerment, see Alexandra Juhasz, "WAVE in the Media Environment: Camcorder Activism and the Making of HIV TV," *Camera Obscura* 28 (1992): 135–50.

41. This argument on increasing access to media production as a democratic right has also been used by media producers working in pubic access in less urban and smaller communities. See, for example, Chris Hill and Barbara Lattanzi, "Media Dialects and Stages of Access," *Felix* 1, no. 2 (1992): 98–106.

42. See Steven Greenhouse, "Praise and Protest on Clinton's Decisions," *New York Times*, January 24, 1993, 6; Adam Clymer, "Abortion Rights Supports Are Split on U.S. Measure," *New York Times*, April 2, 1993, A16; Felicia R. Lee, "On Battle Lines of Abortion Issue: Debates Rages on Outside of Clinics," *New York Times*, May 17, 1993, B1, B4; Felicity Barringer, "Slaying Is a Call to Arms for Abortion Clinics," *New York Times*, March 12, 1993, A1, A17; Alisa Solomon, "Harassing House Calls," *Village Voice*, March 23, 1993, 20.

43. Many feminist theoreticians have advanced similar arguments that reproductive technologies are controlled by men, and thus women's choices are circumscribed and limited. See, for example, Michelle Stanworth, "Reproductive Technologies and the Deconstruction of Motherhood," and Hilary Rose, "Victorian Values in the Test-Tube: The Politics of Reproductive Science and Technology," both in *Reproductive Technologies: Gender, Motherhood, and Medicine*, ed. Michelle Stanworth (Minneapolis: University of Minnesota Press, 1987).

44. I would particularly like to thank Scott MacDonald, Sally Berger, and Kathy High for alerting me to these tapes on reproductive rights. I would also like to thank the distributors of these tapes for their generosity in lending me preview copies. *Spring of Lies* is available from the Media Coalition for Reproductive Rights, P.O. Box 33, Buffalo, NY 14201. *US Bans Abortion* is available from Paper Tiger Television, 339 Lafayette Street, New York, NY 10012; (212) 420-9045. *Access Denied* is available from Women Make Movies, 462 Broadway, Suite k501; or from Video Data Bank, 37 S. Wabash Avenue, Chicago, IL 60603; (312) 899-5172. *S'Aline's Solution* is available from The Kitchen, 512 W. 19th Street, New York, NY 10011; (212) 255-5793.

5. Pirates of the New World Image Orders

1. Pirate Editorial, "So You Want to Be a Pirate?" in *High Noon on the Electronic Frontier: Conceptual Issues in Cyberspace*, ed. Peter Ludlow (Cambridge: MIT Press, 1996), 110. I thank Chuck Kleinhans for provoking my thinking on piracy by asking me why PBS and CPB matter anymore for political documentary.

2. Gordon Graham, "Progress in a Quiet War," *Publishers Weekly*, January 12, 1990, S4.

3. Guillermo Gómez-Peña, "The Subcomandante of Performance," in *First World, Ha Ha Ha: The Zapatista Challenge*, ed. Elaine Katzenberger (San Francisco: City Lights, 1995), 90–91.

4. "Statement of Subcomandante Marcos," satellite broadcast, *Freeing the Media Teach-In*, organized by the Learning Alliance, Paper Tiger Television, and FAIR in Cooperation with the Media and Democracy Congress, January 31, 1997, New York.

5. Guillermo Gómez-Peña, "The Free Trade Art Agreement/El Tratado De Libre Cultura," in *The New World Border* (San Francisco: City Lights, 1996), 12.

6. John Fiske, "Popular News," in *Reading the Popular* (Boston: Unwin Hyman, 1989), 185–97.

7. Quoted in Kenneth B. Noble, "Defying Airwave Rules and Exporting the Way," *New York Times*, January 2, 1996, A10.

8. Zeke Teflon, *The Complete Manual of Pirate Radio* (Tucson, Ariz.: See Sharp, 1993), 5.

9. Douglas Rushkoff, *Media Virus! Hidden Agendas in Popular Culture* (New York: Ballantine, 1994), 258–316.

10. Dawn Ades, *Photomontage* (New York: Thames & Hudson, 1973), 12–13; see also Douglas Kahn, *John Heartfield: Art and Mass Media* (New York: Tanam, 1985).

11. David Cordingly, *Under the Black Flag: The Romance and Reality of Life among the Pirates* (New York: Random House, 1995), 1–75.

12. Ibid., 96.

13. Jacques Derrida, *Archive Fever: A Freudian Impression*, trans. Eric Prenowitz (Chicago: University of Chicago Press, 1996), 68.

14. Paul Gilroy, *The Black Atlantic: Modernity and Double Consciousness* (Cambridge: Harvard University Press, 1994), 12, 73–106, 190–200.

15. Ibid., 100–106.

16. Ibid., 200–202.

17. Michel de Certeau, *The Practice of Everyday Life* (Berkeley: University of California Press, 1984), 23–25.

18. Ibid., 117.

19. Ibid., 26.

20. Michael Spector, "Latest Films for 2: Video Piracy Booms in Russia," *New York Times*, April 11, 1993, A3; Celestine Bohlen, "In Russia's Free Market, Cultural Piracy Thrives," *New York Times*, July 2, 1993, A4; Matthew Brzenzinski, "New Polish Law Takes Aim at Copyright Piracy," *New York Times*, June 1, 1994, D6; Clyde H. Farnsworth, "Negotiations Concluded over the U.S.-Soviet Trade," *New York Times*, May 29, 1990, A6; Steven Erlanger, "Thailand Is the Capital of Pirated Tapes," *New York Times*, November 27, 1990, C15; Adam Florance, "Legit Vid Sales Up 30% after Piracy Clampdown," *Variety*, July 11–17, 1994, 39; Kenneth Bradsher, "U.S. Cool to China Proposal; Dispute on Piracy Continues," *New York Times*, January 11, 1992, I33–34; Thomas L. Friedman, "China Faces U.S. Sanctions in Electronic Copyright Piracy," *New York Times*, July 1, 1994, D2; Douglas Jehl, "Warning to China on Trade; U.S. Adds It to List of Product Piracy," *New York Times*, April 30, 1994, I34; Clyde H. Farnsworth, "China Called Top Copyright Pirate," *New York Times*, April 20, 1989, D7; Seth Faison, "Razor, Soap, Cornflakes: Pirating Spreads in China," *New York Times*, February 17, 1995, A1, D2; Seth Faison, "U.S. and China Sign Accord to End Piracy of Software, Music Recordings and Film," *New York Times*, February 27, 1995, A1, D6.

21. Derek Elley, "China: Trick or Treaty?" *Variety*, March 6, 1995, 1, 78. See also Stephen Engelbaerg, "Polish Pirates' Booty: Bootleg Tapes," *New York Times*, L1, L52; Bradsher, "U.S. Cool to China Proposal," I33, I44; Gregory Stanko and Nisha Mody, "Chinese Pirates Sail the Potomac," *New York Times*, May 5, 1994, A27; "A Smart Move on China," *New York Times*, February 6, 1995, A16; Seth Faison, "Fighting Piracy and Frustration in China," *New York Times*, May 17, 1995, D1, D5; Robert Hurtado, "With Sanctions Set, Companies Rethink Their China Plans," *New York Times*, February 6, 1995, A1, D2.

22. World Commission on Culture and Development, *Our Creative Diversity: Report of the World Commission on Culture and Development* (Paris: UNESCO, 1995), 115–17.

23. Richard J. Barnet and John Cavanaugh, *Global Dreams: Imperial Corporations and the New World Order* (New York: Simon & Schuster, 1994), 1–160.

24. Cees J. Hamelink, *Trends in World Communication: On Disempowerment and Self-Empowerment* (Penang: Southbound, 1994), 37–75.

25. Herbert I. Schiller, *Information Inequality: The Deepening Social Crisis in America* (New York: Routledge, 1996), 59–75. For an extended discussion of the impact of computers and digitization on the moving image, see Philip Hayward and Tana Wollen, eds., *Future Visions: New Technologies of the Screen* (London: British Film Institute, 1993).

26. Janet Wasko, *Hollywood in the Information Age* (Austin: University of Texas Press, 1994), 37–39.

27. See Justin Wyatt, *High Concept: Movies and Marketing in Hollywood* (Austin: University of Texas Press, 1994).

28. Jon Lewis, *Whom God Wishes to Destroy: Francis Ford Coppola and the New Hollywood* (Durham, N.C.: Duke University Press, 1996).

29. Wasko, *Hollywood in the Information Age*, 187–210.

30. See Eric Smoodin, ed., *Disney Discourse: Producing the Magic Kingdom* (New York: Routledge, 1994).

31. For discussions of the corporate media's antipiracy campaigns, see "Piracy Costly for Hollywood," *New York Times*, March 27, 1989, D4 ; Will Tusher, "U.S. Losses to Global Piracy Fell 25% in '89, per Valenti," *Variety*, January 10, 1990, 13, 21; "A Scourge of Video Pirates," *Newsweek*, July 27, 1987, 40–41; "Disney Sues over Cassettes," *Wall Street Journal*, August 15, 1989, D15; Christine L. Ogan, "Developing Policy for Eliminating International Video Piracy," *Journal of Broadcasting and Electronic Media* 32, no. 2 (1988): 163–82; Jeremy Coopman, "Industry Report Warns of Deeper Piracy Woes," *Variety*, January 21, 1991, 89; Florance, "Legit Vid Sales"; Will Tusher, "MPAA Bans the Sale of U.S. Pictures to USSR," *Variety*, June 10, 1991, 8; Elisabeth Malkin, "Declaring War on the Pirates," *Business Week*, October 2, 1994; Willliam E. Schmidt, "A Third World Rule on Video: Copy It and Sell It," *New York Times*, August 18, 1991, A1, A12.
32. Wasko, *Hollywood in the Information Age*.
33. David E. Sanger, "Trade Agreement Ends Long Debate, but Not Conflicts," *New York Times*, December 1994, 1, 32; Michael Williams and Rex Wiener, "Deep Thaw in Beaune: US, French Bury GATT Hatchet," *Variety*, November 6, 1995, 31; "Valenti Working on Plan to Counter EC's Quota on TV Programming," *Variety*, September 6, 1989, 4.
34. Ronald V. Bettig, *Copyrighting Culture: The Political Economy of Intellectual Property* (Boulder, Colo.: Westview, 1996), 5.
35. DeeDee Halleck, "Research: *The Gringo in Mananaland*" (press release), fall 1995; DeeDee Halleck, "Film Censored by NEA Featured at Venice Film Festival" (press release), August 29, 1995.
36. bell hooks, *Black Looks: Race and Representation* (Boston: South End, 1992), 21–39.
37. Quoted in Teresa Riordan, "Writing Coypright Law for an Information Age," *New York Times*, July 7, 1994, D1.
38. Bettig, *Copyrighting Culture*, 2.
39. Jane M. Gaines, *Contested Culture: The Image, the Voice and the Law* (Chapel Hill: University of North Carolina Press, 1991), 9–29, 60–70, 121–30.
40. Bettig, *Copyrighting Culture*, 12–13.
41. Ibid., 100–107; Gaines, *Contested Culture*, 83–103.
42. See Bettig, *Copyrighting Culture*, 90–120; Gaines, *Contested Culture*, 39–50.
43. Martha Buskirk, "Commodification as Censor: Copyrights and Fair Use," *October* (spring 1992): 84.
44. John Browning, "Africa 1 Hollywood 0," *Wired*, March 1997, 61.
45. For further examples of how the debate between copyright maximalists and copyright minimalists has foregrounded a new set of power relations based on control of digitized information, see Riordan, "Writing Copyright Law," D1, D5; Sabra Chartrand, "Patents: The Promise of a Multi-media Revolution Is Creating a Giant Copyright Headache for Some Companies," *New York Times*, March 28, 1994, D3; "Copyright Changes Urged for Electronic Networks," *New York Times*, September 6, 1994, D4 ; Thomas J. Galvin and Sally Mason, "Video, Libraries and the Law: Finding the Balance," *American Libraries*, February 1989, 110–19; Sally Mason, "Copyright or Wrong: The Public Performance Dilemma," *Wilson Library Bulletin*, April 1992, 76–77; Roger Cohen, "Software Issue Kills Liberal Amendment to Copyright Laws," *New York Times*, October 13, 1990, A1, A11.
46. Peter H. Lewis, "160 Nations Meet to Weigh Revision of Copyright Law," *New York Times*, December 2, 1996, A1, D12.
47. Pamela Samuelson, "Big Media Beaten Back," *Wired*, March 1997, 61.
48. See ibid., 61–64, 178–84; Browning, "Africa 1 Hollywood 0," 61–66, 185–88; David McCandless, "Warez Wars," *Wired*, April 1997, 132–35, 178–81; Anne W. Branscomb, "Common Law for the Electronic Frontier," in *Electronic Culture: Technology and Visual Representation*, ed. Timothy Druckrey (New York. Aperture, 1996), 376–83.
49. Howard C. Lincoln, "Huge China Market, a Mirage," *Wall Street Journal*, March 23, 1994, A14.
50. Jim McCue, "Who Cares about Dickens' Heirs?" *Spectator*, February 25, 1995, 23.
51. Margot Lovejoy, *Postmodern Currents: Art and Artists in the Age of Electronic Media* (Upper Saddle River, N.J.: Prentice Hall, 1997), 228.
52. John Perry Barlow, "Selling Wine without Bottles: The Economy of Mind on the Global Net," in *High Noon on the Electronic Frontier: Conceptual Issues in Cyberspace*, ed. Peter Ludlow (Cambridge: MIT Press, 1996), 14.
53. Bill Nichols, "The Work of Culture in the Age of Cybernetic Systems," in *Electronic Culture: Technology and Visual Representation*, ed. Timothy Druckrey (New York: Aperture, 1996), 123–43. See also David Tomas, "From the Photograph to the Postphotographic Practice: Toward a Postoptical Ecology of the Eye," also in *Electronic Culture*, 145–53.
54. Pierre Levy, "The Art of Cyberspace," in *Electronic Culture: Technology and Visual Representation*, ed. Timothy Druckrey (New York: Aperture, 1996), 367.
55. See Lee Marshall, "The World According to Eco," *Wired*, March 1997, 15–18, 193–95.
56. Tricia Rose, "A Style Nobody Can Deal With: Politics, Style and the Postindustrial City in Hip

Hop," in *Microphone Fiends: Youth Music and Youth Culture*, ed. Andrew Ross and Tricia Rose (New York: Routledge, 1994), 85.

57. See Richard Parker, *Mixed Signals: The Prospects for Global Television News* (New York: Twentieth Century Fund Press, 1995).

58. See Christine L. Ogan, "Media Diversity and Communications Policy: Impact of VCRs and Satellite TV," *Telecommunications Policy*, March 1985, 63–73; Douglas A. Boyd, "Third World Pirating of U.S. Films and Television Programs from Satellites," *Journal of Broadcasting and Electronic Media* 32, no. 2 (1998): 149–61.

59. Brian Springer, e-mail correspondence with the author, April 10, 1996.

60. iEAR Studio, Rensselaer Polytechnic Institute, "Performance Art Pioneer Gómez-Peña to Commandeer Airwaves," "Tune In and Talk Back," and "Celebrate the Art of Community Television and Aztechnology" (press release), October 1994.

61. A partial transcript of *El Naftazteca: Cyber Aztec T.V. for 2000 A.D.* has been published in Guillermo Gómez-Peña, *The New World Border* (San Francisco: City Lights, 1996), 111–25.

62. Copyright Act of 1976, Section 107, as cited in Michael Fox, "Take the Image and Run," *Independent*, December 1995, 35. For a legal interpretation of the fair use provision, see Volunteer Lawyers for the Arts, "Guide to Copyright for the Visual Arts: Painters, Sculptors, Photographers, Graphic Artists" (pamphlet), 1995, 6–7.

63. Ivan R. Bender, "Copyright Law and the Newer Technologies," *Wilson Library Bulletin*, June 1993, 44–47; Robert L. Jacobson, "College Media Group Issues Draft Rules on Copyright and 'Fair Use,'" *Chronicle of Higher Education*, September 29, 1995, A48–50; "Congress Acts to Clarify the Fair Use Doctrine," *Publishers Weekly*, October 19, 1992, 10; "House Passes Bill to Clarify Fair Use; More Debate Likely," *Publishers Weekly*, August 31, 1992, 21; "Court Reverses Fair Use Ruling on Hubbard Bio," *Publishers Weekly*, June 15, 1990, 13–14; "House Gets Bill on Unpublished Fair Use," *Publishers Weekly*, March 30, 1990, 10; "Eight Publishers Sue Photocopying Chain," *Publishers Weekly*, May 12, 1989, 100.

64. Negativland, "In Fair Use Debate, Art Must Come First," *Billboard*, December 25, 1993, 15.

65. For a more extensive discussion of the arguments for expanding the Fair Use Doctrine and for copies of the original court cases related to the Island Records suit against Negativland as well as copies of faxes and letters between the defendants and the record company, see Negativland, *Fair Use: The Story of the Letter U and the Numeral 2* (Concord, Calif.: Seeland, 1995).

66. See Jon Pareles, "Parody, Not Smut, Has Rappers in Court," *New York Times*, November 13, 1993, I13, I18; Ronald Sullivan, "Judge Rules against Rapper in 'Sampling' Case," *New York Times*, December 17, 1993, B2; Kurt Andersen, "The Freedom to Ridicule," *Time*, December 13, 1993, 93; Linda Greenhouse, "Court Enters New Era in Rap Copyright Case," *New York Times*, March 30, 1993, A16.

67. Ronald Sullivan, "Appeals Court Rules Artist Pirated Photo of Puppies," *New York Times*, April 3, 1992, B3; Constance L. Hays, "A Picture, a Sculpture and a Lawsuit," *New York Times*, September 19, 1991, B12.

68. Martha Buskirk, "Commodification as Censor: Copyrights and Fair Use," *October* (spring 1992): 101–6.

69. Mark Dery, "Culture Jamming: Culture Jamming, Hacking, Slashing, and Sniping in the Empire of the Signs" (pamphlet), Open Magazine Pamphlet Series, Westfield, N.J., 1993, 7.

70. Immediast Underground, "Seizing the Media: A Treatise" (pamphlet), Immediast International, New York, 1994, 3.

71. Anonymous policy analyst, Benton Foundation, telephone interview with the author, April 11, 1997.

72. Patricia Aufderheide, *Communications Policy and the Public Interest: The Telecommunications Act of 1996* (New York: Guilford, 1998), 80–109.

73. Tom Frank, "Hip Is Dead: The Howl of Unreflective Consumerism," *The Nation* April 1, 1996, 16.

74. Frank Rich, "Mixed Media Message," *New York Times*, March 6, 1996, A19.

75. Media and Democracy Conference program, San Francisco, February and March, 1996.

76. Rich, "Mixed Media Message," A19.

77. Michael Moore, "What You Can't Get Away with on TV," *The Nation*, November 18, 1996, 10; Doron P. Levin, "Tweaking the Captains of Industry in Prime Time," *New York Times*, July 13, 1994, D3, D5; John J. O'Connor, "New Targets Lined Up for a Deadpan Deadeye," *New York Times*, July 19, 1994, C15, C18; Laurie Mifflin, "The Rib Tickler's Approach to Social Provocation," *New York Times*, July 16, 1995, sec. II, p. 24; Matt Rush, "Newsmag Nirvana, Moore or Less," *USA Today*, July 19, 1994, D3.

78. Andrew Ross, "Hacking Away at the Counterculture," in *Technoculture*, ed. Constance Penley and Andrew Ross (Minneapolis: University of Minnesota Press, 1991), 132.

79. For a more lengthy explanation of image flows and local spaces, see Rob Wilson and Wimal Dissanayake, "Introduction," and Matsuhiro Yoshimoto, "Real Virtuality," both in *Global/Local:*

Cultural Production and the Transnational Imaginary, ed. Rob Wilson and Wimal Dissanayake (Durham, N.C.: Duke University Press, 1996).

80. Arjun Appadurai, *Modernity at Large: Cultural Dimensions of Globalization* (Minneapolis: University of Minnesota Press, 1996), 3–10, 159–88.

81. Salman Rushdie, *The Wizard of Oz* (London: British Film Institute, 1992), 57.

82. Gilles Deleuze and Félix Guattari, *Nomadology* (New York: Columbia University/Semiotext[e], 1986), 34.

83. Ibid., 52.

84. See, for example, Angelika Bammer, ed., *Displacements: Cultural Identities in Question* (Bloomington: Indiana University Press, 1994); David Morley and Kevin Roberts, *Spaces of Identity: Global Media, Electronic Landscapes, and Cultural Boundaries* (London: Routledge, 1995); Jonathan Friedman, *Cultural Identity and Global Process* (London: Sage, 1994); Avery F. Gordon and Christopher Newfield, eds., *Mapping Multiculturalism* (Minneapolis: University of Minnesota Press, 1996).

85. Arif Dirlik, "Global in the Local," in *Global/Local: Cultural Production and the Transnational Imaginary*, ed. Rob Wilson and Wimal Dissanayake (Durham, N.C.: Duke University Press, 1996), 1, 42.

86. Appadurai, *Modernity at Large*, 176–98.

87. Caren Kaplan, *Questions of Travel: Postmodern Discourses of Displacement* (Durham, N.C.: Duke University Press, 1996), 159–85.

88. For an example of the debates about the privatization of public space, see Bill Kovach, "When Public Business Goes Private," *New York Times*, December 1, 1996, A29.

89. For descriptions of the Gap Campaign and the Disney Alert, see National Labor Committee, Gap Campaign press kit, 1995, and Disney Alert press kit, 1996. The National Labor Committee can be reached at 275 Seventh Avenue, New York, NY, 10001; (212) 242-3002.

90. Trinh T. Minh-ha, *Woman, Native, Other: Writing Postcoloniality and Feminism* (Bloomington: Indiana University Press, 1989), 134.

Index

ABC/Capital Cities, Disney and, xvi, 46

Abdallah, Anouar: on Rushdie affair, 19

Abortion: access to, 139, 143; advertisements against, 127–28; female body and, 141, 151, 152; freedom of speech and, 140; health care and, 143; ideological exorcism on, 149–50; illegal/botched, 145; images/symbols of, 125; media and, 136–37, 139; radicalized site of, 149; signification and, 126; television and, 134, 135

Abortion clinics, attacks on, 119, 141

Abortion discourse, 30; public sphere and, 134; suppression of, 132

"Abortion Film Wars, The" (Cooper), 125

Abortion: Stories from North and South, 136

Abrash, Barbara, 6

Access Denied, 91, 146; described, 144–45; scene from, 121 (photo); screen grab from, 145 (photo)

Accuracy in Media, independent documentary and, 3

Achebe, Chinua, 12

ACLU. *See* American Civil Liberties Union

Activist media: defense by, 21; interactive mode of, 98

ACT UP, 139, 184; piracy and, 157; protest by, 33, 100 (photo); video about, 32

Acuff-Rose Music, 180

Aesthetics, xvii, xx, 80

"Aesthetics and Anesthetics: Walter Benjamin's Artwork Essay Reconsidered" (Buck-Morss), 79

AFA. *See* American Family Association

Affirmative action, 16, 119

AFL-CIO, funding controversy and, 50

Afrocentrist essentialism, black nationalist pluralism and, 161

Agitprop, 8, 10

AIDS, xxii, 51, 139, 157; media and, 136; videos on, 99–101

Air: nation-states and, 89; war and, 57–60, 77

AIVF. *See* Association of Independent Video and Filmmakers

A.K.A. Don Bonus, 38 (photo)

Akomfrah, John, 12

Alchemy Cabinet, 134

Alexander, Jane: on endowment costs, 44

Alive from Off Center, 7

Allen, Austin: *Claiming Open Spaces* and, 195

All That the Law Allows, 132

Alpert, Jon, 49, 60; *Chiapas* and, 90; *Hard Metals Disease* and, 92

Alternative media, 159–60, 185, 188; dominant media and, 123–24

American Civil Liberties Union (ACLU), *Rust* decision and, 140

American Dream, 11, 89

American Family Association (AFA), 8; independent documentary and, 3; offensive by, 32; privatization and, 46; *Roe* movie and, 135; suit against, 29

American Family Research Council, injunctions by, 140

American Film Institute, grants for, 37

American Library Association, 139, 171

Amnesty International, 81

Anderson, Kelly: *Out at Work* and, 49, 50

Antiabortion agendas, 125, 131, 150; avant-garde art and, 134; video on, 189; visual front and, 126

Antigay agendas, 51; video on, 189

Antiwar movement, 20, 142

Appadurai, Arjun, 191; on locality, 194

Aquino, Cory, 53

Archaeology of Knowledge, The (Foucault), 127

Archives, 168; regulation/policing of, 166

Armey, Dick: public broadcasting and, 45

Aronowitz, Stanley, 40

Arresting Images (Dubin), on abortion discourse, 134

Arthur S. DeMoss Foundation, commercials by, 127–30, 132, 152

Artistic Freedom under Attack (People for the American Way), 31

Art Lessons, 33

Arts: democratizing, 31; nation-state and, 46; war against, 27

marketing/advertising in, 165; pirating of, 162–70

Holocaust, 78; signification and, 126; testimonies about, 63

Holy Terror, 136

Homelessness, xxii, 51, 93, 94; photo of, 94

Home video, 189; Disney and, 165–66

hooks, bell: on speech/history/identity, 60

Hoop Dreams, xx, 11

Horowitz, David, 5, 7; conspiracy theory and, 9; on independent documentary, 8; on public television, 9; witch-hunt by, 9, 10

Hosler, Mark: photo of, 183

Housing Problems, 62, 63, 64, 93

Hudson, Rock: archival trace of, 166–67

Hughes, Holly, 27, 46

Human Rights Festival, 73

Human Rights Watch, suit by, 29

Hunter, Holly, 135

Hutcheon, Linda: on postmodern art, 133

Hybridity, 84, 159; piracy and, 179

Hyde, Henry, 188

Hyde Amendment, 143

Iannacone, Linda: on reception, 108

Identities, 91; collective, 181; female body and, 150; heterogeneous, 120; national, 27, 202n40; piracy and, 192; pluralization of, 98, 102; speech and, 60

Identity politics, 41; cultural battle about, 17; solidification of, 15

Ideological warfare, 56; shift from, 122

Imagery: aerial, 101; computer, 165; family, 115; fetishes and, 59; healing through, 111–12; male nationalist, 76; national, 4; piracy and, xviii, 161; pro-life, 129; regulation/policing of, 166; as texts, 184; transnationalizing, 48, 162–70; war, 53, 77–78, 80, 87, 115; water, 112

Immediast Underground, copyright manifestos by, 181–82

"In a Word, with Technology" (Rensselaer), 177

Independence Day, pirating from, 162

Independent documentary, 34–35, 50, 53; conscience/consciousness and, xix; cost of, 36; criticism of, 7, 20; as endangered species, 197; forms of, xviii, xx; marginality of, 10–16; as negations, 52; new world order and, 154; nonprofit sector and, 13; piracy and, 186, 192; politics of, 21; producers of, 5–6; public funding and, 13; real in, 54; social justice and, 24–25; spaces and, xx, 7, 9, 13; state and, 4, 55; thinking about, xx, xxiii; transnationalized media and, 4, 12, 104–5; war and, 53, 55, 60

Independent Documentary Fund (WNET), 22–23

Independent Feature Project, suit by, 29

Independent film: agitprop, 10; avant-garde, 10; as counterdiscourse, xix; described, xviii–xix; political correctness of, 8; radical discourse of, xix

Independent media: corporate media and, 104, 160; division of labor in, 137; funding for, 25–26; public sector and, 25; reconnaissance by, 105; transnationals and, xix, 186

Independent Television Service (ITVS), 8, 9, 19;

documentary and, 20–23; funding for, 44; independent production and, 36; subsidies by, 6

Institute for Alternative Journalism, Media and Democracy Conference, 185

Intellectual property rights, 164, 166

Interactive mode, 92, 102

International Trade Act (1988), 19–20

International War Crimes Tribunal: *Calling the Ghosts* and, 75; on rape, 73, 74

International Women's Day Video Festival, The, 109

Internet, 185, 189; communication and, 27; controlling, 32; distribution on, 165; narrowcasting and, 186

Internment camps, xxii, 67, 68–70, 71–72

In the Land of War Canoes, 114

In vitro fertilization (IVF), 146, 147–48

Island Records, suit by, 182–83, 215n65

"I Still Haven't Found What I'm Looking For" (U2), 182

It Is a Crime, 192; scene from, 191 (photo)

ITVS. *See* Independent Television Service

Ivens, Joris: *Spanish Earth* and, 88

IVF. *See* In vitro fertilization

Iwasaki, Akira, 79

Jacobson, Mandy, 73

Jameson, Fredric: on deregulation/globalization, 47

Japanese American internment, xxii, 67, 68–70, 71–72

Japanese Relocation, 71–72

Jarvik, Laurence, 5, 7; communist bashing by, 10; conspiracy theory and, 9; on independent film, 8, 10; on public television, 137

Jelincic, Karmen, 73

Jenik, Adriene: *El Naftazteca* and, 177

Jesus Christ Condom, 32

Jimenez, Lillian, 185

Joan Does Dynasty, 106

Joan Sees Stars, 167; scene from, 168 (photo)

Jones, Philip Mallory, 10, 84–85; *Dreamkeeper* and, 85–86

Juhasz, Alexandra, 99

Just Say No!, 109

Kahn, Douglas, 183

Kaplan, Caren: on local/plural, 194; on politics of location, 88

Kaplan, E. Ann, 124, 128–29

Karkal, Malina, 148

Kasem, Casey: *Sonic Outlaws* and, 182

Katz, Esther, 6

KCET (Los Angeles), Gulf Crisis and, 109

Khomeini, Ayatollah: Rushdie and, 18, 19

Kimball, Roger: on public funding, 38

King, Larry, 175, 176

King, Martin Luther, Jr., 114

King, Rodney, 53, 101, 175, 177

Kinoy, Peter: *Take Over* and, 93

Koons, Jeff, 180, 181

Kopple, Barbara, 11, 89

KQED (San Francisco), Gulf Crisis and, 109

Kramer, Hilton, 8; on good art, 40; on grants, 39; on popular culture, 38; on public funding, 38
Kruger, Barbara, 153

Language, 77; exile of, 60; testimony and, 76; verbal, 76; war in, 53
Lanzmann, Claude: *Shoah* and, 63
Las Madres: The Mothers of Plaza de Mayo, 64; nation-state and, 66; scene from, 67 (photo); testimonies in, 65–67
Latino Public Broadcasting Project (LPBP), 36
Laub, Dori, 65, 71; on reexternalization, 67; testimonies and, 63, 76
Legal Services Corporation, 43
Leibman, Nina: on Production Code, 134
Lesage, Julia, 124; feminist filmmaking and, 62
Letterman, David, 101
Levy, Pierre: on digitality, 172
Lewis, Jon: on Coppola, 165
Liberators: Fighting on Two Fronts in World War II, 5–6
Lila Wallace Foundation, grants from, 35
Limbaugh, Rush: on public broadcasting, 39
Lincoln, Howard C.: on piracy, 171
Lines in the Sand, 109
Listen to Britain, 78
Locations: pluralization of, 98; politics of, 88
Los Angeles rebellion, xxii, 51, 209n25
Los Angeles Times, 106
Lovejoy, Margot: on copyright/digital technology, 172
LPBP. *See* Latino Public Broadcasting Project
Lubiano, Wahneema: on narrative, 200n20
Lyotard, Jean-François, 138

MacArthur Foundation, 21, 26; grants from, 6, 35
MacNeil-Lehrer Report, The, 7
Madigan, Amy, 135
Madonna, 29, 155
Mahmuljin, Velida, 75
Making Sense of the 60s, 6
Manufacturing the Enemy, 109
Man with a Movie Camera, 77, 183
Mapping World Communication: War, Progress, Culture (Mattelart), 56
Mapplethorpe, Robert, 16, 27, 29, 34, 46; controversy over, xvii, 37; funding for, 17
Maquiladoras, 187, 195
Marcos, Subcommandante, 90, 155; on independent media, 156
Mare, Aline: *S'Aline's Solution* and, 149
Margaret Sanger: A Public Nuisance, 6
Market economy: democracy and, 164; traditional family and, 43–44; transnational communications and, 48
Marquis, Alice Goldfarb: on endowments, 33
Massachusetts House Ways and Means Committee, Council on the Arts and Humanities and, 30
Matsushita, MCA/Universal and, 46
Mattelart, Armand: on communication systems, 56
McCarthy, Joe, 104

McCorvey, Norma, 135
McCue, Jim: on copyright law, 171
MCRR. (New York Media Coalition for Reproductive Rights), 141
Media: activist, 21, 98; alternative, 123–24, 159–60, 185, 188; collapsing of, 123; cheap, 109; concentration of, 34, 46–47, 185, 186; copyright and, 171; decentralization/democratization of, xiv, 31, 139; democracy and, 139, 184; dominant, 7, 123–24; elite and, 39; female body and, 134–37; feminism and, 138; Gulf War and, 56, 110–11; matrix of, 194; political oppositional, 120; politics/consciousness and, 124; postmodernism and, 133; radical, 15, 197; reproductive rights and, 138, 139; transnational capital and, 4; underground, 8; wartime control of, 55–56. *See also* Independent media; Transnationalized media
Media and Democracy Conference, 185
Media arts: funding for, 35; transnational corporate networks and, 35; vulnerability of, 35
Media Arts Centers, 36, 37
Media piracy, 161, 183, 184, 186; corporatized speech and, 180; as counterdiscourse, 155; defining, 154–55; exchange value/use value and, 156; fair use and, 179; image and, 157, 166; space and, 162. *See also* Commercial piracy
Media production, 212n41; landscape of, 138; spectatorship and, 144
Media technology, 183, 197; pirate media and, 186
Media transnationals: ideological control by, 24; independent documentary and, 4; piracy and, 163–64; public discourse and, 3; telecommunications bills and, 185
Media Virus!, 157
Medunjanin, Sadeta, 75
Memory: media and, 142; technology and, 178
Mendoza, David: on public funding, 45
Mercer, Kobena: on independent media, 25
Meta Mayan, 81–82
Michelman, Kate, 130
Mickey Mouse Goes to Haiti, 195–96
Miles, William, 5
Millennium Film Workshop, 31
Miller, Branda: *El Naftazteca* and, 177
Miller, Mark Crispin, 186; on national entertainment state, 4
Milner, Sherry: on cheap media, 108
Minh-ha, Trinh T., 54; displacement and, 84; on documentary/war, 55; on independent film, 10; on *Meta Mayan*, 81; on narrative/story, 197; on Western culture, 14
Minnesota State Arts Board, grant from, 30
Minority Broadcasting Consortia, 36, 44
Miranda, Carmen, 169
Mita, Merata: on filmmaking, 95
"Mixed Media Message" (Rich), 185
Miyoshi, Masao: on transnational corporations, 4
Mobil Oil, underwriting by, 47–48
Monopoly, copyright and, 170, 171
Moore, Michael, 186, 187; *Roger & Me* and, 11

Mootoo, Shani, 191–92
Morgan, Tracy: Title X and, 142, 143
Moritsugu, Jon, 6
Morrison, Toni, xviii
Motherhood and Representation (Kaplan), 128–29
Mother Machine, The (Corea), 148
Mothers of the Plaza de Mayo, 65–67; photo of, 67
Motion Picture Association of America (MPAA), 155, 164
Mouffe, Chantal, 88; on AIDS videos, 100
Mowlana, Hamid: on deregulation, 47
MPAA. *See* Motion Picture Association of America
MTV, 164, 187; Pixelvision and, 24
Mukherjee, Bharati: pirate ship image and, 160
Multiculturalism, xvi, xxii, 13, 38, 72, 185
Muñoz, Susana: *Las Madres* and, 65
Murdoch, Rupert, 174, 186
Murphy Brown: abortion issue and, 136; Quayle criticism of, 136
Murrow, Edward R.: legacy of, 103, 104
Muwakkil, Salim, 185
Mythmaking: The Balkans, 72

NAATA. *See* National Asian American Tele-communications Association
NAFTA. *See* North American Free Trade Agreement
Nagasaki, 57, 78
Nanji, Meena: *It Is a Crime* and, 191–92
NAPT. *See* Native American Public Telecommunications
Narrative: maternalizing, 132–33; story and, 197; women and, 137
Narrowcasting: institutional space and, 189; Internet and, 186; piracy and, 186
Narrowcasting: Technology and the Rise of the Christian Right, 188–89, 190
Nation, culture and, 27, 28
Nation: Frank in, 185; funding controversy in, 50; on national entertainment state, 4
National Archives of Guatemala, 168
National Asian American Telecommunications Association (NAATA), 21, 36, 45
National Association of Public Television Stations, 21
National Black Programming Consortium (NBPC), 36
National Endowment for the Arts (NEA), xvii, 16, 30, 31, 34, 35; budget for, 45; Catholic Church and, 32; criticism of, 40–42; defending, 44; de-funding, 32; federal budget for, 43; *Film in the Cities* and, 32; grants from, 6, 30, 36, 37, 138; media activists and, 21; media arts centers and, 36; opposition to, 43, 45; privatization of, 43; public broadcasting and, 8, 37
National Endowment for the Humanities (NEH), 34, 41; criticism of, 40, 42, 43; defending, 44; defunding, 32; grants from, 6, 35, 36; media activists and, 21; offensive against, 43; public broadcasting and, 8, 37
National Endowments: A Critical Symposium, The (Vieth), 39
National Enquirer, 106

Nationalism, xvi, xxii; cultural affirmation of, 27; representation and, 202n40; Serbian, 72; transnationalism and, xx
National Labor Committee: Disney campaign by, 196 (repro.); media campaigns of, 195
National Public Radio (NPR), 6, 185
National Services, grants for, 37
Nation Erupts, The, 101–2
Nation-state: air and, 89; arts and, 46; culture and, 5, 14; documentary and, 61; fantasy construction of, 7; female body and, 123; war and, 54
Native American Public Telecommunications (NAPT), 36
NBC, 184, 186; documentaries on, 36; General Electric and, 104; pirating news from, 158
NBPC. *See* National Black Programming Consortium
NEA. *See* National Endowment for the Arts
Negativland, 184; copyright law and, 180; Fair Use Doctrine and, 180; suit against, 182–83, 215n65
NEH. *See* National Endowment for the Humanities
Nervous System, 112
New Criterion, 40
News: corporate downsizing of, 25; deregulation/privatization/liberalization and, 48; expository ethic of, 103–4; participatory, 156; transnational control of, 174–75; wartime, 55–56
News Corporation, 186; Fox and, xvi
Newsreel collectives, 6, 8, 143, 160
News World Order, 109
New world image order, xxii, xxiii
New world order, 16, 50, 94; art and, xviii; copyright and, 179; gender/sexuality in, 124; independent documentary and, 154; pessimism about, 110; technology and, 110
New York City Department of Health: abortion issue and, 143; demonstration at, 142
New York International Festival of Lesbian and Gay Film, 32
New York Media Coalition for Reproductive Rights (MCRR), 141
New York State Council on the Arts (NYSCA), xviii, 30; abortion and, 136; film/media division of, 31
New York Times, 59, 106, 184; on art/politics, 16; on Clinton/abortion, 130; on documentaries, 11; on Dunifer, 157; on nationalist civil wars, 28; op-ed pieces in, 196; on Reproductive Rights March, 136; Rich in, 185
Nicaragua: Report from the Front, 5
Nichols, Bill, 53, 104, 189; on digitality, 172; on discourse of sobriety, xxi; on documentary, 210n8; on *History and Memory,* 70; on inter-action, 92; on testimonials, 63
Night and Fog, 78–79
Nixon, Richard: public television and, 47
Nonprofit sector, xx, 35–36; arts budgets and, xvi; economic destabilization of, 27; independent documentary and, 11–12; undermining of, xxi
"No Place to Hide" campaign (Operation Rescue), 122

Norris, Christopher, 57; on Gulf War debate/postmodernism, 110
North American Free Trade Agreement (NAFTA), 90, 155, 177, 187
Not Channel Zero, 36, 101
NPR. *See* National Public Radio
Ny, Sokly "Don Bonus": photo of, 38
NYSCA. *See* New York State Council on the Arts

Obsessive Becoming, 111–12; imaging in, 115; political history of wars in, 114; reconnaissance in, 115; scene from, 113 (photo); testimony in, 113
O'Connor, John J., 32, 33
O'Connor, Rory, 6
Ohio v. Akron Center for Reproductive Health (1990), 130
"Oh, Pretty Woman," Fair Use Doctrine and, 180
Omarska, 65, 75
"101 Sweatshops" (National Labor Committee), 196 (repro.)
Onwurah, Ngozi, 12
Operation Disobedience, 109
Operation Rescue, 144–45; blockades by, 119, 141; campaign by, 122
Orbison, Roy: Fair Use Doctrine and, 180
Out at Work, 49, 50; postcard announcing, 49 (repro.)

Pacific Islanders in Communication (PIC), 36
Panama Deception, The: described, 103, 105
Paper Tiger, 36, 72, 139, 189, 185; Deep Dish and, 109; documentaries by, 105–7, 109; Gulf War programs by, 60; *Narrowcasting* and, 188; *Panama Deception* and, 103; piracy and, 186; screen grabs from, 107 (repro.); *US Bans Abortion* and, 142
Paper Tiger West, KQED and, 109
Paramount Communications Inc., 46, 166; Viacom and, xvi
Passin' It On, 6
PBS. *See* Public Broadcasting Service
Penley, Constance, 123
People for the American Way, 43; annual volume by, 31; suit by, 29
Perestroika, 17, 182
Performing arts, 187; vulnerability of, 35
Perot, Ross, 124, 176
Petchesky, Rosalind: on anti-abortionists, 125, 126
Philip Morris, international masters and, 46
Photography: aerial dimensions of, 57; attacks against, 32
PIC. *See* Pacific Islanders in Communication
Picasso, Pablo, 46
Piracy, 174, 186, 189, 190, 191, 196; copyright and, 155, 163, 164, 166; defining, 154–55; democracy and, 194; documentary and, 182, 192, 197; hybridity and, 179; identity and, 192; images and, 161; manifesto for, 183; mercantilism and, 160; new formations of, 155; as new media strategy, 161; performing, 178; plagiarism and, 154–62; satellite dishes and, 175; telecommunications and, 164; theorizing, 161; transnational

media and, 165–66. *See also* Commercial piracy; Media piracy
Pixelvision, 59, 91, 184; MTV and, 24
Planned Parenthood, 122, 210n5
Planned Parenthood v. Casey (1992), 130, 136
Polan, Dana, 59, 60
Police brutality, 98, 101
Political documentary, 16; formations of, 97–98; textuality/contextuality in, 125
Politics, xvii; aesthetics and, 80; collapsing of, 123; culture and, 26; discourse and, 99; media and, 124; pluralization of, 98; radical, 123; sexual, 62. *See also* Identity politics
Portillo, Lourdes: *Las Madres* and, 65
Postcolonialism, xxii, 10
Postmodernism, xx, 38, 41, 157, 190; as artistic strategy, 133; culture and, 133; as descriptive, 133; Gulf War and, 110; media and, 133
Poston, internment at, 71–72
Poto and Cabengo, 92
P.O.V., 7, 49; *Stop the Church* and, 32
Practice of Everyday Life, The (De Certeau), 161
Pravda, 106
Prelude to War, 53
Presley, Elvis, 169
Private sector, 15; funding increase from, 48; public affairs and, 50
Privatization, xviii, xxi, 13, 28, 42–50, 97, 137, 190; advocacy of, 47; aggressive, 154; copyright and, 180; criticism of, 42–43, 44–45, 46; defunding and, 29–30; economic, 27; family values and, 43
"Problem moment" structure, 62
Pro-choice: cognitive/political arguments of, 126; visual terrain and, 125
Production: access to, 141; landscape of, 138
Production Code, 134
Pro-life, 122, 131; imagery, 129
Propaganda, 60; psychological warfare and, 56
Proximities: distance and, 92; genealogy and, 92–93
Psychology Today, 106
Public: demolition of, 42–50; transnationalization and, 14–15
Public Access (Berube), 38
Public affairs programming: deregulation/privatization/liberalization and, 48; hearings on, 21–22; private enterprise and, 50; public space for, 20–23; public television and, 47; reductions in, 138
Public broadcasting: critics of, 22–23; privatizing, 8; transnational corporations and, 19; war against, 27
Public Broadcasting and the Public Trust (Horowitz and Jarvik), 8
Public Broadcasting Service (PBS), 47, 87; criticism of, 5, 23, 37–38; defending, 44; defunding, 137, 138; documentaries on, 49; Gulf Crisis and, 109; privatization of, 44, 137; subsidies by, 6
Public culture, xviii; closing down, 18
Public funding: attacking, 8, 26, 32–33, 37, 38, 41,

14; independent documentary and, 12; media sector and, 4

Transnational corporations, xviii; copyright and, 170; media arts/documentary and, 35; public broadcasting and, 19; public space and, 195. *See also* Media transnationals

Transnationalism, xvi, 5, 24, 27; corporate, xv, xx–xxi; corporate consumer culture and, 41; cultural policies and, 46; documentary and, 48–49; economic, 15; expansion of, xvii–xviii; impact of, 4; nationalism and, xx, xxi; public and, 14–15; public space and, xx–xxi; rumblings of, xvi; sources for, 34; state/culture and, 48; technology and, xvi

Transnationalized media, 24, 190, 202n48; democracy and, xvi; disenfranchisement by, xix; independent media and, xix, 104–5, 186; piracy and, 165–66; technosubculture and, 181

Traveling shot, 150

Triumph of the Will, aerial shots in, 58

Tropic Zone, 169; pirating from, 168

Truth or Dare, 11

Turner, Frederick: on arts funding, 41

Turner, Ted: CNN and, 174

Turner Broadcasting, Time Warner and, 46

TV Guide, xx, 106

"TV Intervencion Pirata, A," 178

TV Nation, 36, 187; piracy and, 186

20/20, 186

Twist Barbie, 106

2 Live Crew, 29; Fair Use Doctrine and, 180

Tyler, Stephen: postmodern ethnography and, 93–94

Underexposed: Temple of the Fetus: reproductive technologies and, 146–47, 148, 149; scene from, 147 (photo)

Under the Black Flag (Cordingly), 160

UNESCO, on media ownership concentration, 164

United Auto Workers, funding by, 49

United Fruit Company, bananaland and, 169

US Bans Abortion, 142; camcorder strategy of, 143; female body and, 144

U.S. Marine Archives, 168

U.S. National Archives, 168

U.S. Supreme Court: abortion issue and, 130, 152; *Bray* and, 119

Unsere Afrikareise, 77

Unzipped, 11

Updike, John, 17

U2, Negativland and, 182

Vaid, Urvashi, 185

Van Dyke, Barbara, 79

Vanishing Nation: The Inside Story of Public Television, The (Day), 22

Variety, 106, 164

Velez, Edin: *Meta Mayan* and, 80

Vertov, Dziga, 92, 184, 188

Viacom, 24; Paramount and, xvi

Victimization, 64, 89, 97, 187; testimony and, 66

Video technology, 80; social relations and, 141

Vieth, Gene Edward, 39

Village Voice: on Gingrich offensive, 42; on Halleck, 106

Virilio, Paul, 53; on war of objects, 57

Visual arts, vulnerability of, 35

Visual Communication, 21

Visual Studies Workshop, 31

Voices from the Front, 100

Waits, Tom, 115

Walljasper, Jay, 185

Wallner, Martha: on Gingrich/privatization, 44

Wall Street Journal: on Mapplethorpe funding, 17; on piracy, 171

War: aestheticizing, 79–80; air and, 56, 58, 60, 77; blockades/embargoes and, 55–57; defined nation and, 54; documentary and, 52, 58; horror of, 51–52; human psyche and, 82; images of, 56, 58, 59; independent documentary and, 53, 55, 60; languages of, 77; media/state and, 56; nationalist, xviii, xxii, 28; nation-states and, 54; official imaging of, 87; psychic/imaginary, 53; reconnaissance during, 103–11; state-manufactured image of, 59; technologies of, 57–58

War and Cinema (Virilio), 57

War and Television (Cummings), 51

War Crimes Tribunal, 76

Wark, MacKenzie, 104

Warner Communications, 46; Time and, xvi, 17

War, Oil and Power, 109

War on the Home Front, 109

War rape, 73, 74, 75–76

War We Left Behind, The: described, 87

Washington Week in Review, 21

Wasko, Janet, 165; on media/entertainment sector, 166

Waugh, Thomas, 88–89; on committed documentary, 200n14

Webster v. Reproductive Health Services (1989), 130; abortion/freedom of expression issues and, 139; *Access Denied* and, 145; *Roe* movie and, 135

Weddington, Sarah, 135

Weiss, Marc N., 42

Welfare, xxii; for artists, 40; reform, 34, 40

WHAM!. *See* Women's Health Action and Mobilization

When Billy Broke His Head . . . and Other Tales of Wonder: described, 95–97; scene from, 96 (photo)

When the Mountains Tremble, 187

White male patriarchy, recentering, 137, 138

Who Killed Vincent Chin?, 61

Wildmon, Donald: *Film in the Cities* and, 32; *Roe* movie and, 135; suits involving, 28, 30

Will Be Televised, described, 109

Williams, Raymond, 40

Wilson, Pete: arts council funding and, 30

Winston, Brian, 62, 104; on *Triumph,* 58

WIPO. *See* World Intellectual Property Organization

WIPO Diplomatic Conference, 171

With a Vengeance, 136

PATRICIA R. ZIMMERMANN is professor of cinema and photography in the Roy H. Park School of Communications at Ithaca College. She is the author of *Reel Families: A Social History of Amateur Film* and coeditor with Erik Barnouw of the special monograph issue of *Wide Angle* titled "The Flaherty: Four Decades in the Cause of Independent Cinema." Her essays have appeared in *Afterimage, Wide Angle, Cinema Journal, Journal of Film and Video,* and *Screen,* among others. She has also served as guest curator with the Robert Flaherty Film Seminar as well as with museums and film festivals.